Carved in Stone, Etched in Memory

Despite the recent history of violence and destruction, Bosnia-Herzegovina holds a positive place in history, marked by a continuous interweaving of different religious cultures. The most expansive period in that regard is the Ottoman rule that lasted there nearly five centuries. As many Bosnians accepted Islam, the process of Islamisation took on different directions and meanings, only some of which are recorded in the official documents. This book underscores the importance of material culture, specifically gravestones, funerary inscriptions and images, in tracing and understanding more subtle changes in Bosnia's religious landscape and the complex cultural shifts and exchange between Christianity and Islam in this area.

Gravestones are seen as cultural spaces that inscribe memory, history and heritage in addition to being texts that display, in image and word, first-hand information about the deceased. In tackling these topics and ideas, this study is situated within several contextual, theoretical and methodological frameworks. Raising questions about religious identity, history and memory, the study unpacks the cultural and historical value of gravestones and other funerary markers and bolsters their importance in understanding the region's complexity and improving its visibility in global discussions around multiculturalism and religious pluralism. Drawing upon several disciplinary methods, the book has much to offer anyone looking for a better understanding of the intersection of Christianity and Islam, as well as those with an interest in death studies.

Amila Buturovic is Associate Professor of Humanities and Religious Studies at York University, Toronto.

Carved in Stone, Etched in Memory
Death, Tombstones and Commemoration in Bosnian Islam since c. 1500

Amila Buturovic

ASHGATE

© Amila Buturovic 2015

All rights reserved. No part of this publication may be reproduced, stored in a retrieval system or transmitted in any form or by any means, electronic, mechanical, photocopying, recording or otherwise without the prior permission of the publisher.

Amila Buturovic has asserted her right under the Copyright, Designs and Patents Act, 1988, to be identified as the author of this work.

Published by
Ashgate Publishing Limited
Wey Court East
Union Road
Farnham
Surrey, GU9 7PT
England

Ashgate Publishing Company
110 Cherry Street
Suite 3-1
Burlington, VT 05401-3818
USA

www.ashgate.com

British Library Cataloguing in Publication Data
A catalogue record for this book is available from the British Library

The Library of Congress has cataloged the printed edition as follows:
Buturovic, Amila, 1963–
　Carved in stone, etched in memory : death, tombstones and commemoration in Bosnian Islam since c. 1500 / by Amila Buturovic.
　　pages cm
　Includes bibliographical references and index.
　ISBN 978-1-4724-3260-5 (hardcover) – ISBN 978-1-4724-3261-2 (ebook) – ISBN 978-1-4724-3262-9 (ePub) 1. Muslims–Bosnia and Herzegovina–Social life and customs. 2. Death–Social aspects–Bosnia and Herzegovina–History. 3. Death–Religious aspects–Islam–History. 4. Sepulchral monuments–Bosnia and Herzegovina–History. 5. Memorials–Bosnia and Herzegovina–History. 6. Islamic funeral rites and ceremonies–Bosnia and Herzegovina–History. 7. Material culture–Bosnia and Herzegovina–History. 8. Bosnia and Herzegovina–Religious life and customs. 9. Islam–Relations–Christianity–History. 10. Christianity–Relations–Islam–History. I. Title.
　DR1674.M87B88 2015
　305.6'970949742–dc23

2015007105

ISBN: 9781472432605 (hbk)
ISBN: 9781472432612 (ebk – PDF)
ISBN: 9781472432629 (ebk – ePUB)

Printed in the United Kingdom by Henry Ling Limited, at the Dorset Press, Dorchester, DT1 1HD

Contents

List of Figures   *vii*
Acknowledgements   *xiii*

Introduction   1

1   Constructing Authenticity, Ensuring Continuity:
    Death, Dying and Commemoration in Bosnian Islam   13

2   Remembering the Dead and Marking the Deathscape   59

3   Converting the Stone: Text and Images in
    Early Ottoman Bosnia   109

4   Islamising Memory, Framing the Community: Funerary Text
    in the Religious Imagination   165

Conclusion   203

Appendix   *209*
Bibliography   *229*
Index   *237*

List of Figures

I.1　Old Muslim cemetery in Vidimlije, Glamoč.
　　Photo by Velibor Božović　　12

1.1　Tombstones of Ayni Dede and Shamsi Dede in Sarajevo.
　　Photo by Velibor Božović　　22
1.2　Muslim cemetery in Travnik.
　　Photo by Velibor Božović　　31
1.3　Muslim cemetery in Blažuj, Tomislavgrad.
　　Photo by Velibor Božović　　40
1.4　Old stones fighting for space with new ones, Sarajevo.
　　Photo by Velibor Božović　　48
1.5　Dobrun, eastern Bosnia. One of the earliest Ottoman Muslim cemeteries in Bosnia and Herzegovina.
　　Photo by Velibor Božović　　58

2.1　Ajvaz Dede's rock.
　　Photo by Velibor Božović　　73
2.2　*Turbe* in Ustikolina.
　　Photo by Velibor Božović　　78
2.3　Ajvaz Dede's *turbe* in Prusac.
　　Photo by Amila Buturović　　79
2.4　Ostružnica shrine with 1171 AH/1758 CE etched in the stone. Visible in the middle are the traces of stone scrapings used for curative powers.
　　Photo by Amila Buturović　　80
2.5　Inside ruins of the *turbe* in Glamoč.
　　Photo by Velibor Božović　　81
2.6　Cephalophore martyr, Turovi.
　　Photo by Amila Buturović　　86
2.7　Cephalophore martyr, Lukavac.
　　Photo by Amila Buturović　　87

2.8 Bones upon bones: old and new in competition for space, Sarajevo.
Photo by Velibor Božović 94
2.9 Sarajevo Roses, two blasts side by side.
Photo by Velibor Božović 106
2.10 A typical tombstone of a fallen Bosniak soldier, depicting fleur-de-lis as the State insignia (bottom), the *Fātiḥa* (top) and the Qur'anic quote affirming martyrdom: 'And do not say for those who are killed for the cause of God they are dead; nay, they are alive, but you do not perceive them' (2:154).
Photo by Amila Buturović 107
2.11 Kovači 1992–95 war cemetery in Sarajevo in the background; an old Ottoman cemetery in the foreground.
Photo by Velibor Božović 108
2.12 Srebrenica Potočari memorial to civilian casualties, with inscriptions stating the same martyrdom verse from the Qur'an (Q2:154).
Photo by Amila Buturović 108

3.1 Medieval *stećak* necropolis, Kupres.
Photo by Velibor Božović 113
3.2 *Stećaks* under a blanket of moss. Ladjevina, Rogatica.
Photo by Velibor Božović 113
3.3 *Stećak* at Gornje Ravno. Human representation.
Photo by Velibor Božović 118
3.4 Zoomorphic representation, detail. Bitunja.
Photo by Velibor Božović 119
3.5 Human representation, detail, Bitunja.
Photo by Velibor Božović 119
3.6 Detail from a *stećak* in Fatnica. A man and a woman.
Photo by Velibor Božović 121
3.7 Man's tombstone with a turban.
Photo by Velibor Božović 126
3.8 Woman's tombstone.
Photo by Amila Buturović 127
3.9 Solitary tombstone from the period of Ottoman conquest, Trnovo. Photo by Velibor Božović 130
3.10 Tombstone from the period of Ottoman conquest, with a crescent and hemispheres, Sokolac.
Photo by Amila Buturović 131
3.11 The *biljeg* of Suleiman Oškopica, Dumanjići, with inscription in Bosančica.
Photo by Amila Buturović 136

3.12a	Cemetery in the village of Žunovi, with the *stećaks*, Orthodox tombstones, and an early Ottoman Muslim *nišan*. Photo by Velibor Božović	142
3.12b	Žunovi. Photo by Velibor Božović	142
3.13	The tombstone of Hasan (and Ahmet) in Čadovina, with inscription in Bosančica. Photo by Amila Buturović	145
3.14	A mosque with the *harem*, Sarajevo. Photo by Amila Buturović	149
3.15	Female face, Šišići, Trnovo. Photo Velibor Božović	153
3.16	Raised hand, Džindići. Photo by Amila Buturović	153
3.17	Zoomorphic representations, Vragolovo, Rogatica. Photo by Velibor Božović	153
3.18	Human figure, Turovo. Photo by Velibor Božović	153
3.19	Muslim *nišan* with a cross, Imamovići. Photo by Amila Buturović	158
3.20a	Muslim *nišan* with a cross, Kalimanići. Photo by Amila Buturović	159
3.20b	Recto, a crescent and a bird, Kalimanići. Photo by Amila Buturović	161
3.21	Catholic cemetery with amorphous, cross-shaped tombstones ('*bosanski križ*') in the foreground and a Muslim cemetery below. Both cemeteries still active. Brajković, Vitez. Photo by Velibor Božović	162
3.22a	Solitary cross/crescent tombstone at Janjići, Zenica, recto. Photo by Amila Buturović	164
3.22b	Solitary cross/crescent tombstone at Janjići, verso. Photo by Amila Buturović	164
3.23	A tombstone at the 'Wedding Martyrs' cemetery, with a cross and a downward crescent on the same side. Rostovo, Novi Travnik. Photo by Velibor Božović	164
3.24	A downward crescent arches above a solar sign; an anthropomorphic cross below. Muslim cemetery in Lisac, Novi Travnik. Photo by Velibor Božović	164

4.1	Year 1003 AH/1593 CE, Podvinjci.	
	Photo by Amila Buturović	172
4.2	Year 975 AH/1567 CE, Hlapčevića brdo.	
	Photo by Amila Buturović	172
4.3	Year 976 AH/1568 CE, Podvinjci.	
	Photo by Amila Buturović	172
4.4	Deer image, 1015 AH/1606 CE, Seonica.	
	Photo by Amila Buturović	172
4.5	Vefāt Ahmed, 1080 AH/1669 CE, Džindići.	
	Photo by Amila Buturović	174
4.6	*Shahada*, 1144 AH/1731 CE, Fojnica.	
	Photo by Amila Buturović	176
4.7	*Shahada*, n.d., Visoko.	
	Photo by Amila Buturović	176
4.8	*Shahada*, n.d., Janjići, Zenica.	
	Photo by Amila Buturović	176
4.9	*Shahada*, 1027 AH/1618 CE, Glamoč.	
	Photo by Velibor Božović	176
4.10	'The resident of this spot (*maqām*) is Aisha', 1177 AH/1753 CE, Ćatići.	
	Photo by Amila Buturović	178
4.11	'The resident of this is Mustafa Aga … ', 962 AH/1555 CE, Šetići.	
	Photo by Amila Buturović	178
4.12	'The resident of this *nišan* is sheikh Hajji Ibrahim, the imam and preacher … ', year 1132 AH/1719 CE, Uskoplje.	
	Photo by Amila Buturović	178
4.13	'The resident of this grave (*qabr*) is Osman b. Salih Beg … ', n.d., Fojnica.	
	Photo by Amila Buturović	178
4.14	'Kara Osman *marḥūm*', n.d. Kopčić, Bugojno.	
	Photo by Amila Buturović	180
4.15	The gigantic tombstone of Omer Aga Bašić in Jakir, Glamoč (4.35m tall, turban alone 2m). The inscription reads: 'The year of death of the deceased and pardoned (*marḥūm wa maghfūr*) is 1213 AH/1798 CE. [Say] the *Fātiḥa* for his soul'.	
	Photo by Velibor Božović	184
4.16	'He is the Ever-living, the Ever-lasting', executed in the form of the Imperial Monogram, Fojnica.	
	Photo by Amila Buturović	187
4.17	(left) 'Woe upon us is death', a 'secular' elegiac invocation on Ottoman Islamic gravestones, usually replacing a divine name.	
	Photo by Amila Buturović	191

4.18	Old Ottoman tombstones in Sarajevo's central park. Photo by Amila Buturović	192
4.19a and 4.19b	Alhamiado inscription, erected in 1924 by Ibrahim Haki Galijašević to commemorate the execution of 12 landlords during the first incursion into Bosnia by Eugene of Savoy in 1110 AH/1697 CE, Tešanj. Photo by Velibor Božović	199
4.20	Stylised Alhamiado from Mostar: 'Here lies … (*ovde leži*)', 1969(?). Photo by Amila Buturović	200
4.21	'With God's mercy (*Allah rahmet ile*)', in Cyrillic script. Vragolavi, Sokolac. Photo by Amila Buturović	201
4.22	*Al-Fātiḥa*, in transliteration. Sarajevo. Photo by Velibor Božović	201
4.23	'He is the Creator, the Everlasting. Death is a drink that all shall taste; the grave is the door that all shall pass through; [Say] *Fātiḥa* for her soul'. Faletići. Photo by Amila Buturović	201
4.24	*Al-Fātiḥa* in Bosnian translation. Sarajevo. Photo by Velibor Božović	201
C.1	Old turbans mushrooming in Travnik. Photo by Velibor Božović	207
A.1	Ravne Bakije, Sarajevo	210
A.2	Malo Polje, Blagaj	211
A.3	Dobro, Livno	212
A.4	Jakir, Glamoč	213
A.5	Presjeka, Goražde	215
A.6	Jazići, Kalinovik	216
A.7	Varošnice, Jajce	217
A.8	Alifakovac, Sarajevo	218
A.9	Šetići, Rogatica	219
A.10	Dobrače, Rogatica	220
A.11	Fatnica, Bileća	221
A.12	Rostovo, Novi Travnik	222
A.13	Lisac, Novi Travnik	223
A.14	Tomislavgrad	224
A.15	Dujmovići, Bjelašnica	225
A.16	Božine, Rogatica	226

Acknowledgements

I am grateful for the support I received from many individuals and institutions in preparing this book. The financial and administrative assistance from York University and the Social Sciences and Humanities Research Council of Canada enabled me to carry out fieldwork in Bosnia and Herzegovina and conduct library research at home and overseas. I sincerely appreciate the generous intellectual engagement of many colleagues and friends, in Canada, Bosnia and Herzegovina, Turkey, the U.S. and elsewhere, who offered valuable feedback and provided me with the opportunity to present the material at different academic and public venues and in front of diverse audience. Their comments and recommendations were paramount for the successful completion of the book, but any shortcomings in it are exclusively mine.

Special thanks are extended to Selma Zečević, Snježana Buzov, Hande Solakoğlu, Irvin C. Schick, Andras Reidlmayer, Asya Hekimoğlu, Michael Porretta, Edina Bećirević, Mark Auslander and Paul Szeptycki for their helpful suggestions and encouragement; the Ashgate Publishing team, especially Thomas Gray, Tricia Craggs and Johanna Robinson, for their efficient editorial guidance in preparing the manuscript; and the anonymous readers for their rigorous criticism and insightful comments on the manuscript.

The book would not have acquired its present form if it had not been for Velibor Božović: his skill in perceiving and visually recording the stone memorials steered the book in a direction not initially considered. His friendship and engagement during our field trips, some animated by delightful discoveries and others tedious and even treacherous because of the elements, land mines and unfriendly flora and fauna, encouraged me to visit locations to which I would not have ventured on my own. To Velibor, this book owes much more than its visual enrichment.

Finally, I extend gratitude to my dear ones who had already crossed to the other side but kept me steady company as I did research and wrote this book. *Nur içinde yatsınlar.*

Introduction

This study is a product of two simultaneous journeys. The first one was motivated by a personal reconnection to the place of my birth and youth, which I had lightheartedly left nearly 30 years ago in pursuit of graduate studies in Canada. Little did I know that the departure would take a turn of no return, that Yugoslavia to which Bosnia and Herzegovina had belonged as a constituent federal republic would shatter into nothingness and take some of my most beloved people with it. The newly formed state of Bosnia and Herzegovina was barely a month old when it became enveloped in war and genocide drawn along ethno-religious lines. Even as the conflict raged on, dividing families and friends and the neighbourhoods and cities they inhabited, the idea of conflict and loss amidst the most palpable reality of both seemed unfathomable. The mind sometimes refuses to accept. In the aftermath of the war I readily sided with those who imagined a new modernity unfolding rapidly from the ashes of destruction in which Bosnia and Herzegovina, once again, would prosper as a complex society where neither religion nor ethnicity would define the boundaries of what mattered. Where, against the foibles of the 1995 Dayton Peace Accords, which ended the violence but reinforced the violence-induced partition, the arteries connecting all those who believed in a unified civil society would flow freely with cosmopolitan energy, democratic aspirations and strong social ethics. Such Bosnia would, truthful to its long historical legacy, once again defy all impositions of uniformity and allow its Muslims, Catholics, Orthodox Christians, Jews and others to jointly shape and nurture a productive society, as they had done over many centuries. After all, history could only be progressive and, despite a(nother) violent episode, the sum of all good actions would secure full closure and proper healing to the survivors, justice for war crimes and a global recognition of Bosnia's importance in the aftermath of the 1992–95 genocide and culturecide.[1]

---

[1] Some parts of this text appear in A. Buturović, 'Bosnia and Herzegovina, Between Loss and Recovery', *Descant* 156 (Spring 2012), 10–15.

Regrettably, the post-war rebuilding has proven to be much more precarious and retrograde than even the worst sceptics had assumed. The events that occurred between 1992 and 1995, though ideologically evocative of previous expressions of nationalist violence in the region, are also differentiated from them by many significant factors, of both local and international nature. We may have relived the past but that past is now set in a different global context and orchestrated by players who possess new perilous forms of power and capital and corresponding mindsets. Moreover, the basic necessity of resettling the displaced population that counts over a million, rebuilding the economy, configuring a government and setting up the most rudimentary framework for the functioning of civil society is hindered by the Dayton Agreement due to its inherent contradiction of both empowering divisive identity politics and asking those responsible to overcome the same. To make things worse, the very international community that set the Dayton in motion has over the years withdrawn the support necessary for its proper implementation. Democracy can hardly be introduced under such conditions.

In the labyrinth of walls obstructing the path to a better future, another one has been erected, standing in the view of Bosnia's historical and cultural heritage, or whatever is left of it in the aftermath of the war. In an age where the past keeps unfolding through multiple channels of global connectivity to the extent that it has become everyone's business and not just that of the historians to reconstruct it, it is very difficult to assess the meaning of specific historical moments, events and places without being influenced by the multiplicity of voices, many of them ideologically motivated, trying to appropriate the past, rewrite it or deny it. This is where my other journey is located, in the academic environment geared to listening to cultural and religious history, making sense out of it as it unfolds into the present and moves forward into the future.

As an Islamicist and cultural historian, I am specifically fascinated by locative permutations of Islamic teachings. Especially intriguing are the ways in which teachings and practices converge over time, and how historical processes affect them. The idea that religion is an immutable and discrete phenomenon is not sustainable in any context, particularly not in an environment like Bosnia and Herzegovina where plural religious teachings and customs routinely cohere. Bosnian Islam, as I approach it, includes evolving commitments and observances, teachings and embodied practices, and constrictive and expansive qualities. I find gratification in unravelling the strands of a complex cultural canvas that makes Bosnian Islam at once exclusive and inclusive, universal and idiosyncratic, stagnant and dynamic, and parochial and cosmopolitan. Navigating through those variations and occasional paradoxes has never failed to produce creative but also unruly energy. I thus locate my work within the overarching principle that religious culture is never just one definable phenomenon and that it requires both text and context to express itself and be understood.

The genesis of the subject matter of this study – death and its embodied rituals and markers – was occasioned by a visibility of the dead across the Bosnian landscape. Travelling through this country, one encounters both urban clutter, where structures huddle together like a frightened flock, and long stretches of vacuous space that seem to be devoid of any import, other than perhaps the one of disconnecting the 'flocks' from each other. In both cases, the presence of the dead is striking. Around human dwellings, gravestones poke through the grass, dirt and even asphalt, in expected and unexpected places – cemeteries, playgrounds, parks, backyards, orchards, schoolyards and so on. Often there seems to be no rhyme or reason to their placement but they appear keen to participate, if only from the sidelines, in the life around them. In the countryside and away from human activity, the dead appear in a different way. They rest in uninhabited and untamed stretches of land and in deep pristine forests where light reaches only halfway down tree canopies to give bare visibility to the gravestones. Whether embedded in open fields, tucked away among the trees or overgrown with vines and moss, the dead seem disengaged and inconsequential, abandoned to the elements and passage of time. Here their markers dot the empty landscape, branding it quietly and somewhat randomly. Was it their choice to be removed into such raw and inhospitable environment?

It is within such contemplations over many road trips that my academic prejudices sprang to life: as contemporary theorists tell us, no space exists as an objective empty reality but always as a contested one.[2] Landscape, including deathscape, is here for us to imagine and interpret. I thought of the importance given to the empty, forbidding landscape of Bosnia and Herzegovina that may have galvanised intervallic waves of violence in the course of the 1900s, culminating in the events of 1992–95. I considered the stories, songs and invocations through which the meaning of these graves-marked environs had been perpetuated over generations, meaning which came to be associated with the readiness to die or kill. I envisioned it in other historical moments as it connected rather than disconnected its people, and as it honoured rather than dishonoured cultural proximity. While in recent decades Bosnia-Herzegovina may have infused popular imagination with the language of violence and destruction, this country also holds a more positive place in history, marked by continuous interweaving of different religious cultures. However, rather than imposing my own answers on the land and its bygone people now resting in (intermittent) peace, I embarked on research

---

[2] P. Sheldrake, *Spaces of the Sacred: Place, Memory, Identity* (Baltimore: Johns Hopkins University Press, 2001), 4–8.

that would lead me to some answers about its complex history by studying its vast deathscape.

This study is a product of that research. At the heart of it stands the assumption that in pursuing historical questions about a local culture we can learn as much from the dead as we can from the living. The paradox of this statement does not escape me: of course the subjects of the historical studies are dead, but our tendency to revive them and speak of them as if they were still alive and available shrouds us in documentary pretence. We purport to have access to their world like spectators at a mise-en-scène, able to scrutinise their actions and analyse their complex relations and ulterior motives without the mediation of historical sources we so painstakingly require. In contrast, we tend to treat those we label as dead subjects of history in a flat, two-dimensional way, paying little heed to their agency and engagement in the world and reducing their relevance to stone markers and related signifiers of their death. This study draws attention to the fact that there is always this other world inside the world we study. This inner world belongs to the dead – the dead twice removed – and possesses its own spry cultural space we commonly refer to as deathscape. I attempt to approach this inner world through its diverse representations and self-representations: the former consists of a selection of religious, folkloric, literary and ethnographic writings that describe and prescribe our relationship to death and at times enable the dead to act as agents in our world; the latter involves combing through epigraphic texts recorded on tombstones, as image and word, where the dead offer a message for posterity. Their stone message is probably the closest we can ever get to first-hand voices of the past, unmediated by chroniclers and historiographers, despite the intercession by masons and close kin. Like other cultural texts, then, the tombstone is treated as a type of primary source that elucidates, in addition to biographical data, broader issues of eschatological, historical and spiritual value. It is always a product of its time and as such sheds light on personal, religious and cultural choices of its residents and creators. Conversely, because of its embedment in a shared landscape, its meaning is equally subjected to historical change and interpretative variations.

In unpacking its meanings, however, we must not lose sight of the tombstone's primary function, which is to commemorate. Tombstone is a material trigger, marker and guardian of memories. As an expression of material funerary culture, it has both a visual and tactile quality, making it possible for the living to anchor their memories and stabilise them for private sentimental needs or public ritual practices. Of course, as personal connections recede with the passage of time, the tombstone either gains a broader cultural function of being an aspect of collective heritage or is abandoned to naturalise in the landscape to become yet another fixture. We are thus urged to look beyond the initial impression of the tombstone's durability – while the artefact and text may remain stable, their meaning does not. Subjectivities interfere, narratives emerge, social change takes place. In its simplicity, a tombstone acquires a new quality and purpose and becomes something different from what those who erected it and used it to express their loss may have intended. Our readings of tombstones as we inherit them from earlier historical epochs require us to take this modification into account as we are reminded to consider their meaning in accordance with their original commemorative function.[3] What kind of memory did they instil and preserve, and what can they tell us about the community that erected them? Tombstones, of course, are not the only material makers, markers and guardians of memory as many types of mementos abound in the face of loss and mourning. However, more than most other mementos tombstones tend to bridge public and private domains of everyday life and recognise both individual and public expressions of loss. The key aim of this book is to examine how funerary markers shape the culture of death in Bosnian Islam, including memory practices and consecration of space. Emphasis is placed on concrete historical practices of funerary commemoration but and also on the representational value given to deathscape, specifically how deathscape is used to construct zones of inclusion and exclusion, religious and gender identification, imperial projections and local self-assertions. Historically, the starting point of reference in the understanding of the culture of death among the Muslims of Bosnia and Herzegovina is related to the transformation of the religious fabric after Bosnia's incorporation into the Ottoman Empire in the mid-fifteenth century. Major religious beliefs and practices – including those surrounding death – are often authenticated by evoking distant origins in new interpretations in order to give them at once historical depth and contemporary relevance. As a result, considerable focus in this study is laid on the formative period of Bosnian Islam associated with the early Ottoman period. At the same time, the study offers a broad brushstroke of both past and present practices, and their synchronic and diachronic connections, drawn from a variety of textual and visual sources. In attempting to reconcile an in-depth, microhistorical examination of the funerary markers in Bosnia and Herzegovina with their long-term perception as enduring, if episodic, foci of cultural memory, the book aims to help loosen the grip of the essentialist claims, made from within and without, about the region's burdensome past and entrapment in an ineluctable fate.

A few words on historiography: the expansion, consolidation and eventual downfall of the Ottoman rule in the Balkans has been extensively addressed in the last two decades in particular, mainly in relation to the precarious and volatile place of modern Balkan nations within European and world history. Partly due to the difference in the trajectories undertaken by Balkan nation

---

[3] E. Hallam and J. Hockey (eds) persuasively underscore this tension between stability and fluidity of memory associated with material objects in *Death, Memory and Material Culture* (Oxford & New York: Berg, 2001), 8–9.

builders from other regions of Europe and partly because of disciplinary differences in approaching the Balkans, scholarly findings on the questions of cultural and religious transformation are often posed in value-laden terms and therefore appear at odds with each other. Were the Ottomans a positive or negative force in the region? Did their presence enhance the gap between Islam and Christianity or did it allow the two religions to better interact and influence each other? What criteria should be applied to measure and assess the Ottoman legacy, including the language on human rights, gender and minority, religious freedom, freedom of expression and such? The region is at once splintered by larger, mutually exclusive theoretical and methodological vocabulary and national frameworks, while kept unified by recurrent geopolitical narratives that 'here lies the edge of Europe' in which history has taken a different, more volatile and regressive route than in the rest of the modernised, progressively minded continent. The fact remains, however, that it is hardly possible to speak about Europe without the Balkans, and about the Balkans as a geographical and geopolitical concept without understanding the Ottoman legacy through which Balkan ethnicities and religions have been configured, politicised and nationalised in pre-modern and modern periods. It is likewise incorrect to speak about Europe without its rich Islamic heritage that has spanned the Iberian Peninsula and the Balkans for the past 14 centuries. Because of that, in looking at the processes of cultural and religious exchange in funerary sensibilities, this study refrains from employing dichotomies such as West versus East and Europe versus Islam, that saturate our contemporary discourse on pluralism, cosmopolitanism and cultural values.

In its academic scope, this study inevitably overlaps with social history but because social history is not its primary concern, other methods of inquiry are considered. In tracing the patterns of religious change, specifically conversion to Islam, social history primarily relies on the Ottoman tax and property registers (*tahrir defteri*) to examine social change after the conquest of Bosnia in and around 1463.[4] These are detailed documents, geographically divided into regions and administrative units, containing lists of settlements and taxpayers, and providing periodic revenue overviews to monitor the social and economic state of affairs in the Empire. They encompass the period between the early 1400s and the early 1600s, and appear later only in newly conquered areas or those temporarily 'de-conquered', as well as in villages and communities established as *waqf* charity endowments.[5] Through them historians learn about changes in religious demography thanks to the list of taxpayers introduced by their given and patrilineal names. Widows are also

---

[4] S. Faroqi, *Approaching Ottoman History: An Introduction to the Sources* (Cambridge: Cambridge University Press, 2000), 82–110.

[5] M. Kiel, 'Ottoman Sources for the Demographic History and the Process of Islamisation of Bosnia-Hercegovina and Bulgaria in the Fifteenth – Seventeenth Centuries: Old Sources – New Methodology', in M. Koller and K. Karpat (eds), *Ottoman Bosnia: A History in Peril* (Madison: The University of Wisconsin Press, 2004), 93.

entered as the heads of households. By looking at the first names of taxpayers – specifically the substitutions of Christian names by Muslim ones – patterns of conversion can be established within families and within communities, and key periods of religious change can be identified. As Nedim Filipović points out, the Islamisation of Bosnia and Herzegovina was not relevant only for the region but for imperial history at large given the substantial effects conversion had on the affairs of the Empire.[6] Becoming Muslim in the eye of the Ottoman administration was an important statistical matter relevant to demographic shifts, but primarily for a general management of human, monetary and land resources.[7] Among other types of sources that contain references to becoming and being Muslim, there are court documents and registers that record internal disputes and resolutions and add to the general knowledge of Islamisation. For example, a court record in the town of Zenica discusses a case of disputed land in the nearby town of Bobovac in 908AH/1502CE. Several elders were brought in as witnesses because of their knowledge of the original boundaries of the property from before the Ottoman conquest. The elders listed in the document include Živan, and his sons Sarudže and Hasan; Dobrešin, and his sons Alija and Pavle Bogilja; Vukač, and his sons Sarudže and Nikola. Notably, then, the document indicates that the elders were still Christian while some or all of their sons had become Muslim.[8]

However, personal circumstance or socio-cultural consequences of conversion are not the subject matter of these sources. Despite the detailed character and regularity of tax and court records of fifteenth-century and sixteenth-century Bosnia, understanding the qualitative change and its religious and cultural meaning can hardly be extrapolated. In the recent wave of renewed interest in conversion, other sources have increasingly drawn historians' attention: chronicles, conversion narratives and literary sources such as hagiography, biography and poetry. Often treated as mutually connected, some of these sources, such as chronicles, tell tales of conquest and prowess while others, such as conversion and other literary texts, narrate stories of a more personal nature. Together, they provide a more textured account of Ottoman cultural milieux in and after the sixteenth century albeit with some caveats. In the case of chronicles, which are often composed in formulaic and repetitive way, the subjects are conquerors, warriors and often legendary holy figures credited with spreading the faith. As Cemal Kafadar argues, they are likely to have been subject to successive redaction whereby earlier works were rewritten in light of new developments, practically undermining

---

[6] N. Filipović, *Islamizacija u Bosni i Hercegovini* [Islamisation of Bosnia and Herzegovina] (Sarajevo: Armis Print, 2008), 172.

[7] M. Coşgel, 'Ottoman Tax Registers (*Tahrir Defterleri*)', *Economics Working Papers* (2002). Online: http://digitalcommons.uconn.edu/econ_wpapers/200247.

[8] M. Handžić, *Islamizacija Bosne i Hercegovine i porijeklo bosanskih Muslimana* [Islamisation of Bosnia and Herzegovina and the Origins of Bosnian Muslims] (Sarajevo: Islamska dionička štamparija, 1940), 22–4.

the integrity of what may have been written before.[9] Personal narratives have been appreciated for shedding light on the webs of communication, social spaces, and private engagements of the authors/subjects living in different places and under different circumstances.[10] First-hand narratives of this kind have also an eclectic quality in bringing together less canonical modes of literary expression that have both a professional value and descriptive bent – travelogues, diaries, dream-logs, captivity memoirs, epistolary material – but not all can be authenticated as being genuinely personal rather than emulated or projected.[11] To that end, the conversion narratives of the mid-sixteenth century onward have been increasingly criticised for not being sincere and accurate but rather polemical and propagandist, contrived to promote Islam and the Empire's self-image.[12]

While important in tracing the variety of voices from within the Empire as well as establishing connections between internal and external dynamics, the available conversion narratives and other first-hand accounts are not always representative of ordinary conversion experiences. Most converts did not narrate their life into either confessional/polemical or confessional/ autobiographical texts. They did not assume a position that reflected either canonical or non-canonical versions where writers reinterpreted stories or fashioned new identities. Their location in the imperial world as new Muslims was by and large unconcerned with finding an appropriate literary genre to express and define the new identity within. The sources may have documented the converts' new way of self-identification but beyond that, the sources are silent just as most of their subjects are silent, illiterate and for the most part preoccupied with everyday needs and challenges of meeting the demands of history without feeling the obligation to add their stamp to it. But the adjustments must have been dramatic and transformative – changing one's life and the way of being while trying to maintain the cohesion of family and community which, in a broader and more abstract sense, were granted a placement in the imperial structure. New Muslims had to navigate the space between expansive collectivity and trite individuality in a way that had to be meaningful for both levels of identity. In an effort to trace patterns of conversion in everyday life, this study expands the pool of sources to include funerary texts as important primary sources. It seeks to analyse how becoming Muslim affected the way in which death was inscribed on the tombstone and the dead remembered. In other words, it investigates how death was 'Islamised'

---

[9] C. Kafadar, *Between Two Worlds: The Construction of the Ottoman State* (Berkeley and Los Angeles: University of California Press, 1995), 105–10.

[10] C. Kafadar, 'Self and Others: The Diary of a Dervish in Seventeenth Century Istanbul and First-Person Narratives in Ottoman Literature', *Studia Islamica* 69 (1998), 122–5.

[11] C. Kafadar, 'Self and Others', 132.

[12] T. Krstić, 'Illuminated by the Light of Islam and the Glory of the Ottoman Sultanate: Self-Narratives of Conversion to Islam in the Age of Confessionalization', *Comparative Studies in Society and History* 51:1 (2009), 35–63.

and commemorated with the help of the new epigraphic and iconographic vocabulary. In the case of Slavic-speaking Bosnians, this vocabulary entailed a new form of literacy associated with the Ottoman languages (Arabic, Persian, and Ottoman Turkish) and a new set of cultural representations based on the Qur'an and Islamic tenets, all of which required 'translation' into local argot. The funerary text embodies those processes and reflects the new eschatological sensibilities the Muslims of Bosnia acquired as they departed this life and entrusted their memories to those who survived them.

While the goal of funerary inscriptions was to connect the dead with the living, it was also necessary to relate them to a wider community of believers, their history and eschatology. The dead are thus simultaneously bound by their historical moment, location and condition and absolved from the same. The texts and images on funerary artefacts, despite their condensed quality, allow us a glimpse into different aspects of history thanks to their contemporaneity to and intimacy with everyday life: issues of social norms, literacy, religious sensibilities, modes of remembering. On the other hand, having survived to date, funerary artefacts also allow the dead to be released from history, appearing a-historical and static in the landscape against the realities of chronological change. In a sense, the difficulty of producing a linear narrative based on funerary material goes hand in hand with the problem of engaging this material in historical analysis while continued memories and understanding of past deaths subvert it. This tension ought to be acknowledged. It compels us to approach the funerary artefact, including its text and image, as a reflection of its time as much as our own time. In contrast to museum objects collected and sanitised so as to induce an 'objective' view of the past, funerary artefacts *in situ* provide us with the double bind of analysing and understanding their presence in 'our' living landscape as much as 'theirs'.

In order to avoid closing the gap between the past and the present and to help acknowledge the historical shifts of local funerary culture on its own accord, this study investigates first and foremost gravestones found in rural cemeteries and burial sites away from city centres. Whether still active or long abandoned, they survive to date as the most illustrative and authentic examples of the transition to Islam and the slow remapping of ethno-religious relations and identities within Bosnia. While following in the footsteps of Šefik Bešlagić and Mehmet Mujezinović, two Bosnian scholars who, respectively, compiled meticulous catalogues of mediaeval and Ottoman Islamic gravestones half a century ago, this study has expanded its research scope into uncharted areas and compiled evidence in dozens of locations across Bosnia and Herzegovina, paying special attention to the questions of spatial and iconographic continuity. The photographs taken by Velibor Božović during the field trips became an essential aspect of the study thanks to their ability to document the visual intensity of the gravestones *in situ* and to masterfully capture their ephemeral condition between memory and forgetting. They also persuaded me to move the focus out of a conventional textual approach to include a broader perspective on the tombstone as a commemorative object intended for both historical and enduring cultural recognition.

Four chapters comprise this study. Chapter 1 and Chapter 2 contextualise Bosnian Islamic funerary culture within historical and theoretical premises. Chapter 1, which introduces a broader historical and religious backdrop, discusses different strands of Islamic teachings and the multiple sources of authority through which religious knowledge was channelled within nascent Bosnian Muslim communities and around which funerary sensibilities were formed. It identifies key scriptural tenets, found primarily in the Prophetic traditions, and traces their resonances in prescribed local teachings and recorded practices of Bosnian Muslims. Emphasis is placed on the intersections of local sensibilities and Islamic norms, which resulted in the formation of specifically Bosnian Islamic beliefs and practices surrounding death. Chapter 2 focuses on the relationship between the living and the dead. Memory of the dead is key for this relationship to exist and be expressed. Situating it within memory studies at large, memory of the dead is discussed as being formed and sustained through various embodied practices and personal commemorative acts. External markers of memory – tombstones, graveyards, memorials, sites of petitionary prayers, shrines – represent many different locations around which Bosnian Islamic remembrance of the dead is shaped. The chapter traces a typology of commemorative rituals within Bosnian Islam to achieve a wider understanding of how relationships with the dead endure and transform under different historical, ritual, and spiritual conditions.

Chapter 3 and Chapter 4 turn towards funerary markers and texts. As the visible sites of commemoration, funerary texts exhibit important transformations of old forms under the demand of a new funerary culture. How did the first generations of Muslims of Bosnia and Herzegovina remember their ancestors? What kind of translation of religious cultures did the conversion occasion, and how did it affect the collective memory of their dead ancestors? Were the existing forms abandoned, adopted or adapted/translated so as to reflect the convergence of different eschatological systems? In Chapter 3 historical emphasis is placed on the first two centuries of the Ottoman rule (late fifteenth to late seventeenth century), arguing that there was Ottomanisation but hardly Islamisation of commemorative culture. Chapter 4 moves on to discuss important religious shifts occurring in the eighteenth century that manifested as Islamisation of the funerary text and its standardisation along Ottoman Islamic norms. Thus, in contrast to the fascinating patterns of cultural and spiritual intimacy in the first couple of centuries of Ottoman rule, the funerary text of the eighteenth and nineteenth centuries exhibit a clearer separation between Christian and Islamic modes of commemoration. Epitaphs and scriptural invocations bolster an increasingly differentiated sense of group identity and usher the remembrance of the dead into normative, rather than historical or communal channels.

In arguing for the importance of tombstones in mediating the relationship between the living, the dead and the memory that connects them, the study concentrates on the visibility and impact of certain gravestones but not all. The fragility of cultural heritage is in physical destruction but also neglect, wilful or not. This too must be accepted as an aspect of its complexity. While the choices here may have been compelled circumstantially – decay and erasure, an ongoing danger of minefields, physical inaccessibility – they have also been selected by the logic that not all dead tell the story in an equally persuasive way. During our encounters some dead appeared very much alive, pushing me to think beyond the carved epitaph marking their life. They, and many others, came alive again in Velibor Božović's photographs included in this study, prodding me to think contextually about their situation in the current environment. In fact, in many areas completely cleansed during the war or abandoned in its aftermath, the dead were the only evidence of life. Amidst burned houses and levelled buildings, they were often the only welcoming party. On more than one occasion we had witnessed local Christians care for Muslim graves. Except for a few notable instances, graves and graveyards had not been singled out for destruction, although they often constituted collateral damage.[13] Reverence for the dead ironically defied the political brutality of the war and ethnic cleansing. Travelling to these gravesites has thus prompted a search for a perspective as much as a search for historical meaning. In memory of all these dead of Bosnia and Herzegovina who endured and defied historical challenges to compel our reflection on more than their historical placement, we submit our visual journey blog as a companion to this study.[14]

---

[13] There are notable exceptions to this general observation. In 1992, for example, Serb nationalists burned the Naqshbandi Sufi lodge (*tekke*) in the eastern town in Foča and two adjacent shrines, and broke a number of tombstones in the surrounding cemetery. Similarly, in 1993 the Croats destroyed and vandalised the Sufi shrine at Oglavak and desecrated the remains of a Sufi master. More recently, the same *tekke* in Foča has been repeatedly vandalised, including in 2010 when 20 gravestones in its precincts were toppled and broken. http://www.24sata.info/crna-hronika/28716-foca-oskrnavljeno-mezarje-tekija-i-poruseno-20-nisana.html.

[14] StoneSpeaker blog: www.stonespeaker.ca.

Figure I.1 Old Muslim cemetery in Vidimlije, Glamoč. Photo by Velibor Božović

Chapter 1

Constructing Authenticity, Ensuring Continuity: Death, Dying and Commemoration in Bosnian Islam

> They say, there is nothing but our present life; we live, we die and only Fate destroys us
>
> Q45:24

Critical of the pre-Islamic Arab sense of finitude and blind adherence to empirical reality which denies any possibility of the beyond, the Qur'an configures a new cosmology in which the dead are apportioned eternal life according to powerful ethics of right and wrong heeded or ignored in this world. Muslims, like their fellow monotheists Jews and Christians, hold the belief that a responsible and omnipotent God oversees the cycle of life and death with reason and justice, and that dos and don'ts follow a clear divinely mandated logic which paves the road to eternity. No life or death goes unnoticed. Neither living nor dead are subject to the whims of Fate characteristic of pre-Islamic and indeed most secular cosmologies in which life and death are but random events. Of course, in Bosnia and Herzegovina today, much like in many parts of the contemporary world, a variety of opinions circulate regarding the possibility of life after death. The historical presence of three monotheistic teachings coupled with the legacy of secularism and communism in the modern period have left all Bosnians, including Bosnian Muslims, without a unified view as to what to expect in death or from the dead.

Within such a varied map of beliefs and ideas governing even as small a society as Bosnia and Herzegovina, prospects of reaching a tidy conclusion regarding perceptions of death and beyond appear dim. Yet, if we momentarily step back from the eschatological assurances of monotheism and modernist scepticism to probe the question in a hypothetical way, whom could we ask to speak for the dead and what would they say? Is it possible to give the dead a voice without subjecting them to our hopes and fears regarding death's ultimate otherness? It seems we are inevitably bound in our thinking about death by conceptions articulated through philosophy, religion, mysticism, literature, arts and many other intellectual and creative genres, all intended to assuage the unknown and transcend incertitude. Death in representation is constituted by myriad symbols, activities and beliefs. Across all cultures people have created buffer zones to protect themselves from this final exit but also to ease their way into it. While the paths to the exit may be multiple and multifaceted, we have established sedulous ethical, religious and legal norms to buttress our hope of entering death in a morally dignified way. Most cultures have created nuanced mental systems to protect life from life because they cannot protect it from death. Death, as Jon Davies puts it, is the major legacy the dead give to the living.[1] It is death that makes us more assertive, creative and responsible towards life. In death we observe ourselves and through death we seek and find answers about life. It is hardly possible to imagine the dead recovering the human voice to speak about ordinary matters. From our vantage point, the dead are larger than life, utterly transhistoricised and divested of any banality associated with this world. Their objective presence in death has erased their subjectivity in life. In turn, we humble and humanise ourselves before death and allow our emotions, intellect and eschatological imagination to guide our humanity away from death. In our imperfect efforts to understand death we paradoxically distance ourselves from the dead.

Because of the emphasis on the cultural bearings of death in the life of the living, it is helpful to reach out to the language of the social sciences and humanities, which discuss death as the ultimate rite of passage and the universal phenomenon that mobilises the creative imagination and social practices of a community. More than any other transitional experience, death induces multiple responses in us to universal issues of finitude, loss and rupture. It also inspires our counteractive practices and narratives to help repair the trauma of loss and to ascertain a sense of durability and continuity. Peter Berger observes that 'death radically challenges all socially objectivated definitions of reality', which forces religion to fulfil its main and most trying task of counteracting this challenge of death.[2] As the relationship with and to death is simultaneously formed at the personal and public level, many different modes of expression exist for coping with the event of death and memories of the dead. Crucial to this study is the way individuals and communities anchor and utilise memories of the dead to enrich lived space and lend depth to material culture, specifically tombstones in the context of Bosnian Islam. This chapter examines how Bosnian Muslims treat and remember their dead, setting the stage for a subsequent discussion of memory of the dead in reference to historical space, material culture and funerary text. Of course, memory in space as explored on grave markers, while posited as the key interpretative frame through which this relationship is sustained, is just one of the elements that is relevant in the constitution of memory; other interconnected material and immaterial expressions of memorialisation – funeral rites, prayers, rituals, elegies and stories – are also considered to facilitate a better understanding of

---

[1] J. Davies (ed.), *Ritual and Remembrance: Response to Death in Human Societies* (Sheffield: Sheffield Academic Press, 1994), 25.
[2] P. Berger, *The Sacred Canopy* (New York: Anchor Books, 1967), 43.

how the Muslims of Bosnia and Herzegovina position themselves towards death and the dead with whom they share cultural and physical space.

To that end, a word is due on the relevant sources of knowledge that may have generated and guided Bosnian Muslim eschatological sensibilities. How did new Muslims learn about Islamic ways of dying and caring for the dead? What guided their knowledge, cultural and spiritual needs and the preferred modes of representing death, dying and the afterlife? Juan Campo points out that there is an incongruity between what is prescribed and what is performed in Islamic death culture because of the competing voices of religious authority on the one hand and the immediate circumstances and inherent practices of any given social context on the other.[3] In the exemplary case of Bosnia many authoritative recommendations on how to deal with death had already evolved as culturally multifaceted and historically entrenched before Islam ever came to the region. Thanks to the malleability of local culture, which over time integrated different trends and voices from within and outside of the nascent Islamic community into a meaningful set of symbols and practices, the incongruity and tension have by and large been reconciled despite periodic quests for authenticity by the religious establishment.

Islam in Bosnia and Herzegovina: Sources, Teachings, History

Earlier we discussed the question of conversion and its various socio-historical implications. However, more than social, intellectual or political responsibilities associated with becoming a new Muslim in the provinces of the Ottoman Empire, what is of particular relevance here are shifts in day-to-day attitudes and worldview, especially concerning the changes in death culture and related eschatological sensibilities that accompanied acts of conversion. Inscriptions found on Bosnian semi-urban and rural tombstones reflect highly localised customs and practices, betray a variety of interpretations associated with the process of transition into Islam and speak to a certain lack of uniformity in both ritual and textual capacities. If death is the moment when even the least religious individuals embrace God and orthodoxy in order to secure a safer transit into the afterlife and elicit proper remembrance, it would be easy to imagine that the tombstones of the period should reflect uniformity in 'orthodoxy' and 'orthopraxy'. But they do not. Gravestones contain a variety of textual and iconographic choices, making it impossible to conclude what 'orthodoxy' was, or if it could have been imposed in a steadfast, consistent and firm fashion. Who, then, were the messengers

---

[3] J. Campo, 'Muslim Ways of Death: Between the Prescribed and the Performed', in K. Garces-Foley (ed.), *Death and Religion in a Changing World* (Armonk, NY: M.E. Sharpe, 2003), 147–77.

who taught the ordinary people about Islam and what was the message that ensured the integrity and religious growth of the new Muslim community?

WHITHER ISLAM?

As aforementioned, Islam in Bosnia and Herzegovina and indeed in the Balkans at large was established and shaped by Ottoman Sunni Islam of Hanafi legal orientation. While this gave the Empire its unifying quality, there were other pertinent threads in the Ottoman fabric. The confluence between teachings inherited from earlier Muslim religious authorities as exemplified by Hanafi jurisprudence, the influence of a multi-lingual and multi-religious mosaic across Ottoman lands and neighbours and the Ottoman imperial ambitions which produced an intellectual elite resulted in an Islamic formation that was neither an imported finished product nor an indigenous Ottoman creation. Rather, Ottoman Islam evolved as a hyphenated system and remained a work-in-progress for a long period, before and after Ottoman consolidation in the Balkans. Coupled with the formation of the Ottoman Hanafi corpus of knowledge was the perpetuation of Sufi teachings and orders that added more complexity to the religious imperial landscape and offered alternative loci of spiritual authority and knowledge. Public religiosity integrated these different strands of knowledge across Bosnia and Herzegovina into the deeply seated beliefs and practices of its pre-Ottoman Christian and Slavic heritage.[4] Scholars biased towards (or against, in some cases) the notion of normative religion tend to label this an instance of typical 'Balkan syncretism' entailing an informal blending of disparate religious beliefs and practices or a mere reaction against the new religious system imposed through Ottoman conquest and aggressive proselytising activities.[5]

I prefer not to refer to this process as syncretic. 'Syncretism' suggests a lack of authenticity and a certain level of impurity, lack of awareness and even conscious manipulation of official religious norms. It destabilises the idea of religious truth and theological consistency and sheds doubt on the ethics and loyalty of adherents. Moreover, in the Balkans, the language of syncretism is often evoked in ideological terms, as a way of dismissing the validity of one religion in relation to others, especially in the context of

---

[4] A. Handžić, 'Konfesionalni sastav stanovništva u Bosni i Hercegovini u prvim stoljećima osmanske vladavine [Religious composition of Bosnia's population in the first few centuries of the Ottoman rule]', *POF* 42–3 (1992–93).

[5] 'Bosnia', in G. Agoston and B. Masters (eds), *Encyclopaedia of the Ottoman Empire* (New York: Facts on File, Inc, 2009), 91. For more on syncretism in religion, see E. Maroney, *Religious Syncretism* (London: SCM Press, 2006); A. Leopold and J.S. Jensen, *Syncretism in Religion: A Reader* (New York: Routledge, 2005); and more specifically on the Ottoman case, Gilles Veinstein (ed.), *Syncrétismes et hérésies dans l'Orient Seldjoukide et Ottoman, XIVe–XVIIIe siècle*, (Paris: Peeters, 2005).

political relations between majority and minority groups in the nation state.[6] Islam is thus commonly dismissed as alien to the region and appreciated only if it includes considerable borrowings from Christianity. The fact is, however, that most religions have origins in plural environments that compel them to negotiate different forms of religiosity before defining orthodoxy. None of the three Abrahamic religions that spread through the Balkans had pure origins, nor did they emerge as mere syncretic reactions or contrivances. None were defined just internally but also through and against regional influences, extraneous beliefs, customs and both intracultural and intercultural contact. In all these instances, converts always kept a part of the past heritage alive as they moved into the new system. In Bosnia and Herzegovina, the lack of uniform belief within Christian communities before Ottoman times and the institutionalisation of different Christian denominations under the Ottomans also affected how Islam was spread and shaped. Moreover, as Hamid Algar points out, despite intense intermingling with Christian populations, the Muslims in Bosnia and Herzegovina had little taste for syncretic or antinomian forms of religiosity during the Ottoman centuries.[7]

Of course, the phenomenon of dual religiosity, found primarily in the early periods of the Ottoman rule, is important to acknowledge. Earlier, in the Introduction, it was mentioned that a number of early court documents reveal split religious identities within one and the same family, where one brother or more would remain Christian while one or more became Muslim. Similar situations have been recorded in later periods too: for example, Zirojević cites an 1848 source describing a family in the Sandžak area of Serbia where one brother followed the teachings of Muhammad and did the *namaz* and the other believed in Christ and made the sign of the cross while praying. In another family, all sons were Muslims but the father was a Christian, so whenever the holy Bayram came, the source adds, the brothers went to pray at the mosque while the father went to church.[8] Furthermore, there were notable instances of related but different occurrences of the so-called crypto-Christianity whereby individuals would publicly profess Islam but privately remain loyal to Christian beliefs and practices. Documented across the Balkans, as well as Asia Minor, this dual-religiosity or dual faith (*dvovjerstvo*) persisted, according to some accounts, well into the nineteenth

---

[6] For a good survey of relevant publications that include the Balkans, see A. Konstantakopoulou, 'Religious Syncretism and Deviance in Islamic and Christian Orthodoxies', *Turkish Historical Review* 3 (2012), 91–113. See also M. Balivet, *Romanie Byzantine et Pays de Rum Turc* (Istanbul: Isis, 1994), 190–93; M. Hadžijahić, 'Sinkretistički elementi u islamu u Bosni i Hercegovini [Syncretic elements in Islam in Bosnia and Herzegovina]'. *POF* 28–9 (1978–79).

[7] H. Algar, 'The Hamzeviye: A Deviant Movement in Bosnian Sufism', *Islamic Studies* 36:2 (1997), 243.

[8] O. Zirojević, 'Vjerski sinkretizam: Alahovi hrišćani [Religious syncretism: Allah's Christians]', *Montenegrina* online, http://www.montenegrina.net/pages/pages1/religija/vjerski_sinkretizam_alahovi_hriscani_o_zirojevic.html.

century.[9] From very early on, all official religious establishments – Catholic, Eastern Orthodox and Muslim – denounced such practices and insisted on uprooting them but, evidently, without success, especially in remote areas.

This rich tapestry of religious expression in the Balkans, including Bosnia, suggests that Islamic knowledge spread quite rapidly and extensively, but the trajectories and nature of its dissemination are somewhat unclear. Except for some activities of the religious elite, documents recording charity endowments and the teachings of Sufi orders, it is difficult overall to trace these patterns, especially among new Muslims outside the urban areas. Of course, the presence of the religious courts, hierarchically organised lawmakers, lawgivers and administrators, the rise of Ottoman Islamic city culture and values, and the infiltration of Sufi orders all opened up many channels for transmission of knowledge among new Muslims. The effect, as the evidence suggests, was not necessarily cohesive across Bosnia. The development of religious institutions and the centres of learning such as mosques, colleges (*medrese*), primary schools (*mekteb*) and libraries facilitated the propagation and flourishing of Hanafi Islamic teachings throughout Bosnian cities but with uneven intensity across the countryside. As Abdurrahman Atçıl argues in his study of the formation of the Ottoman learned class, the reign of Mehmet II was marked by an increasing emphasis on a stable and mature imperial enterprise with a fully integrated scholarly elite to operate across the Empire, including the Balkans.[10] In the early periods of Ottoman consolidation in the Balkans, nascent urban centres imported the Ottoman learned elite in the absence of local Muslim institutions. Within a century or two, however, Bosnia, like many other places in the Balkans, developed its own religious powerbase that took part in the formulation and transmission of knowledge.[11] Some members of the local *ulema*, the learned class, functioned at high levels of imperial institutions as well, while others, of lesser stature, operated in towns and rural areas, commonly in association with local mosques and *mektebs*, introducing and safeguarding the basic tenets of Hanafi Islam as they understood it. Within this hierarchical stratification of learning there evolved micro-local centres which were not necessarily congruent with each other. While urban Islamic culture that went hand in hand with the establishment of main centres of learning is relatively accessible now thanks to a web of sources associated with the religious and legal institutions, we know considerably less about rural religious life. In addition to the difficulties associated with tracing the spread of ideas and knowledge, it is also extremely challenging,

---

[9] S. Skendi, 'Crypto-Christians in the Balkan Area under the Ottomans'. *Slavic Review* 26:2 (1967), 227–46.

[10] A. Atçıl, 'The Formation of the Ottoman Learned Class and Legal Scholarship (1300–1600)', (PhD Dissertation, University of Chicago, 2010), chapter 4.

[11] S. Zecevic, 'Islamic Law in the Balkan Peninsula', *The Oxford International Encyclopedia of Legal History* (New York: Oxford University Press, 2009), online version. http://www.oxfordreference.com/view/10.1093/acref/9780195134056.001.0001/acref-9780195134056

as Kafadar points out in a cogent imperial context, to differentiate orthodoxy from heterodoxy because many practical considerations, such as local customs, material concerns and existing traditions inhibited the imposition of imperial religious orthodoxy: 'There was even less room,' Kafadar argues, 'for learned definitions and scholarly rigor among those circles that were physically and/ or socioculturally on the margins of institutionalised Islam, though they may have been more sincere in their faith and more aggressive in its promotion'.[12]

To be sure, some of the process of dissemination of religious knowledge outside of urban centres is also traceable through the stipulations contained in the *waqf* endowments.[13] The mechanism of these endowments is explicit and intricate, identifying different types of qualified labour to be deployed in various corners of Ottoman Bosnia. In reconstructing the web of that labour, one notes that it consists of experts in Qur'anic recitations (*tajwīd*), teachers (*muᶜallim*), muezzins, mosque imams, various categories of Qur'anic readers and commentators (*ḥāfiẓ, muᶜarrif, mufassir*), preachers, experts in *hadith*, general caretakers and also Sufis asked to perform certain rituals. Of course, the endowment predicates such appointments on the existence of relevant institutions – schools, mosques, lodges – or the formation of the same by the *waqf* endowment. Educational aims were deeply intertwined with ritual and didactic prescriptions in an effort to circumvent the community as it came of age.[14] Thus, while we may not be able to gain insight into the workings of all these offices and appointments, we can understand their scope and some relevant preoccupations. Job requirements are often formulaic: the *muezzin* who makes daily calls to prayer from the minaret will have a melodic and pleasant voice; the reciters of the Qur'an will be tactful and committed; all appointees at the mosque and schools will be honourable, kind and devout and well versed in all main aspects of Islamic law and customs. In the trust set up by Sinan Beg in 1582, the following is stipulated regarding a teacher in the primary school (*mekteb*) in the town of Čajniče in eastern Bosnia:

> As for the *mekteb* in the town of Čajniče, an appointment should be made for an honourable, hardworking and trustworthy teacher (*muᶜallim*), who is well versed in Islamic regulations, who is devout, knows well the rules of the proper Qur'anic recitation and understands the text of the noble Qur'an and its superior qualities. Let him raise well the children and teach them the Qur'an and if possible Qur'anic grammar, syntax and vocabulary. In his teachings and instructions he should make no distinctions among pupils and should think of them all as his own children. During the school time he should make no excuses for unjustified absence. He ought to treat the children as a true

---

[12] C. Kafadar, *Between Two Worlds* (Berkeley: University of California Press, 1995), 73.
[13] *Monumenta Turcica: Vakufname iz Bosne i Hercegovine* (Sarajevo: Orijentalni institute, 1985).
[14] A. Handžić, 'O formiranju nekih gradskih naselja u Bosni u XVI stoljeću – uloga države i vakufa [On the development of towns in Bosnia in the 16th c. – the role of the state and religious endowments]', *POF* 25 (1975).

caretaker, a merciful father figure and show daily effort and care for them. For his duties he will receive four *akçe* a day. An appointment should also be made for a deputy teacher who will possess all the aforementioned personal qualities, who will also know the glorious Qur'an, be trustworthy and who will review the material with the children so as to clarify it further. He will receive two *akçe* a day.[15]

From such and similar *waqf* stipulations we can get a glimpse of one venue through which transmission of normative Ottoman Islamic teachings around Bosnia and Herzegovina took place and at least partly understand the inter-connections and mobility of relevant personnel. Furthermore, we also detect the involvement of the social elite in learning and the forms of power generated and reinforced through these processes. A seeming uniformity of religious standards understandably contributes to uniformity in expectations across regional distances and differences but this standard provides no clear sense about religious realities. What role local circumstances play in the reception and implementation of Islamic teachings and how we can trace the transformative dimensions of 'Islamisation' in their cultural and not just textual settings must be considered as we chart the effects and spread of the new dominant religious culture across Bosnia and Herzegovina.

Sufism and Sufi Practices Across Bosnia and Herzegovina

As religious scholars proliferated Hanafi tenets across Bosnian cities, towns and villages, Sufi teachings too gained a prominent role in the spread and consolidation of Islam. By the time of the Ottoman conquest of the region, Sufi ideas embedded in the workings of the mystical orders, *tariqas*, had become a powerful instrument of religious expansion across the Islamic world. Ritually malleable and doctrinally meticulous, Sufi orders created important new space for complementary and figurative meanings and even an alternative route to transcendental truth. God could be known more directly, through devotion and spiritual discipline. He could be recalled in ritual evocations of *dhikr* (remembrance of God) and approached with the help of intermediaries, primarily spiritual masters, past and present, around whom Sufi orders were formed and through whom spiritual authority was transmitted. As it identified and consolidated esoteric meanings of the divine message and legal and theological injunctions of ethical and social order, Sufism generated and encouraged diversity in spiritual and ritual expressions under the banner of God's absolute unity. This does not mean that the Sufis offered an entirely different form of religiosity or opposed non-Sufi forms of Islam. Rather, Sufism expanded normative teachings into the realm of personal piety, at times augmenting them and at others unsettling them, while often relying

---

[15] *Vakufname iz Bosne i Hercegovine*, 203.

on regional practices to make the spiritual experience more meaningful for a wide spectrum of followers.

Over time, then, what had begun as a marginalised and isolated quest for a more personal relationship with God evolved, over several centuries, into a widespread social and spiritual force attracting followers from all walks of life and compassing a variety of vernacular practices to meet the devotional needs of the *umma*. The spectrum of Sufi styles encompassed antinomian and puritan expressions, from politically engaged to pacifist; bold and brazen to reclusive and eremitic; from ritually silent and austere to expressive and ostentatious; from Sunni to Shi'i; from elitist to popular; from artistic and stylised to plain and simple. All the while, it showed great vitality in adapting to new circumstances by both adjusting to and absorbing existing types of religious expression so as to bring God closer to the human condition and improve everyday social relations as part of its pietistic mandate.

In Bosnia and Herzegovina, Sufi orders arrived in several waves and left different imprints. Their presence was visible and significant – Evliya Çelebi (d. 1682) mentions 47 Sufi lodges only in Sarajevo – although at times controversial, as it impacted upon both popular religiosity and intellectual life of Bosnian Muslims. There are speculations that Sufism had penetrated the Balkan Peninsula long before the Ottoman conquest, but the sources for such theories are scarce.[16] In the several waves of Ottoman military advances, proto-Sufi groups such as the *akhis/ahis* and *futuwwas/fütüvvet* that accompanied the Ottoman armies spread the ethics of loyalty and commitment to a spiritual leader, missionary zeal and charitable work among the local population. They also infiltrated and began to Islamise extant systems of belief and practice, facilitating conversion to Islam and the dissemination of its teachings. Among the earliest recorded established Sufi groups was the Bektashi order. Originally traced to the teachings of Hajji Bektash, a semi-legendary Sufi saint of thirteenth-century Anatolia, it mainly developed in association with the Ottoman Janissary corps. In Bosnia the Bektashi order had a limited appeal, spreading initially through the activities of two associated dervishes, Ayni Dede and Shamsi Dede, who accompanied Sultan Mehmet II on his military expeditions into the region. It is believed that they settled in central Bosnia, although earlier narrative accounts have it that the teaching may have been first introduced in the thirteenth century by the legendary Sarı Saltık, the

---

[16] H.T. Norris, *Islam in the Balkans* (Columbia, SC: University of South Carolina Press, 1993), 146–55. Other important overviews on the spread of Sufism in Bosnia and Herzegovina include Dž. Ćehajić, *Derviški redovi u jugoslovenskim zemljama* [Sufi orders in Yugoslav lands] (Sarajevo: Svjetlost, 1986); H. Abiva, 'Survey of Sufi Orders in the Balkans', http://bektashiorder.com/sufism-in-the-balkans-1; Dž. Ćehajić, 'Društveno-politički, religiozni, književni i drugi aspekti derviških redova u jugoslavenskim zemljama [Social, political, religious, literary and other aspects of the dervish orders in Yugoslav lands]', *POF* 34 (1984); J.M. Hazen, 'Contemporary Bosnian Sufism: Bridging the East and West', (MA Thesis, Washington DC: American University, 2008), http://eprints.soas.ac.uk/13816/1/Hazen_3369.pdf.

Figure 1.1 Tombstones of Ayni Dede and Shamsi Dede in Sarajevo.
Photo by Velibor Božović

elusive saint hero who had roamed the Balkans and Eastern lands, becoming popular for thaumaturgic, ascetic and shamanistic skills. One of his coffins – and he is believed to have been buried in seven – is allegedly located in the Blagaj *tekke*, the Sufi lodge south of Mostar built in the fifteenth century by the Bektashis. Although popular for their heroic spirit, elaborate oral epic traditions and quite heterodox rituals that integrated Shi'i and Christian elements, the Bektashis never gained as strong an acceptance in Bosnia as they did in Albania. There they carried on through attachments to both rural population and influential landlords, standing in tense relations with the increasingly Sunni configuration of the Ottoman establishment.[17]

Over time, many different orders penetrated into Bosnia: the Hamzevi order preached messianic and highly esoteric hermeneutics of the divine message, having spread across the Middle East and Ottoman Empire into Bosnia where it found popularity primarily in its northern and eastern areas.[18] The order's idiosyncratic and openly subversive teaching challenged many basic premises of the Islamic law, resulting in an alienation and demonisation of the order which culminated in the execution of the order's spiritual leader, Bosnian Hamza Bali (Hamza Orlović) in Istanbul in 1573.[19] A century later, after the execution of another of its leaders, Beshir Aga, the order toned down certain controversial teachings and practices, and declared it was moving closer to Hanafi Islam, attracting some of the highest officials of the Ottoman court and learned elite for its increased adherence to the teachings of the great Sufi master, Ibn ʿArabī.[20] Because of their unconventional and controversial teachings and practices, the influence of Bektashis and Hamzevis declined in Bosnia as more mainstream orders began to pervade its spiritual life. Operating in other parts of the Empire as well, many such orders received tacit acceptance from the Ottoman religious establishment and succeeded in permeating both urban and rural areas of Bosnia from the fifteenth century onward while promoting a more normative style of spiritual edification.

Among the most important was the Naqshbandi order that spread steadily through towns and villages in the fifteenth century. Their first *tekke* was

---

[17] H.T. Norris, *Islam in the Balkans*, 89–99.
[18] I. Mehinagić, 'Četiri neobjavljena izvora o Hamzevijama iz sredine XVI vijeka [Four unpublished sources on the Hamzevis from the 16th c.]', *POF* 18–19 (1968–69), 218–66; M. Hadžijahić, 'Tekija kraj Zvornika – postojbina bosanskih hamzevija [Sufi lodge near Zvornik – the residence of Bosnian Hamzevis]', *POF* 10–11 (1960–61); S. Ilić, 'Hamzevijska i hurufijska jeres u Bosni kao reakcija na političku krizu Osmanske Imperije u drugoj polovini 16. vijeka [The heresy of Hamzevi and Hurufi orders in Bosnia as a reaction to the political crisis of the Ottoman Empire in the second half of the 16th c.]', *POF* 41 (1991).
[19] Y. Toussilis in *Sufism and the Way of Blame: Hidden Sources of a Sacred Psychology* (Wheaton, IL: Quest Books, 2010), 111, wrongfully cites the year of Hamza Bali's execution as 1562. The year was 1573 – see I. Mehinagić, 'Četiri neobjavljena izvora', 218; also Dž. Ćehajić, 'Društveno-politički, religiozni, književni i drugi aspekti derviških redova u jugoslavenskim zemljama [Social, political, religious, literary and other aspects of the dervish orders in Yugoslav lands]', *POF* 34 (1984), 95.
[20] Y. Toussilis, *Sufism and the Way of Blame*, 112.

established in Sarajevo around the time the order spread into Bosnia through the work and preaching of Mulla Abdullah Ilahi (d. 1491), the founder of the Turkish branch. Another Naqshbandi *tekke* in Sarajevo was to be erected in the mid-nineteenth century, but before that, one had been founded in the late eighteenth century in central Bosnia and, somewhat later in the same century, another one in Oglavak, also in central Bosnia. Although the order did not enjoy the same level of popularity and influence over Bosnian Islam in historical periods, it was especially strengthened in the nineteenth century under the spiritual leadership of Sirri Baba (d. 1847), the founder of the Oglavak *tekke*. Among his achievements he counted the effective promulgation of the ethos of piety beyond the Sufi community and in turn infused Sufi spiritual expressions with local cultural and melodic sensibilities. He left an opus of devotional songs, *ilāhiyāt*, which he composed in local Slavic and Turkish languages. They have remained widely popular across Bosnia to date.[21]

In the course of the sixteenth century the Khalwati/Halveti order spread across Bosnia, very much in association with the dominant religious class. Emphasising retreat and isolation (*khalwa* in Arabic), it galvanised personal awareness of God as a complement rather than oppositional force to normative religious authorities. To that end, Ćehajić notes that their main initial goal and success was to curb the spread of the heterodox groups rather than appease the local elite, although *waqf* records show that at least in one case the Halvetis were supported by one of the most influential Bosnian governors of all times, Gazi Husrev Beg (d. 1541), who specifies that the main purpose of the lodge established close to his mosque is for

> Righteous masters who are well known for the honour and piety typical of true mystics, who are dressed in the robe of God-fear and God-reverence, who are steadfast in the *shari'a*, follow the *tariqa* of the previous sheikhs, emulate the saints, always respect the law, are obedient, pray among all Muslims, fast, perform *dhikr*, control their lower ego and respect the ways of all devout and learned people who have travelled the right path. Let one of the best disciples of the Halveti order be appointed at this *tekke*, as he is honourable, devout and God fearing.[22]

While this is clearly a highly favourable endorsement intended to associate Sufi teachings and behaviour with mainstream Sunni Islam, there is in fact a suggestion that such alliances were not always as simple. Ćehajić thus quotes the case of the nineteenth Halveti sheikh of Blagaj *tekke* in Herzegovina who was noted for spying against the local Herzegovinian aristocracy suspected by the authorities to be moving towards greater independence.[23]

---

[21] For a useful survey on Bosnian Naqshbandis see H. Algar, 'Some Notes on the Naqshbandi Tariqat in Bosnia', *Die Welt des Islams*, 13: 3–4 (1971), 168–203.

[22] *Vakufname iz Bosne i Hercegovine*, 55.

[23] Dž. Ćehajić, 'Društveno-politički, religiozni, književni i drugi aspekti derviških redova u jugoslavenskim zemljama', 97.

In the seventeenth century the Qadiri order entered Bosnia and Herzegovina and became influential in the religious life of the region. The order emphasised struggle against the ego with the help of the religious laws and through saintly guidance. Hadži Sinanova Tekija (Hajji Sinan *tekke*) in Sarajevo is the most enduring of legacy of the Qadiri religious architecture. Its most acclaimed disciple, Hasan Kaimi (d. 1691), the great poet and spiritual master, was also remembered for his involvement in political/economic affairs; he participated in deadly protests against the wealthy merchants who withheld selling their goods in the hope of higher prices, as a result of which the local judge and his deputy were killed. In the aftermath, Kaimi was charged with civil disobedience and exiled to Zvornik in eastern Bosnia, where he lived the rest of his days as a spiritual master and poet. As Ćehajić points out, although his reputation exalted him into a reformer and fighter for social justice, he was first and foremost interested in a stricter observance of the Islamic law which the government and the merchants in Sarajevo had not abided by.[24] Kaimi left two important anthologies, *divans*, of devotional poetry in Ottoman Turkish and composed a number of religious odes in Alhamiado, a Bosnian Slavic language in Arabic script. Another Qadiri disciple of great relevance for this study is Mehmed Meyli al-Korani, the renowned poet and calligrapher of the eighteenth century who is credited with the composition of some 50 poignant epitaphs on some of the finest Islamic tombstones in Bosnia.

In contrast to the controversial Hamzevi and Bektashi orders and to an extent the Rifa'i that found wide acceptance for miracle working and healing practices in rural Bosnia, the Naqshbandi, Halveti, Qadiri and especially Rumi-inspired Mevlevi that had spread in the seventeenth century all attached themselves to the educated elite and found support in the establishment. Their status within Bosnia and the Empire at large, however, was never fully free of tension. Over time, several orders and the offshoots of the original ones faded away from the spiritual life of the region, in large because their support diminished or collapsed under the crush of religious traditionalists who commonly held anti-Sufi sentiments. In addition to the aforementioned example of the Hamzevis suffering the wrath of antagonism in the sixteenth century by the Sultan himself, the seventeenth century witnessed more endemic anti-Sufi activities instigated by the puritan Kadizadeler movement, discussed again in Chapter 4, which aggressively defended Sunni Islam against any practices that stood outside their narrowly defined Sunni orthodoxy. Sufis were targeted as the worst manifestation of such deviancies and heresies.[25] In the aftermath of the Kadizadeler's interventions, many orders were required to regroup and position themselves more closely to

---

[24] Dž. Ćehajić, *Derviški redovi u jugoslovenskim zemljama* [Sufi orders in Yugoslav lands] (Sarajevo: Orijentalni Institute, 1986), 25.
[25] S. Shaw, *History of the Ottoman Empire and Modern Turkey* (Cambridge: Cambridge University Press, 1976), 1:206–8.

mainstream institutions, although the opposite is also true as in the case of the Bektashis who, paradoxically, gained more popular support in the southern part of the Balkans in response to Kadizadeler's intolerance.[26]

In post-Ottoman times, the activities of most Sufi orders were greatly affected by the rise of nation states, a general hostility towards the Muslim population and an increased secularisation of the region. Although the Austro-Hungarian Empire that replaced the Ottomans in Bosnia after 1878 did not pursue any active policy directed against Sufi orders, Sufi life did not flourish. In the aftermath of two world wars and the establishment of Titoist Yugoslavia, the orders came under heavy political scrutiny. In 1952, the government closed the *tekkes* in an attempt to centralise Islamic life under the auspices of the government-sanctioned Islamic Community, *Islamska Zajednica*. In the eyes of the Islamic religious leadership, the Sufis stood for superstition and regress. Needless to say, they were also feared as a source of potential rivalry and spiritual decentralisation when the Islamic clerics of Yugoslavia were not in a position to risk such developments. Although officially promulgated, the ban of the *tekkes* only partly impeded the Sufi way of life, as many activities continued in different forms, semi-officially as well as underground. In the 1970s, the Sufis organised their activities into an Association (ZIDRA) intended to revitalise internal affairs but also to re-activate connections with Sufis elsewhere. Between 1992 and 1995, targeted like all other Bosnian Muslims during the campaigns of ethnic cleansing, many Sufis joined resistance against deportation and eradication and participated in social services wherever possible. In the aftermath of the war, Sufi orders rose again to prominence in the religious tapestry of post-war Bosnian Islam, although the relationship with the institutionalised Islamic clergy remains uneasy.[27] However, as Catherina Raudvere suggests, more than the Ottoman legacy, the Sufi orders today face the challenge of global mobility of their membership, the influences of movements abroad, more general shifts in gender relations within the Islamic establishment and a growing attention by otherwise non-practising Muslims, all of which lead to the refashioning of traditional forms of authority and activity.[28]

---

[26] H. Abiva, 'A Survey of Sufism in the Balkans', http://bektashiorder.com/sufism-in-the-balkans-3.

[27] For an insightful analysis of contemporary developments see J.M. Hazen, 'Contemporary Bosnian Sufism', 93–101.

[28] C. Raudvere, 'Claiming Heritage, Renewing Authority: Sufi-oriented activities in post-Yugoslav Bosnia-Herzegovina', *European Journal of Turkish Studies* 13 (2011); also her more general study on the changes in female authority, 'Textual and Ritual Command: Muslim Women as Keepers and Transmitters of Interpretive Domains in Contemporary Bosnia and Herzegovina', in M. Bano and H. Kalmbach (eds), *Women, Leadership and Mosques* (Leiden: Koninklijke Brill NV, 2012).

Sufi Teachings in Non-Sufi Practices

The aforementioned orders that spread through Ottoman Bosnia possessed important internal differences, rendering them separate spiritual centres of belief and action, but they also melded some important unifying features that helped them leave an enduring imprint on religious life outside Sufi circles. To begin with, Sufi emphasis on the absolute unity of God – *tawhīd* – not as an abstract theological concept but as a living reality assumes that the indivisible oneness of God is exemplified in its multiple historical forms. Human beings, as God's representatives on earth, are outward aspects of that multiplicity but they also carry within themselves His quintessential unity. As representations of the divine essence their mandate is to remember, without a slip of forgetfulness, the primordial reality of oneness. Hence the need for ritual remembrance, *dhikr*, and derivative acts of remembrance in everyday thought and action. As the Hamzevi and Bektashi cases demonstrate, some mystics paid little attention to religious laws, considering them as only rudimentary methods of remembering God, to be re-interpreted and re-cast when one is on the path to God in accordance with the Sufi quest.

This quest requires the presence of a mentor. Drawn along the Qura'nic narrative of Khidr, the mysterious guide who led Moses through the test of commitment when the latter appeared confused, the idea of spiritual mentorship is divinely mandated to prevent misperceptions or a sense of loss and confusion in the world of transient forms. If Moses, the prophet of God, had trouble navigating through this world of half-truths to the point that God gifted him with a guide, then all initiates must rely on someone who has reached high spiritual stations to aide them as they delve into hidden truths. Notably, trust in the master (*shaykh, pir*) must be unequivocal. The masters are, after all, truer in their knowledge than average people, including the religious elite who may be well acquainted with the word of God, but not with God Himself. In His grace, God befriends those who search for him selflessly in every action and every thought, those who do not succumb to the duality inherent in everyday existence and reinforced by human forgetfulness. These special individuals, the *awliya/evliya* or saints, achieve such levels of intimacy with God that they can facilitate, in life and death, the spiritual progression of others with surety and competence.

The greatest guide of all (and archetype of the rest) is the Prophet Muhammad. In most Sufi ruminations he stands as the primordial wayfarer who was able to attain, beyond the achievements of previous prophets, the mysteries of divine knowledge. Not only did he deliver the Word, he also transcended it: his beatific vision, achieved on God's invitation to visit Him at the Highest Abode as scripturally enunciated in the story of Mi'raj (Q17:1), is the apex of the spiritual quest. In the Qur'anic and Sufi teachings, Muhammad is the only prophet who was graced with that gift. From its beginnings, the

Sufi tradition reflected on this special status of Prophet Muhammad in the cosmological order. Muslims in general venerate Muhammad as the final prophet whose mission was to deliver the last and complete message of divine guidance. For the Sufis, he is also the archetypal Sufi, the ultimate exemplar whose insight into divine realities posits him as equally present in the transcendental realm and this world. He is thus the perfect human being, *al-insān al-kāmil*, to be celebrated, emulated and cherished through pure devotion and reverence. Importantly, many members of the Prophet's family, especially his son-in-law Ali, his daughter Fatima and other members of the immediate family, enjoy reverence by the Sufis, which often engenders misguided perceptions of the orders as denominationally Shi'i. The Bektashis are one such order, which, in the increasingly Sunni solidification of the Ottoman Empire, generated repeated tensions and conflicts, especially in light of the imperial rivalry between the Sunni Ottoman and Shi'i Safavid dynasties.

Sufi teachings were disseminated in different forms and genres of mystical expression. Oral tradition infused with apocryphal stories about early masters and saints travelled with the Sufis across the Islamic world and beyond, expanding and changing so as to blend in with and appeal to regional sensibilities. These were live and fluid texts, possessing stable salvific cores intimating divine rewards for heroic and selfless acts. Many great heroes and saints were celebrated through such oral narratives, often subsuming the stories of local heroes, as was the case with aforementioned Sarı Saltık. In poetry, Sufi speakers of Arabic, Persian, Turkish, Urdu and other languages skilfully blended secular themes of love, intoxication, devotion, remembrance and other common tropes to create sacred love poetry that was neither spotlessly spiritual nor wantonly mundane, but contained familiar elements inspired by universal human emotions and their ethos and pathos, across cultural boundaries. These narrative permutations lent Sufis a stronger and more organic powerbase wherever they moved. In written tradition, specifically prose, Sufi literature expanded in varied disciplinary directions: philosophical, exegetical, theological and even legal. Some of the writings were abstruse, inaccessible and complex enough to rival the most sophisticated of intellectual undertakings. In fact, many great Sufi masters were exactly that – astute commentators of theosophy, Qur'anic exegesis, authors on cosmology, ethics, theories of the soul and other complex subjects.[29] Other teachings were simple and transparent, delivered in short and didactic narratives, parables, fables and folk expressions. Sufi poetry inspired by the rich poetic traditions of Arabic and Persian culture infused local poetic sensibilities with a new spiritual force and became a ready medium for many Sufis to express their innermost thoughts and experiences to which the legacy of the great poets such as Rumi, Hafez, Ibn al-Farid, Yunus Emre, al-Hallaj and others testifies.

---

[29] R. Hafizović, 'A Bosnian Commentator on the *Fusus al-hikam*', *Journal of the Muhyiddin Ibn ʿArabi Society* 47 (2010).

In Ottoman Bosnia, Sufi teachings found both a receptive audience and creative ground. Bosnian Sufis became well acquainted with the currents in Persian, Arabic and Turkish mystical verse and thought, as their polyglot contributions evidence. From very early on, they engaged in the mystical discourse and literary expressions, usually reflecting their order's specific teachings but also participating in the shared idiom and themes. Acquainted with the works of great Sufi masters from around the Muslim world, Bosnian Sufis disseminated that heritage in meetings, learning circles, home workshops, *tekkes* and other private and public venues.[30] Their work, like the Sufi works elsewhere, were saturated with themes of sacred love, allegories of life and death, ethical issues, metaphors expressing our relationship with the world and God, and many other themes that depict rich and ephemeral connections between this and divine realms of existence. Exemplary cases include Fevzi of Mostar (d. 1747) whose *Bulbulistan* is a comprehensive, didactic medley of poetry and prose animated by the rich heritage of Persian poetry and composed in Persian, but with a distinct touch by this Bosnian author. There was also Ahmed Sudi Bosnevi (d. 1579), another authority on the Persian mystical verse of Hafez, Rumi and Saadi, who is remembered as a superb commentator and interpreter of great Persian works into Turkish, exhibiting full mastery of the linguistic culture that produced such complex and refined spiritual poetry. Abd al-Rahman Sirri (d. 1847) wrote in Turkish and Bosnian, promulgating the Naqshbandi emphasis on strong ethics, austere lifestyle and vigilant self-reflections through daily meditation. His poems in Bosnian, while didactically addressed to the Sufi wayfarers, also have a proselytising tone for potential initiates into the Sufi path and many words of advice about the importance of the Qur'an, so they became widely recited and sung outside Sufi circles.[31] Hasan Kaimi (d. 1691), remembered for his heroic protest against the manipulations of the local commercial elite for which he was exiled from Sarajevo, authored numerous mystical poems that resonate with the teachings of Ibn ʿArabī. In Kaimi's rendering, truth is synonymous with God and language must be transcended if one is to know God. God is thus unspoken, everything that is not God is a passing reality and must therefore be negated: 'Know Truth by means of Truth, for only Truth can know Itself,' wrote Kaimi.[32] Ibn ʿArabī, influential that he was across Sufi intellectual history, left a mark on another acclaimed Bosnian mystic of the late sixteenth century, Mulhid Vahdeti. While there has been some confusion as into which order Vahdeti may have been initiated, it is commonly accepted that he adhered to certain monistic notions characteristic of Bektashi,

---

[30] M. Handžić, *Književni rad bosansko-hercegovačkih muslimana* [Literature of the Muslims of Bosnia and Herzegovina] (Sarajevo: Državna štamparija, 1934).

[31] Š. Sikirić, 'Pobožne pjesme (ilahije) šejh Abdurrahmana Sirrije [Devotional songs of sheikh Abd al-Rahman Sirri]', *Glasnik Islamske Vjerske Zajednice* 9: 11–12 (1941), 362–73.

[32] Cited in Dž. Ćehajić, 'Društveno-politički, religiozni, književni i drugi aspekti derviških redova', 106.

Hamzevi and Hurufi orders. His anthology abounds with ecstatic and subtle meditations on the unity of creation and being and evokes common metaphors of 'the drop that becomes the sea' to intimate the sense of metaphysical union that Sufi initiates can have in their quest for God. The message that we all participate in being with God, that we must look into the mirror if we wish to see God, elevates the ontological status of human beings in a way that most religious establishments would scornfully reject as blasphemous and indeed Vahdeti refers to the proponents of the mainstream religious establishment as 'the villains of their times'.[33]

The last but not the least unifying quality of the Sufi orders was a charitable presence in the broader community. 'The faithful is the mirror of the faithful' is the Prophetic dictum that inspired practical Sufi involvement with the community at large,[34] especially by assisting the poor, the disadvantaged, travellers, orphans and anyone else in need of assistance. The *tekkes* usually included spare rooms to accommodate wandering dervishes and other travellers and public kitchens were set up to meet the demands of the poor, all usually funded from a *waqf* endowment, as recorded for a number of *tekkes* in Bosnia.[35] Thus, the fifteenth-century kitchen of the Skender Pasha *tekke* founded in Sarajevo was required through its *waqf* foundation to bake *fodul* bread loaves every day to serve to its visitors and on the eve of every Friday to cook a rice pilaf and *zerde*, a rice dish sweetened with honey, almonds and cinnamon, to be distributed among all the lodgers, the employees at the endowment fund, the travellers, the poor and the disabled.[36] Other *tekkes* across Bosnia performed similar roles in their own communities, some including bakeries that catered for the community on a daily basis, others on special days and yet others served the people by combining regular day work with night shifts.[37] All this testifies to the commitment Sufi orders had to charitable work regardless of their location or orientation, because the idea of food for the soul was countenanced alongside practical social realities. The human requirement of material nourishment was satisfied by the Sufis in the form of sustenance, healing and general hospitality.

Many aspects of Bosnian Islam contain Sufi resonances. Partly for historical factors involving popular religiosity and intimacy with Christian practices and partly because of the Sufi tendency to absorb eclectic cultural material and re-cast it through Islamic spirituality, different spheres of cultural and

---

[33] H. Abiva, 'The Poems of Mulhid Vahdeti', http://bektashiorder.com/poems-of-mulhid-vadeti.

[34] A. Schimmel, *Mystical Dimensions of Islam* (Chapel Hill: The University of North Carolina Press, 1975), 228.

[35] A. Handžić, 'O ulozi derviša u formiranju gradskih naselja u Bosni u XV stoljeću [The role of dervishes in the formation of towns in Bosnia in the 15th c.]', *POF* 31 (1981).

[36] Dž. Ćehajić, 'Društveno-politički, religiozni, književni i drugi aspekti derviških redova', 98.

[37] Dž. Ćehajić, 'Društveno-politički, religiozni, književni i drugi aspekti derviških redova', 99.

Figure 1.2 Muslim cemetery in Travnik.
Photo by Velibor Božović

religious expressions in Bosnia exhibit Sufi influences. When it comes to death culture, although it is exceedingly difficult to separate Islam's different strands, it is important to acknowledge that funerary customs bear strong marks of both Sufi and mainstream Sunni teachings and practices, in addition to elements derived from the local social context. In what follows we will explore the beliefs and rituals which have proven to be especially durable and meaningful as indicators of interaction between normative and non-normative, religious and secular, spiritual and material, formal and poetic, comforting and distressing and other responses to death in Bosnian Islamic culture.

Death and Dying in Islam: General Remarks

Common Bosnian Muslim views and beliefs about death are predictably eclectic considering the diverse means employed to spread Islam across the region. Local customs carried over from pre-Ottoman times and still practised by both Bosnian Muslims and Christians are a source of additional complexity. Thus, the culture of death that crystallised within Bosnian Islam drew on customs from imperial and local contexts, reflecting not only the Islamic ethos, but also a connection to a particular environment and its resources.

In fact, this weaving of multiple ideas and practices characterises the development of most religious death culture. In his detailed study on death rites in the nascent Arabo-Islamic community, Leor Halevi argues that the process of Islamisation of such rituals was not only slow but also multidirectional, involving emulation as well as modification of Christian, Jewish, Zoroastrian and other cultural practices active in the same space. The pressing question for early Muslims, as Halevi postulates, was not related to eschatological issues alone, since the belief in a scripturally defined afterlife was comprehensively articulated in the Qur'an from the very beginning; rather, the pressing question was how to translate burial practices that had existed before Islam among the Arabs alongside those common to non-Muslims into uniquely Islamic forms. In this process, divergent views appeared along regional, theological and legal lines, reflected myriad reactions against existing practices such as the washing of the corpse, gender participation, burial dispositions, tombstone inscriptions, expressions of mourning and bereavement and others. Halevi describes early Islamic funerary laws as partly 'adaptive' and partly 'reactive', having risen 'in opposition to underlying practices' rather than in a mental vacuum.[38] In that sense, Islamic customs surrounding death reflect a society as it comes of age and as it exteriorises, through rituals as well as art and architecture, new and more subtle religious sensibilities towards the deceased and navigates a broader religious environment. An earlier and probably most comprehensive study on the subject goes even further as it locates the

---

[38] L. Halevi, *Muhammad's Grave* (New York: Columbia University Press, 2007), 10–11.

Qur'anic attitude towards death both in Muhammad's own evolving interest in the subject of death, which explains the subject's increasing presence in the Medinan period, and in parallel Syriac old Semitic attitudes on life and death, which became reworked in an original and expansive fashion in the Qur'an. In other words, while Qur'anic death is not unrelated to the broader beliefs and practices of the region, it should be appreciated for its own distinctive reflections.[39] In a similar vein but more focused on contemporary practices, Juan Campo discusses the discord between prescribed rules governing the Islamic way of dying and the performed practices that are often driven by immediate conditions and experiences that may stand in opposition to what is prescribed. Emerging thus 'in a conjunctive discursive space, a space infused with incongruity', Campo argues, Islamic beliefs and practices related to death point to an 'interplay of the prescribed, formal requirements with the specificities and arbitrariness of history, culture, imagination and experience'.[40] We can observe similar patterns in Bosnia and elsewhere in the Balkans, though a broader comparative perspective on death rites in the Ottoman Balkans and elsewhere in the Islamic world is yet to be undertaken.

Early on, classical Muslim scholars developed a set of injunctions to deal with death, dying and memory of the dead in response to internal and external norms. As a subject of divine discourse, death is heavily infused with apocalyptic imagery. Scripture abounds with eschatological references to eternal reward and punishment. The Qur'an explains death first and foremost as the beginning of eternal life and not as an existential terminus. If anything, life and death are part of one and the same continuum, broken apart by human perception rather than reality. Death brings about binary divine justice expressed in either a punitive or rewarding fashion, with nothing in between. Scripture pays meagre heed to death as the biological end of this life. Rather, it focuses on the issue of continuity of life in another form, which is made possible by the crossing of a boundary – *barzakh* – after the interment of the body. *Barzakh* is a cryptic Qur'anic term, explained as a fixed, non-porous divide, akin to a strip of land that separates sweet and salt waters and prevents them from mingling (Q25:53; 55:20), to be dismantled only at the Day of Judgement. [41] Once they cross to the other side of the *barzakh*, the dead can no longer return to rectify their predicament by performing good deeds (Q23:99–100), nor can they maintain sensorial relations with the living (Q35:22). Even the martyrs who do not really die are placed beyond our sensory reach (Q2:154; 3:169) while God provides for them (Q3:170–71). The quality

---

[39] T. O'Shaughnessy, *Muhammad's Thoughts on Death: A Thematic Study of the Qur'anic Data* (Leiden: E.J. Brill, 1969), 80–83.

[40] J. Campo, 'Muslim Ways of Death: Between the Prescribed and the Performed', in K. Garces-Foley (ed.), *Death and Religion in a Changing World* (Armonk, NY: M.E. Sharpe, 2003), 149.

[41] For more on *barzakh* in the context of Qur'anic death see L. Halevi, *Muhammad's Grave*, 202–7.

of the *barzakh* is somewhat ambiguous: neither explicitly defined as space nor time, the *barzakh* severs the cord and inaugurates afterlife. Spatially, however, the Prophetic tradition clarifies that the grave (*qabr*) is the first station of the afterlife.[42] It therefore coincides with the *barzakh* in many significant but not unambiguous ways. As a result, medieval Islamic theological writings about afterlife resorted to using the *barzakh* synonymously with the grave, as a 'zone' transcending the grave's primary spatial connotation so as to incorporate those Muslims whose corpses were not laid into the grave for some reason but who nevertheless must undergo the same fate as buried bodies.[43] Because death occurs at a time and place determined only by God – 'wherever you are, death will find you out' (Q4:78) – religious scholars found it important to emphasise that all dead, regardless of the fate of their bodies, were all set on the same trajectory thanks to the correlation of the *barzakh* with the grave. No deceased Muslim is granted a reprieve from the transactions of the afterlife.

The Qur'an recognises that for human beings the moment of death is never easy. The soul, it informs us, will leap from the throat (Q56:83) and will be taken away by the angel of death (*malak al-mawt*) and delivered to God (Q32:11). This view of death as the separation of the soul from the body was upheld previously by the Arabs of the pre-Islamic times.[44] According to classical Islamic interpretations, this act causes agony to those who live a godless existence and the resultant misery will be apparent to anyone who observes such brutal suffering of an unbelieving soul which will be scorched by the Fire (Q56:94). In contrast, a devout and virtuous soul shall slip out gently. Such souls will be welcomed to Paradise upon their separation from the body (Q56:89; 16:32). Notably, the condition of death following the soul's detachment has little narrative presence in the Qur'an. Until the Day of Reckoning, when the soul is to be reunited with the body for the purposes of resurrection and judgement (Q6:36), the Qur'an leaves us with a narrative vacuum, or interruption, until eternity sets in. Instead, the main emphasis is placed on God's power to later return the dead to life – mainly after the Day of Judgement but in some cases in this world as well (Q2:55–6; 3:49). This power is attributed to the fact that He is the only one among the living who never dies (Q25:58).

Over the centuries and with the help of the Prophetic *hadith* where death and burial-related traditions are compiled under the category of 'funeral compendium' (*kitāb al-janā'iz*), Islamic scholars elaborated the course of post-burial events, supplementing the scriptural gaps and choreographing a post-mortem itinerary for the soul and its abandoned body until their

---

[42] Ibn Majah, *Sunan* 37:4408. Online: http://sunnah.com/urn/1293700.
[43] R. Eklund, *Life between Death and Resurrection according to Islam* (Uppsala, Almqvist & Iksells, 1941), 55.
[44] J. Waardenburg, 'Death and the Dead', in J.D. McAuliffe (ed.), *Encyclopaedia of the Qur'ān* (Leiden: Brill, 2001), 1: 507.

salvific reunion. For Islamic theologians, whose main goal was to elucidate the nature of God, it was important to detail His behaviour towards the dead as an affirmation of His consistency and justice, even when God Himself left things unsaid.[45] For legal scholars, on the other hand, it was the proper social behaviour towards the dead, including funerary rituals, which required explication and specification. Finally, in the Muslim necrological imagination, death and its different aspects led to a proliferation of both descriptive and didactic eschatological literature that, combining canonical and popular attitudes, rationalised death within the Islamic worldview.

Succinctly put, the appointed time arrives when the angel of death, ʿIzrāʾīl/Azrael, executes God's command to take away the soul. Azrael, who is not mentioned by name in the Qur'an but only by his title, personifies death in some accounts, but in each they are inexorable: there is no death without Azrael and there is no Azrael without death. The location and precise moment of death are known to God alone. In a popular narrative, the mother's womb, at the moment of conception, is sprinkled with the soil from the place where the child is destined to die.[46] In a primordial way, then, dying is the ultimate homecoming: to the location of non-historical creation and to the creator. Popular narratives do not focus much on the idea of nostalgia that may haunt all living beings towards the predestined territory of death. The nostalgic focus is rather articulated as a return to God, in accordance with Q2:156: 'Surely we belong to God and to God shall we return' – a maxim to which the Sufis add their own share of spiritual imagination by evoking the return as the key quest in one's spiritual journey, in life and not only death. Perhaps it is this confluence of historical birth and death with non-historical birth and death that can elucidate a somewhat ambiguous Qur'anic statement, as discrepancies in the mainstream exegetical literature indicate, that we in fact live and die twice (2:28; 40:11). As Waardenbur puts it, 'death has been designed as a part of creation and is put to use to attain creation's aim; God wants human life – understood as service to him – not to end but to receive eternity in paradise'.[47]

In order to confirm his or her sense of religious focus, the dying person ought to utter the *shahada*, or the statement of witness that God is one and that Muhammad is His (last) prophet. The pronouncement of the *shahada* serves as an individual and collective affirmation of belonging. It is also the decisive utterance made in the act of conversion as one transitions into Islam by bearing witness to the divine and Prophetic truth. Self-awareness of becoming and being a Muslim is a weapon against forgetfulness of one's placement in the world. In the moment of dying the articulation of that awareness eliminates

---

[45] J. Smith and Y. Haddad, *The Islamic Understanding of Death and Resurrection* (Oxford: Oxford University Press, 2002), 30.
[46] J. Smith and Y. Haddad, *The Islamic Understanding of Death and Resurrection*, 35.
[47] J. Waardenburg, 'Death and the Dead', 1:508.

anxiety, both the basic anxiety about mortality and the fear of God's wrath while sojourning in the grave. In popular and scholarly discourse on the condition of the Muslim corpse, which the Qur'an treats as both lifeless and possessing some form of identity (Q35:9; 17:49), much ink was spilled to reconcile the notion of material insentience with animate responsiveness before the burial and within the grave. The Qur'an mentions some form of punishment for wrongdoers before the Day of Judgement (Q6:93; 32:21; 52:47), suggesting that the corpse is not entirely lifeless or insentient. In non-scriptural, dramatic rendering by classical and medieval Muslim thinkers, two monstrous angels by the name of Munkar and Nakir appear to the dead and question them about their faith and loyalty to the Prophet and his message; in another, stemming from the Prophetic *hadith*, the angel called Ruman is first to arrive at the corpse, asking it, in a less terrifying fashion than Munkar and Nakir, to record his or her good and bad deeds.[48] Many great Muslim theologians detail the various aspects of life in the grave/*barzakh*, postulating that torture and punishment can occur because the spirit swiftly returns to the corpse after death takes place. The soul, on the other hand, is retained by God, as per repeated Qur'anic injunctions, while the spirit, *rūḥ*, is restored into the corpse. As a result, the dead continue to have some semblance of awareness of self and others after the burial. The channels of communication are not fully severed. In the Prophetic *hadith*, this awareness is indicative of the possibility of restoring communication between the dead and the living, albeit on new and ethically enhanced grounds, so as to diminish the vulnerability of the corpse as it lies in the grave. As Smith and Haddad persuasively demonstrate, the classical and medieval Islamic imagination developed ways of combating notions of life's end that threatened to reduce people to a materiality of bones. It offered a human response to looming nothingness. Although it attached horror to the grave, post-Qur'anic Islamic tradition attributes vulnerability, comfort, anxiety and all other states typical of worldly emotions to the dead too.[49]

In line with such considerations in the realm of ideas, Islamic jurists sketched out appropriate legal injunctions regarding funerary practices. Deriving from religious and historical foundations in the Qur'an, Prophetic traditions and theological discourse, they addressed different aspects of the process of dying, being handled, buried and remembered as a Muslim. As with many other aspects of legal practice governing everyday life, death-related regulations have been subjected to variances of opinion among legal schools and often within the same one, as well as in accordance with denominational teachings. For the most part, however, the jurists agree on the necessity to attend to the dying person and his/her body down to the minutest detail so as to prevent any excess punishment or mistreatment in the grave. The aim, therefore, is not

---

[48] J. Smith and Y. Haddad, *The Islamic Understanding of Death and Resurrection*, 42–3.
[49] J. Smith and Y. Haddad, *The Islamic Understanding of Death and Resurrection*, 63–98.

to interfere with the Final Judgement, but to ensure favourable conditions in the grave and forgo the damnation of the deceased. Halevi's research shows that already by the late eighth century a host of ritual acts had evolved to relieve the deceased from the punishment of the grave.[50]

In accordance with a detailed Prophetic guidance preserved in the *hadith* corpus,[51] prescribed ritual acts are set in place. The dead are promptly to be washed and prepared for the burial. The martyrs, on the other hand, like the ones at the battle of Uhud, can be buried immediately in their clothes and no prayer ought to be said over them.[52] The martyrs are not only the ones who die in the battle. The Prophet identified seven additional categories: one who dies of plague; one who drowns; one who dies of respiratory illness; one who dies of internal complaint; one who burns to death; one who is killed by a falling structure; and women who die in pregnancy.[53] All otherwise deceased Muslims whose bodies can be retrieved, handled and attended to, ought to be washed and shrouded with plain white cloth.[54] If possible, before the onset of death, the dying person, as mentioned earlier, should be encouraged to say the *shahada*[55] and the attendants and visitors should recite *Yā-Sīn* (Q36) in their presence.[56] When a person dies, the attendants should close the eyes of the deceased[57] and the person performing the ritual washing of the corpse (*ghusl*) should take a bath after performing the act.[58] The Prophet encouraged that 'the honest ones should wash the dead', and stated that the one washing the corpse and preparing it for the burial regains his/her utmost purity.[59] Similarly, the persons carrying the corpse to the grave ought to perform ablution.[60] The ritual washing ought to be done in odd numbers: thrice, five times, or seven times and is to start from the right side.[61] Three rows of praying men need to accompany the bier in order to ensure favour in Paradise,[62] but the one who takes his or her own life will receive no prayer.[63] The procession ought to follow the bier, not be followed by it. The bier should be carried on men's shoulders,[64] the pace should be neither too fast nor too slow and must be

[50] L. Halevi, *Muhammad's Grave*, 229.
[51] The *hadith* material regarding death, dying and caring for the dead is extracted primarily from Abu Dawud, *Sunan: kitāb al-janā'iz* (vol. 20), online http://www.sunnah.com/abudawud; al-Bukhari, *Saḥīḥ: kitāb al-janā'iz* (vol. 23), online http://sunnah.com/bukhari; and Ibn al-Majah, *Sunan: kitāb al-janā'iz* (vol. 6), online http://www.sunnah.com/ibnmajah.
[52] Abu Dawud, *Sunan*, 20: 3128; 3129; Bukhari, *Saḥīḥ*, 23: 427.
[53] Abu Dawud, *Sunan*, 20: 3105.
[54] Abu Dawud, *Sunan*, 20: 3014, 3144 (which mentions 'Yemeni' cloth); 3145. Bukhari, *Saḥīḥ*, 23: 354; Ibn Majah, *Sunan*, 6: 1539.
[55] Ibn Majah, *Sunan*, 6: 1512.
[56] Ibn Majah, *Sunan*, 6: 1515.
[57] Ibn Majah, *Sunan*, 6: 1522.
[58] Abu Dawud, *Sunan*, 20: 3155
[59] Ibn Majah, *Sunan*, 6: 1529.
[60] Abu Dawud, *Sunan*, 20: 3155.
[61] Bukhari, *Saḥīḥ*, 23: 345, 346, 349.
[62] Abu Dawud, *Sunan*, 20: 3160.
[63] Abu Dawud, *Sunan*, 20: 3179.
[64] Bukhari, *Saḥīḥ*, 23: 402.

dignified and muted.[65] Those who see a procession go by must stand up and wait until the bier is either put down or out of sight,[66] even if the deceased is not a Muslim.[67] Upon the placing of the bier, first the *basmala* is uttered,[68] then four *takbirs*.[69] In addition, a sincere supplication prayer ought to be said over the bier,[70] asking for forgiveness on behalf of 'those who are living and those who are dead, those who are present and those who are absent, our young and our old, male and female'.[71] The funeral prayer should be said at the grave after the completion of the burial,[72] and the Prophet's preferred choice of recitation was *al-Fātiḥa*, the opening chapter of the Qur'an.[73] Also, a prayer is said to ease the punishment in the grave and grant the dead a quick access to Paradise.[74] Forgiveness for the dead ought to be pleaded at the gravesite, because the questioning begins promptly upon the burial.[75] There ought to be no weeping at the grave, for the dead may be tortured for it.[76] Women should therefore not visit the graves,[77] but men should go so as to be reminded of the Hereafter.[78] The graves need to be slightly raised and singular, but if necessary two or three bodies can be placed together into one and the same grave,[79] as the Prophet had done with the Uhud martyrs.[80] The graves ought to be deep and sufficiently spacious,[81] marked with a rock and containing no structures or writing.[82] One must tread carefully among the graves, lest the noise of the heels disturb the dead.[83] One must not desecrate or defile the graves, no matter who occupies them.[84] The dead are mourned for three days, except widows who should mourn their husbands for four months and 10 days.[85]

Of course, in light of the variations between schools of jurisprudence regarding interpretations of the *hadith* in the matter of death and burial as well as the demands of specific cultural and social circumstances, funerary rituals do not exhibit uniformity across all Muslim societies. Here, the emphasis will be placed on the Hanafi position as manifest in Bosnian Islamic beliefs and

---

[65] Abu Dawud, *Sunan*, 20: 3178.
[66] Bukhari, *Saḥīḥ*, 23: 394, 397.
[67] Bukhari, *Saḥīḥ*, 23: 398, 399.
[68] Abu Dawud, *Sunan*, 20: 3207.
[69] Abu Dawud, *Sunan*, 20: 3188; Bukhari, *Saḥīḥ*, 23: 405, 406.
[70] Abu Dawud, *Sunan*, 20: 3193.
[71] Abu Dawud, *Sunan*, 20: 3195
[72] Ibn Majah, *Sunan*, 6: 1598.
[73] Bukhari, *Saḥīḥ*, 23: 419; Ibn Majah, *Sunan*, 6: 1561, 1562, 1563.
[74] Abu Dawud, *Sunan*, 20: 3196.
[75] Abu Dawud, *Sunan*, 20: 3215.
[76] Bukhari, *Saḥīḥ*, 23: 377, 378, 391; also Ibn Majah, *Sunan*, 6: 1663.
[77] Ibn Majah, *Sunan*, 6: 1643; 1650.
[78] Ibn Majah, *Sunan*, 6: 1637.
[79] Ibn Dawud, *Sunan*, 20: 3209.
[80] Bukhari, *Saḥīḥ*, 23: 429.
[81] Ibn Majah, *Sunan*, 6: 1627.
[82] Ibn Majah, *Sunan*, 6: 1629, 1630, 1631.
[83] Abu Dawud, *Sunan*, 20: 3224.
[84] Ibn Majah, *Sunan*, 6: 1633, 1634.
[85] Bukhari, *Saḥīḥ*, 23: 370, 371.

practices. Like other legal scholars, Abu Hanifa, the founder of the school of law that would dominate the Ottoman Empire, including Bosnia, set out some basic principles of handling and attending to the dead in response to the *hadith* corpus and broader eschatological views. In Abu Hanifa's words, 'the questioning in the grave shortly upon death by Munkar and Nakir is a fact. The rejoining of the spirit [*rūh*] with the body [*jasad*] of the servant is a fact. The tightening of the grave and the punishment in it affecting all unbelievers and some sinful believers is a fact'.[86] As a result of these fundamental views, it is incumbent on the living to cultivate a level of ritual care in attending those who are about to be carried into the grave. Over the centuries, Hanafi jurists elaborated many different aspects of funerary rituals that deviated from other schools of law, although most of the differences were relatively minor. For example, specific to the Hanafis is the prohibition of the husband on washing the body of his wife unless there is no female present to do the ritual. In contrast, the wife can wash her husband's body. A Muslim can wash the corpse of a non-Muslim, which is especially relevant for first-generation converts. As regards the funeral prayer for a woman, the father, not the husband, should lead it. While women do not attend the burial, they can perform funerary prayers in such a way that they form a single group with the female imam seated rather than standing at the front.[87] These and a few other Hanafi injunctions may have been modified within the parameters of their legal foundations, as can be particularly seen in the reciting of the Qur'an in funerary prayers and using it for tomb inscriptions, which Abu Hanifa opposed. In Bosnia, like in other parts of the Ottoman empire, these injunctions were rendered and applied by the religious scholars in both strict and flexible ways, growing out of the normative principles in combination with the existing beliefs about death and the dead in a way which suggests the reactive and adaptive paradigm, though not in the same measure or in all aspects of ritual practice.[88] This, of course, should come as no surprise. Many contemporary ethnographic writings point to an uneven application of legal rulings surrounding death across Muslim cultures and a necessity to maintain both interpretative and ritual fluidity between macro and micro levels of religious life.[89] After all, as many examples above have demonstrated, this interplay began from the early days of Islam, expanding and shaping the ritual canon without jeopardising the power of Islamic eschatological narratives.

---

[86] Abu Hanifa, *Al-fiqh al-akbar*, in I. Ninowy (trans.), online http://fahadmahdi.webs.com/Other%20Books/Fiqh%20e%20Akbar%20By%20Abu%20Hanifa.pdf, 17.

[87] As summarised in L. Halevi, *Muhammad's Grave*, 28; 61–3; 69; 131, 175–7.

[88] A useful reference for the period in question is the work of Ottoman Hanafi jurist Ibrahim Halebi (d. 1549), compiled in *Mevkufat Islam Fıkhı* (Istanbul: Sağlam yayınevi, 2003), 2 vls.

[89] See, for example, H. Granqvist, *Muslim Death and Burial: Arab Customs and Traditions Studied in a Village in Jordan* (Helsinki: Helsingfors, 1965); C. Venhorst, *Muslims Ritualizing Death in the Netherlands* (Zurich: LIT, 2013); L. Abou-Lughod, 'Islam and the Gendered Discourses of Death', *International Journal of Middle East Studies* 25:2 (1993).

Figure 1.3 Muslim cemetery in Blažuj, Tomislavgrad.
Photo by Velibor Božović

Death and Dying in Bosnian Islam: Local Norms, Foreign Accounts

In light of the questions of how normative teachings about death are enacted in everyday life, we are bound to straddle the dilemmas of generalisation and particularisation. While the assumption that dying as a Muslim is universally understood thanks to the detailed corpus of the Prophetic *hadith*, the language and acts deployed in any cultural setting reveal a level of ethnocentricity associated with death rituals and beliefs thereof. Knowledge about death and death rituals is more readily gained from direct participation rather than theological dictums. Death, after all, is an aspect of ritual life whose continuity relies on communal presence and engagement more than theoretical prescriptions. In addition, there is often a cumulative aspect to this knowledge that draws from many different ideas and practices accrued over time and intricately woven into complex ritual patterns. Often, it is outside observers who detect and describe these complexities and contingencies; insiders, especially in pre-modern times, often do not reflect on them or concern themselves with describing what or how they 'construct' death. In the case of Bosnian Muslims, textual sources on ritual and commemorative practices of the Ottoman times are practically non-existent. A treatise on graves visitation by eighteenth-century author al-Aqḥiṣārī, to be addressed later in the book, tackles the matter from a prescriptive rather than descriptive angle, expressing scepticism about some specific acts but mainly reifying normative Sunni

Islamic teachings. What one does to dispose of and mourn the dead, organise the family and friends and facilitate their grief and memory comprises the knowledge handed through generations and across the community. There are a few notable exceptions related to the provisions set up by charity endowers who specify the conditions for their own commemoration but these are primarily driven by legal and testimonial motivations. One other pertinent exception is worthy of note here: in his treatise dispensing advice on proper religious behaviour, piety, ethical values and good etiquette, Abdulvehhab Ilhami (d. 1237 AH/1821 CE), a prominent scholar and Sufi, includes a section on 'remembering death' in which he dramatises his own death, describing the fateful moment in detail and instructing his friends and family how to act so as to make his departure more meaningful and the prospects of his salvation more promising. In other words, Ilhami writes as if he were about to lie on his deathbed, moving from a hypothetical to realistic prose: he first awaits death, then enacts the moment of taking the last breath, receives his friends' forgiveness and prayers, delivers a homily and finally dies. His 'death' coincides with the end of his treatise, which he dates to the month of Muharram in 1216 AH/1801 CE:

> At the moment of death, remind me to say the *shahada* lest I am hurried out of this world faithless. Close my eyes so that I scare off nobody. Let the imams tie my feet so they do not move. Let my body not smell much. Let my friends not be overcome. May this be done smoothly so that the mourners do not get bored of my burial. If I was bad, do not condemn me. If I did wrong, do not scorn me. If I was good, God knows it. If I was bad, He knows that too. Immediately ask for forgiveness. Say prayers as you can. Forgive my faults. I have already forgiven you all. Don't be petty. Do not abandon Muhammad's community.
>
> Aza'il [sic., Azrael] has arrived, brothers. Shed tears out of fear of God. Quit chatting about this world now. Open Abdulvehhab's lips with a toothpick so that he may be able say, *'lā illāh illa Allah, Muhammad rasūl Allah'*. Say a prayer, oh believers, from the verses on God's mercy (*rahmet ayetleri*). My soul is going through duress. Say something pleasing for it. The Almighty is causing pain in my head. I will not shed a tear for this world. Nor I will not stick to its goals. I have already passed through the gates of transitional space (*dār barzakh*). Until this moment I had fights with my grave. Now, let me love it ... .[90]

In addition to evoking a sorrowful and didactic self-eulogy, the author's words evoke important aspects of ritual action performed around the dying person and register the basic etiquette set out in the Prophetic traditions. Condensed in a brief concluding paragraph of the treatise, Ilhami's recommendations hint at longue durée currents in Bosnian Islamic culture

---

[90] MS page printed in K. Dobrača, 'Tuhfetul-musallin ve zubdetul-haši'in od Abdul-Vehaba Žepčevije Ilhamije [A gift and treat for those who pray to God by Abdul-Vehhab Ilhami of Žepče]', *Anali Gazi Huserv-begove biblioteke* 2–3 (1974), 65. Translation from Ottoman Turkish mine.

of grief and bereavement and related normative and idiosyncratic attitudes and customs. He reiterates them as ordinary knowledge and lists them as if implying that they are commonly performed in such moments. As such they give us a first-hand insight into how death was 'done' and what expectations and actions were associated with the ritual.

Nearly a century after Ilhami's work, the Austro-Hungarian schoolteacher Antun Hangi similarly describes, in a detailed and rich narrative, complex ritual, emotional and cultural practices of Bosnian Muslims in caring for, burying and grieving the dead. In contrast to Ilhami, Hangi's is an outsider's account and therefore prone to distortions that any narrative, especially colonialist, is vulnerable to – ideological, gender, class and so on. Hangi's microscopic observations, however, are equally valuable for several reasons: first, the author does not presuppose that what he describes is anything more than the Islam of Bosnia, embedded in a regional culture and practised by the people who make it tangible. Hangi's occasional formulary statements and generalisations about 'Bosnian Mohammedans' are far from being attempts at reaching an objective view of all of Islam and do not offer a final word on all Muslims. Rather, his narrative is poised between objective conditions and subjective reflections, rather than formulated as a specific value system. After all, his presence in Bosnia coincides with the transfer of imperial power from the Ottomans to Austria-Hungary, so the Muslims he observes and narrates represent an internal 'Other' that ought to be demystified rather than alienated. Second, Hangi's text intimates that the observed subjects of his narrative and of his Empire inhabit a real, meaningful and complex world of which he, with the Austro-Hungarian imperial administration, may be in political control, but which can at other levels be neither easily grasped nor completely decoded. Hangi approaches his subjects with a series of small questions to create a broader picture. His long-term presence in the region and unwavering curiosity make it possible to weave a narrative that is neither pretentiously on the inside nor the outside. Instead, Hangi astutely positions himself between the two imperial cultures, central European Catholic and Ottoman Islamic, so as to render Bosnian Muslim lifestyle palatable and sufficiently intriguing in its spiritual, cultural and ritual range. As he conveys the richness and occasional oddities of observed reality he avoids qualifying them as superstitious, profane or backward. Thirdly, Hangi often evokes Bosnian folk tradition, poetic heritage and a broader anecdotal material as components of the same holistic continuum of local culture, which he evidently considers to be as relevant as the religious canon. His access to the canon is through the practices and beliefs that surround him. It is thanks to this combination of fundamental Islamic norms surrounding death and the detailed attention to Bosnian Islamic culture that we can appreciate how local tradition negotiates and occasionally changes the prescribed forms of a religious system.

In Hangi's account, reduced here to the sequence of core events, death culture among Muslims of Bosnia consists of a fascinating set of beliefs and actions that testify to the importance of the community as much as the centrality of this rite of passage. Close relatives and friends continually visit and attend to the dying person.[91] Women, men and children are segregated at this time, in accordance with the conventional gender norms governing domestic space, which can be momentarily disrupted only if so wished by the dying person. A dying woman is visited by female and male relatives, but not by men outside the immediate familial circle. The visitors, Hangi notes, do not pray for the person to get better as they do in his own culture, but to alleviate his or her passage into the other world. The testimony of God's oneness – *shahada* – is intermittently uttered by everyone in the room. By this time, the last will is likely to have been completed, as it is customary to write it down with the help of a scribe and a judge (*qadi*) when the sick person is sufficiently bedridden or presumed too ill to recover. The last will also includes specifications of the sum to be allocated for erecting the tombstone 'so as to make it clear, until the Day of Judgement, where the person shall rest'.[92] This is also the time to be generous towards the loved ones and members of the community, neighbours, friends and all others who have acted kindly towards the dying person. One should also distribute pocket money to local children as an act of generosity. In case one dies without a will, the law stipulates that the immediate and extended family takes care of any outstanding debts as well as burial expenses. To this end, Hangi mentions the bill of 1884, set in place by the Austro-Hungarian administration and implemented by local Bosnian authorities, whereby such matters are both validated and expanded to accommodate the new regulations.[93]

The *shahada*, Hangi continues, ought to be said by the dying person or those who surround him at that moment. Preparations should begin for burial the moment the person dies, properly and solemnly, without disturbance to the departed spirit which longs to reunite with the body, and without excessive weeping that may appear as a challenge to the Lord who has summoned the person at his/her destined hour. As the visitors themselves utter the *shahada* they also ease the person's passage into death by forgiving bad deeds, in a form of deathbed confession, if any have been committed by the dying person. '*Halali mi*', ('forgive me') is pleaded before death's door, if the afflicted party can speak. '*Halal ti bilo. Halali i ti meni*', answer the visitors rhetorically, one after another, as they bid farewell: 'I forgive you and may you forgive me too.' This ritual exchange ends with a cup of coffee offered

---

[91] A. Hangi, *Život i običaji muslimana u Bosni i Hercegovini* [Lifestyle and customs of the Muslims of Bosnia and Herzegovina] (Sarajevo: Naklada Daniela Kajona, 1906), 288–9.

[92] A. Hangi, *Život i običaji*, 290.

[93] Referred to as 'Erläuternde Bemerkungen zum Entwurfe eines Grundbuchsgesetzes', in A. Hangi, *Život i običaji*, 297.

to each visitor before they leave the house.[94] When death arrives, prayers must be said and announcements made. The eyes are closed and the mouth, if open, is shut. The body is wrapped in a cloth and carried on the *tabut*, the bier, into the house courtyard and protected from the view with a screen. The muezzin announces from the minaret of a nearby mosque that death has arrived, evokes appropriate sacred verses and ends with salutations to the Prophet Muhammad.[95]

As the narrative progresses, Hangi mentions the ritual washing in a way that resonated with the aforementioned norms: the washing is performed by a local religious leader, *hodža*, and if the corpse is female, it is the *hodža*'s wife or a female family member who does the washing. Once washed, the corpse is placed on a different kind of stand, *tenešir*, on which a large white wrap, *ćefin*, is spread, used to fully and comfortably wrap the corpse in lieu of a casket. Here Hangi quotes a traditional Bosnian *sevdalinka*, a woman's love song, as he often does as if to legitimise his observations with the help of a broader cultural milieu. In this song, a young woman is cursing her unfaithful lover with, 'Now you are dressed in a clean white shirt; tomorrow may that be a clean white *ćefin*.'[96]

Pieces of heavy cotton are placed on the palm of each washed hand, the forehead, between toes, on the knees, to symbolically protect those parts of the body which make contact with the ground during prayer. The body is then sprinkled with fragrant water, or the water from the Meccan Zamzam well, a long sleeveless shirt is put on and, finally, the body is wrapped into the *ćefin* and transferred directly onto the bier. Muslims do not use caskets. The bier has handles on four ends to be carried by four adult men. In some parts of Bosnia, Hangi tells us, a colour-coded wooden board is planted vertically at the bier's front end to demarcate gender and marital status of the deceased.[97] In the olden times, he continues, when young unmarried men had long braids, the braid would hang down the bier and identify the corpse as such. By Hangi's times, this was no longer the case because the braids were out of fashion so few young men wore them and if they did, the braids were cut off before the burial with increasing frequency because of the fear that snakes and bugs might be hiding in the braids to suck out the dead person's eyes. As a terrified poet in a *sevdalinka* laments, 'Look, my sweetheart has turned into a snake, hiding in my braids, she sucks on my eyes.'[98]

Once the bier is prepared and set to go, communal support, of neighbours in particular, is essential to maintain the dignity of the procession. All this must be carried out without wailing or excess emotion. 'In Bosnia,' Hangi adds,

---

[94] A. Hangi, Život i običaji, 300.
[95] A. Hangi, Život i običaji, 307.
[96] A. Hangi, Život i običaji, 309.
[97] A. Hangi, Život i običaji, 309–10.
[98] A. Hangi, Život i običaji, 315.

'neighbours are very attentive to each other because 'there can be no greater misfortune than a neighbourly impasse'.'[99] The *hodža* repeats the *takbir* – God is great [*Allahu akbar*] – several times while leading the prayer, then all present quietly recite the opening chapter of the Qur'an, al-Fātiḥa, the men approach the bier, lift it on their shoulders and, followed by the rest of the procession, move slowly towards the graveyard. Men take turns in carrying the bier, for which each one will receive a divine reward.[100]

In front of every cemetery there is a stone chiselled into a rectangular or human shape known as the burial stone. The corpse is laid onto it, with the face positioned to look at Mecca. The *hodža*, standing ahead of the procession and facing the body and Mecca, initiates the final funerary prayer with another *takbir*, the evocation of God's greatness and several designated prayers. At the end, he turns towards the rows of attendees and asks: 'Was this man, or woman, a good person?'; 'Yes, [she/he was] good,' answers everyone unanimously. God loves those who speak well of the dead, Hangi explains, who forgive them from the bottom of the heart, because they too will need God's forgiveness some day in a similar fashion.[101]

This completed, the body is taken to the grave pit where two close relatives or friends await to receive and deposit the body, making sure the face is tilted towards Mecca. Then they untie the wrap and begin placing the wooden boards, one by one, over the corpse, starting from the feet and moving towards the head, lest the soil fall directly onto it. If a woman is being buried, the bier is laid in directly, because men should not touch a deceased female body just as they should not touch a living one. Once the boards neatly cover the corpse, the shovels start their work. Everyone attending should throw in a shovel-full of earth, because God counts that too as a good deed. Once the burial itself is over, the *Fātiḥa* is said at least one more time before the crowd disperses. The gentle and generous treatment of the dead at their burial is both an altruistic and selfish act, Hangi implies, for one should treat another's body the way one would want to be treated in their own appointed time. Another traditional song is evoked here, capturing a poetic dialogue between a mother and her departed son:

> My dear child, Šećer Salih Aga
> Does the soil press heavy down on you?
> Are you at ease with the blessed earth on you?
> Do the cedar boards crush down on you?
> Oh does the dirt smother your fair eyes?
> The son replies deep from within his grave,
> 'By God, my sweet loving mother,
> The soil does not press heavy down on me,

---

[99] A. Hangi, *Život i običaji*, 312.
[100] A. Hangi, *Život i običaji*, 314.
[101] A. Hangi, *Život i običaji*, 317.

> I'm at ease with the blessed earth on me,
> Cedar boards do not crush down on me,
> And the dirt does not smother my fair eyes,
> It is my tears that weigh so down on me.[102]

It is believed, Hangi reports, that before the crowd gets a chance to take even 40 steps from the grave, the questioning of the dead has already commenced. The corpse springs back to life, though not the same life it had enjoyed in this world, but some form of animate awareness necessary to answer the questions. Munkar and Nakir, known as *sulvadžije*, are the interrogators. The questions they pose are quick and direct, all pertaining to one's faith, belief and deeds, beginning with the three most important ones: 'Who is your god? What is your *qibla* (direction of prayer)? Who is your prophet?' Meanwhile, above the surface, the *hodža*, or any close relative of the deceased, assists the animated body by crying out correct answers, for this is a moment of great anguish and even the most devout of bodies may feel too dumbfounded to enunciate clear and correct words. The questioning continues for a while longer in great distress and ends with the soul being delivered graciously to the gardens of Eden or tossed contemptuously into the fires of Hell. They say that the earth around the grave shakes and painful cries are heard during the questioning. Not being left on his or her own gives a great comfort to the corpse, so the *hodža* or a close relative must wholeheartedly cheer on the body not to be frightened.[103]

Many a Bosnian song, Hangi informs us, laments the cries of dead daughters, sons and beloved ones during their interrogation, while the *hodža* or a relative helplessly shouts words of support. In one such song, a departed fair lady, on the advice of her father, pre-empts the questioning by telling the interrogators about her virtues:

> By God, oh Mighty Interrogators
> I did five prayers just before I died
> And did five readings of our Great Book.
> The interrogators give her a reply:
> But God has still sent us to you,
> To visit you and question you, why
> You mistreated many poor children,
> Gave so little for the public good,
> Never joined neighbourly events
> Offered nothing on high holidays?
> The doors of Hell opened right there and then
> The fair lady was hurled straight through them.[104]

---

[102] A. Hangi, *Život i običaji*, 325.
[103] A. Hangi, *Život i običaji*, 319–21.
[104] A. Hangi, *Život i običaji*, 322.

As suggested above, the composition of Hangi's narrative contains holistic elements drawn from folk tradition, religious texts, anecdotes and various common practices he observed during his sojourn in Bosnia. Importantly, based on the examples he provides from personal interactions, most of his subjects seem to have come from the urban class, were affluent and influential, and were likely to convey to him aspects of funerary practice that he may not have witnessed but rather learned second-hand, through conversations and interaction. While this may make his observations more filtered and more biased towards Bosnian Muslims' learned and social elite rather than ordinary people, it does not make the world he describes any less real. Religious beliefs are typically affected by specific domains of practice and action and are embedded in material forms possessed by the group that enacts them. 'Unofficial' Islam, away from such urban and prescriptive settings, does not necessarily contain different elements; rather, it processes and realises the same ideals in accordance with its own scale and logic of action. Moreover, 'official' and 'unofficial', 'urban' and 'rural', 'popular' and 'learned' are binary forms that are open and porous to each other rather than exclusive and impermeable. The universalising, prescriptive tendencies of the Islamic funerary canon are an element present in all localised forms, including Hangi's. His narrative therefore carries an important historical and cultural value for a better understanding of the centripetal tendencies of that canon, its continuity, durability and malleability in the face of local conditions and practices.

Nearly a century later, in 1972, the Bosnian Islamic theologian, Sinanuddin Sokolović, published a manual on how to care for, attend to and bury Muslims.[105] This publication followed in the footsteps of many treatises and articles on the subject disseminated by Islamic scholars in the early and mid-twentieth century. The end of Empire and the change in political regimes in the aftermath of the First and Second World Wars generated a need to preserve and safeguard Islamic practices against secularisation, but also to make them more acceptable and regulated in light of the new political culture whereby loyalty to the nation replaced loyalty to religion, and where Islam became a minority religion. Perceived as less progressive than the Christian majority and distrusted for allegedly perpetuating 'the Ottoman yoke', the Muslims of the region were pressured to align their beliefs and practices with the values of these new nation states. In most of them, religion – Islam in particular – posed as an obstacle to full modernisation and secularisation. The Islamic religious elite's increasing emphasis on pure, simple and moderate Islam was juxtaposed against superstition, magic, witchcraft and other extreme practices in the publications of the *VIS*, the headquarters of the Bosnian Islamic Community and related press. Publications such as *Gajret*,

---

[105] S. Sokolović, *Islamski propisi o čuvanju zdravlja, posjeti bolesnika i sahrani umrlih Muslimana* [Islamic regulations on maintaining health, visiting the sick and burying deceased Muslims] (Sarajevo: Ahkam al-Islam, 1972).

48 CARVED IN STONE, ETCHED IN MEMORY

Figure 1.4 Old stones fighting for space with new ones, Sarajevo.
Photo by Velibor Božović

Glasnik, Takvim, Behar, Preporod and *Islamski Svijet* became inundated with such texts, especially in reference to the beliefs and customs governing the main rites of passage, including death. In contrast to present day attempts by traditionists to rid Islam of non-Islamic influences so as to assert its original purity and superiority, this was an attempt to make Islam more rational and more compatible with 'modernity and progress'.

Sokolović's is thus not the only study that deals with the subject. The growing literature has in time also acquired an important ethnographic and sociological value of weeding out elements of the religious practice that have deeper historical or socio-cultural roots, and intersect with other religious practices in the region. Continuities and discontinuities abound in this regard, indicating that, while some may be engaged in an ongoing struggle to identify and eliminate 'superstition' from Bosnian Islam, others have acknowledged the important interweaving of popular and official Islam or the persistence of ancient Slavic customs in the religious beliefs of both Christians and Muslims.[106] In all cases, a search for some form of authenticity seems to underline the efforts. Sokolović himself introduces the subject matter with a plea that the religious duty of Bosnian Muslims is not directed only to God and Islamic ethics, but to the community at large, including non-Muslims with whom space and resources are shared.[107] Organising his recommendations around 40 short chapters, the author reiterates in detail the *hadith* material concerned with death and dying by emphasising the avoidance of excess in any aspect of private and public life and the adoption of general hygiene to uphold general social health as prescribed and promoted by the Socialist Yugoslav platform: *u zdravom tijelu zdrav duh* – *mens sana in corpore sano*. Like Hangi, Sokolović too reaches out to the broader Bosnian cultural tradition by quoting poetry, legends, sayings by influential men and women and personal anecdotes to reach a holistic perspective on the subject. His book is not descriptive like Hangi's, but prescriptive, tailored to promoting healthy living and healthy dying according to a well-established paradigm of Islamic ethics and the broader context of a modern society free of superstitious and regressive behaviour, which he labels un-Islamic. As a religious scholar, Sokolović is careful to quote appropriate legal and theological sources within which Bosnian Islam is grounded and his references to the *hadith* corpus are equally thorough. A sense of continuity is established with the normative tradition, yet in a sanitised and modernised way so as to highlight its compatibility with modern demands.

---

[106] Such works include S. Ibrišević, *Pravi put i stranputice* [The true path and wrong paths] (Sarajevo n.p., 1990); M. Busuladžić, 'Nekoliko protuvjerskih običaja kod nas [A few of our superstitious practices]', *Novi Behar* 3 (1945); M. Hadžijahić, *Predislamski elementi u kulturi bosanskih muslimana* [Pre-Islamic elements in Bosnian Muslim culture], (Sarajevo: Institut za društvena istraživanja, 1973), H. Đozo, *Fetve* (Srebrenik: Ilmijja BiH, 1996), and others.

[107] S. Sokolović, *Islamski propisi*, 3.

This last section of the book is of particular interest, dedicated to the practices that have persisted against Islamic teachings. 'Although,' Sokolović remarks, 'we, the Muslims of Bosnia and Herzegovina, can be pleased with a continued decrease in superstitious practices and beliefs, especially in the areas where I personally work as a religious cleric and have first-hand knowledge of what is Islamic and what is not, I fear there are still places where various forms of superstition dominate. Among them are fortune telling, witch crafting, mirror reading, rosary counting, beans and coffee tasseography, palm reading and many others, all of which we must fiercely combat because they have nothing to do with Islamic teachings. On the contrary, they are entirely anti-Islamic in character'.[108] To substantiate his criticism, Sokolović lists numerous examples of such practices, most of which are not free standing: his denunciations pertain to authentic Islamic deeds performed incorrectly. For example, Sokolović recommends that, when the corpse is first turned towards Mecca and covered with cloth, no candles should burn in a bowl of wheat above the corpse's head. That wheat, Sokolović warns against the prevailing belief, will not bring fortune to anyone. The interlocking presentation of normative and non-normative practices is quite significant in that it captures the incongruity mentioned earlier whereby the prescribed and performed norms diverge because of material circumstances surrounding death or competing religious voices. Here, they are fused in ways that make the prescribed norms more meaningful. Other examples include:

- Domestic cats need not be kept away from the room where the corpse lies. If a cat jumps over it, the body will not turn into a vampire.
- One should not be afraid of the dead for they do not turn into vampires. One should be more afraid of the living, as they can be more dangerous.
- One should not knead flour, salt and bran under the armpit of the deceased and feed it to livestock. The animals will not produce more milk or eggs for it.
- One should not collect the water from the corpse's ritual wash. Drinking that water will not ease grief, resolve marital problems or wean alcoholics from drinking. It is entirely wrong to drink soapy water from ritual bathing of the corpse under any circumstances, especially if the dead person had been sick or had developed bedsores.
- One should not sacrifice a ram and carry it over the corpse. The livestock will not be healthier for it. Likewise, one should not carry the body to the stable with the livestock before taking it to the cemetery. The animals will gain no health benefits from it.
- One should not break a finger of an uncircumcised dead boy.
- One should not break glass or pitcher behind the funeral procession believing that no other tragedy will afflict the same family.

[108] S. Sokolović, *Islamski propisi*, 71.

- One should not prevent the husband from carrying his wife's bier, for they are still legally wedded.
- One should not leave a glass of water for 40 days on the windowsill for the soul to drink, because the soul shall not do that, even though the sojourn in the grave is dry and thirsty. There is also no need to leave the water in the grave or pour it over the body.
- One should not light a candle for 40 nights on end after the burial for the soul to be able to see and feel welcomed.
- Most importantly, one should avoid the Christian custom of serving hard brandy to the visitors when they pay their final respects to the dead, either at home or at the gravesite.[109]

The transgressions cited in *Islamic Regulations* are identified as unofficial, non-normative customs persisting as undesirable and unnecessary blemishes to the solemn simplicity of Islamic burial culture and as such warrant disdain. In juxtaposing them to 'orthodoxy', the book sheds light on a widespread set of practices otherwise obscured from historical and theological view; some of those practices are clearly rooted in local folklore and shared with non-Muslim neighbours and others in the local economy, involving livestock and crops as elements of everyday life. What is especially striking in the description of these customs, however, is the interdependence of normative and non-normative elements, making it very hard to disentangle them from each other in function and purpose. Each clarifies the other – the non-normative, popular forms reinforce and perpetuate the official ones, rather than challenge them, constituting new layers of a meaningful expression of grief and mourning on the one hand and, on the other, contributing to renewal in the cycle of life of which death is a key component. Thus, the dead are cared for by all, and they in turn care for all those who belong to the productive life cycle – livestock and crops, rich and poor, old and young. While there is something anti-modern about the focus on communal participation rather than on discreet private burials and remembrance, the canonical material as exemplified by the *kitāb al-janā'iz* corpus is based precisely on group rather than individualistic experiences of death. The ethical spectrum at the root of this process is constituted through the participation of the community, and not its exclusion. The spiritual, material and symbolic elements of such engagement provide a sense of comfort in the face of loss and a feeling of connection at the final separation. Antun Hangi himself had detected and depicted this characteristic of Bosnian Islamic burial culture at the turn of the century, making it possible to imagine the continuity of such practices through different epochs precisely because they had no autonomy from other aspects of everyday life.

---

[109] S. Sokolović, *Islamski propisi*, 71–4.

Sufi Influences on Death

An important dimension of death culture finds no scriptural support in the *hadith* nor is it directly derived from local traditions; rather, it draws from Sufism, which permeated local and official conceptions of death. Historically, as seen above, Sufism infiltrated rural and urban Muslim life, promoting teachings that at times strengthened and hyper-spiritualised common Islamic rituals and at others militated against normative Islam. In the context of memorial culture, the most interesting example of the weaving of local and Sufi teachings related to the concept of *'dobri'*, the 'good' ones. Writes Antun Hangi:

> Muslims believe that the dead can appear in one's dream to pass on news, ask for a favour or perhaps offer to say a prayer for the living. The dead can also inform the living of God's expectations, forewarn them of a pending disaster or bring news of joy to come. Only good spirits can make an appearance and people call these spirits *dobri*. These are the people who inhabit the Heaven because they passed while in the mercy of God. That the *dobri* can appear to people in a dream is confirmed by many a song ... I had a dear friend, a noble young man (*beg*) from Banja Luka, who grew up in an affluent household. This is what he once told me: 'An aunt of mine was a widow. After the death of her husband she tried to build a new house but was forced to stop halfway because she had run out of money. One night a *dobri* appeared in her dream and advised her to dig under the left beam of the old house, for that was where the money had been buried. At first she did not believe him and she felt bad about doing damage to their old house. But after the second and third visit by the same *dobri* she began digging, exactly where he had indicated and she found a clay jug full of money. This is where our good fortune began.[110]

The term *dobri* is part of popular idiom, currently used in a somewhat romanticised way to refer to the members of the Bosnian Church or medieval Bosnians in general. In pre-Ottoman times, the term *dobri* may have possessed a titular function in reference to Bosnian nobility. In various official documents of the medieval Bosnian state, the term is coupled with Bosnian – *i nostri boni Bosnensi* – evidently to designate an aristocratic lineage and, in some situations, to differentiate Bosnians from other inhabitants of the medieval state.[111] While this indeed may not have had a confessional application as occasionally argued,[112] epitaphs found on medieval Bosnian tombstones often contain the attribute *'dobri'* in reference to the dead. The same is true of other cultural texts, folk poetry and proverbs in particular. In other words, the term referred to Bosnians who may not have belonged to the nobility but commanded respect and some kind of spiritual clout in the cultural imagination long after

---

[110] A. Hangi, *Život i običaji*, 230–31.
[111] P. Ćošković, 'Veliki knez bosanski Tvrtko Borovnić [The great Bosnian duke Tvrtko Borovnić]', *Croatica Christiana Periodica* 20: 37 (1996), 63.
[112] P. Ćošković, 'Veliki knez bosanski Tvrtko Borovnić', 64.

the disappearance of the medieval nobility and, in fact, it remains in sporadic use to date. In a parallel fashion, as earlier discussed, Sufism developed the notion of a *wali/awliya*, God's friends and protégés, the saints who bridge the cosmological opposites of this world and the afterlife, God and creation, and visible reality and invisible truths. Thus, God's friends are not separated from Him or the world in either life or death, and are instead able to exist in both realms, enacting their powers in pure sincerity and benevolence. After all, the Qur'an confirms that 'surely, the friends of God shall feel no fear or loss' (Q10:62). It is through the blessing of these saintly figures that comfort can be reached, knowledge gained, fortune acquired and evil thwarted. While doctrinally Sunni Islam does not purport the idea of intercession, the saints de facto satisfy this function in a way that occasionally deviates into cult worship. In Bosnian Islam, the Sufi notion of sainthood intermeshes with the concept of *dobri*, expanding it to include all virtuous individuals rather than only nobility or Sufi saints. In fact, in popular poetry the word *dobri* and *dervish*, a wandering Sufi, are sometimes used synonymously, as in this example: 'When Pasha lay down to sleep/ a *dobri* appeared in his dream/ by Pasha name the *dervish* called him'.[113] The good ones appear usually in dreams, since their physical location is indeterminate and heterotopic, moving from physical visibility and anchor in the grave, to invisibility and movement in one or many locations at once. Dreams are thus common channels for the *dobri* to manifest themselves in an intensely real fashion, act on their own volition and create connections and relationships across physical and historical distances. This enhances parallels with Islamic *walis* who, according to an old account, are also 'roamers and not restricted to their graves, they come and go'.[114] Another parallel has been made with that of the martyrs, *shahids*, whose ontological status is equally complex, as they are not dead in the conventional sense but aware and present through God's protection and grace. Unlike the martyrs with whom they are frequently fused in popular nomenclature, the *dobri* are not bestowed with a thaumaturgic function. Some *dobri* act and continue good deeds in significantly more enhanced, clairvoyant, even miraculous ways than when they were still alive. Most, however, persist through a benevolent but discreet presence, inspiring trust and protection and reinforcing individual and collective memory and bonds.

In addition to this aspect of death culture related to spiritual mediation through saints/good ones, other death rituals also exhibit Sufi influences. The most notable example is in the ritual of *tevhid* (from Ar. *tawḥīd*), which involves a commemorative gathering, usually female, but sometimes with men, to pray for the soul of the deceased and facilitate his or her safe passage to eternal life. *Tevhid* is a ritual derivative of the Sufi practice of *dhikr*, or

---

[113] A. Hangi, *Život i običaji*, 305.
[114] J.S. Trimingham, *The Sufi Orders in Islam* (Oxford and New York: Oxford University Press, 1998), 225.

remembrance of God's absolute unity and transcendence, which helps focus the mind and the body on the achievement of spiritual ecstasy. Like *dhikr*, *tevhid* involves liturgical chanting, evocation of God's unity and meditative engagements. It provides at once a social connection with other participants and a spiritual one with God, operating thus at both external and internal levels. If involving men, *tevhids* take place in mosques or Sufi lodges. Over time, however, they have increasingly become home-based rituals allowing female members of the family and community to partake in commemorative mourning not typically possible due to the women's debarment from burials.

The origins of the *tevhid* ritual and its transformation into a hybrid, Sufi and non-Sufi, form have not been fully elucidated. As discussed, a number of state officials, charitable endowments and religious scholars favoured Sufi teachings and permitted Sufis their own space for ritual participation close to mosques and religious schools. Especially interesting, if somewhat cryptic, is the historical connection between Muslim women and this distinctly Sufi ritual. While we know that many women were Sufi, their access to and participation in ritual life is difficult to assess. Sufi proclivities of many Muslim women were recorded only sporadically and the most notable is movement or spiritual association known as the 'Sisters of Rum' (*Bacıyan-ı Rum*), with roots in Asia Minor and mentioned in incomplete references across Bosnia and Greece. In Bosnia, they were locally known as Badžijanije and anecdotes about their lives in hagiographical literature date back to the seventeenth century. Badžijanije are referred to as spiritual masters, influential educators, even eccentrics. As late as the mid-twentieth century, a prayer to 'Seven Sisters' who were part of this movement was included in mourning ceremonies in some parts of Bosnia. One of the 'Seven Sisters' was the wife of the aforementioned sheikh Hasan Kaimi in Sarajevo of the seventeenth century. She herself worked as the sheikh of Kaimi's auxiliary lodge that was later specified for use by women.[115]

It is plausible that in early days Sufi masters were invited into homes to perform various forms of ritual, including those of mourning at the house of the deceased. While men attended the burial and performed funerary prayers outside the home, women engaged in the Sufi way of ritual grieving and memorialisation and gradually adopted it as their own practice. The ritual of *tevhid* is repeated several times: first on the day of the burial, followed by one on the seventh day, the fortieth day and subsequently six months and one year after the death. The ritual is led by professional *bulas*, the graduates of religious colleges for women. Their responsibilities include attending and supervising various religious ceremonies, most importantly *tevhids* and the festive celebrations of *mevlud* (Ar. *mawlūd*). The *bulas* lead prayers, recite

---

[115] M. Hadžijahić, 'Badžijanije u Sarajevu i Bosni', in *Anali Gazi Husrev-begove biblioteke* 7–8 (1982). A. Buturović, 'Sufi Orders and Movements: Balkans', *Encyclopedia of Women and Islamic Culture* (Brill Online, 2014). <http://www.paulyonline.brill.nl/entries/encyclopedia-of-women-and-islamic-cultures/sufi-orders-and-movements-balkans-COM_0149a>.

appropriate verses from the Qur'an and appoint other present women to carry out parts of the liturgy. Every liturgical section is followed by a collective petitionary prayer, for the soul of the dead and some for the soul of their dead relatives as well. At the final prayer, women collectively evoke the 99 Beautiful Names of God and eulogise Prophet Muhammad.

We can thus see the similarities between *tevhid* and Sufi *dhikr* in that the former emulates many meditative aspects of the latter, including a frequent use of large prayer beads (*tasbīḥ*/*tespih*) similar to those used in Sufi rituals and rhythmic movements of the body. Specifically, the ritual formulae of common *tevhids* involve a repetition of both Qur'anic and non-Qur'anic recollections of God. The *tahlil* formula that 'there is no God but God' is repeatedly uttered, as are some of the Beautiful Names (the Merciful, the Benevolent, the Creator, the Resurrect or, so on). In some places, notably in Sarajevo, women also perform the so-called *yetmiş bin tevhid* (Turkish for 'seventy-thousand *tevhids*'), the prerequisite for which is to have a minimum of 70 (female) participants, who must repeat the *tahlil* utterances at least one thousand times each, in the sum total of seventy thousand *tahlils*.[116] References to the *yetmiş bin tevhid* are present in early Ottoman Bosnia. For example, in the 945 AH/1538 CE testament (*vasiyetname*) of a wealthy landlord in Sarajevo, Kemal beg, it is stipulated:

> When I die ... six-thousand *akçe* should be taken aside from my estate to remunerate those who will in my name perform the pilgrimage to Ka'ba; five-thousand *akçe* to be distributed for the prayers I failed to perform; one-hundred *akçe* should be paid to the one who will recite the articles of faith (*talqīn*) at my grave the day I am buried. Five *akçe* should be paid to each of the forty men selected to go ahead of my body at the funeral procession and repeat loudly, 'He was a good man, may God forgive him;' that a three-year old mutton be sacrificed at my grave during my funeral, in the value of hundred-and-twenty *akçe*, and its meat and hide be distributed to those attending it; two-hundred *akçe* should be paid to the one who will bathe my corpse; one-hundred *akçe* to the one who washes off my corpse; one-hundred *akçe* to the one who lowers my body into the grave; five-hundred *akçe* to be given to those who dig my grave, one-thousand *akçe* to be distributed to the poor once I am buried. As I am being buried and after I am covered [with earth], one-thousand *akçe* should be given those who will offer *yetmiş bin tevhid* for my soul.[117]

While this document speaks to Kemal Bey's concern to compensate fairly those who will ensure his burial is done properly and somewhat ostentatiously, and to even compensate for his own negligence in religious matters, it also indicates his desire to recognise this deeply spiritual and comprehensive form of *tevhid* as an important part of his commemoration. The ritual resonates

---

[116] E. Mulahalilović, *Vjerski običaji Muslimana u Bosni i Hercegovini* [Religious customs among the Muslims of Bosnia and Herzegovina] (Tuzla: Hamidović, 2005), 212.

[117] S. Kemura, *Sarajevske džamije i druge javne zgrade turske dobe* [The mosques of Sarajevo and other public buildings from the Turkish period] (Sarajevo: n.p., 1913), 261.

with the liturgical and spiritual exercise of Sufi *dhikr* through which the mind and the body work together to produce a heightened state of intimacy with the divine. The ritual is also inter-textual, moving between Qur'anic and non-Qur'anic incantations to create a sense of depth and continuity with the spiritual tradition at large (as common in Sufi rituals), the community of mourners and the deceased. Although the liturgical component does include certain complex passages, many are sufficiently accessible to be learned spontaneously with the help of musical cadence. For example, one phrase that stands out during the ritual of *tevhid*, rhythmically repeated 33 times to correspond to the number of beads on a standard string, says 'you are the Guide, you are the Truth, there is no truth, other than Him' (*anta al-hadi anta al-haqq; laysa al-hadi illa hu*). While the phrase is not strictly Qur'anic, it has a strong Qur'anic basis, evoking all key scriptural affirmations of God's absolute unity and transcendence on the one hand and proximity and commitment to humankind on the other. Negation ('there is no') leads to confirmation ('but'). As Hamid Algar points out, remembrance through negation is a common form of *dhikr* among Sufi orders, especially Naqshbandis, whereby 'the negation empties and purifies the heart that it may become a fit receptacle for the divine and capable of receiving the impress of the Supreme Name'.[118] It is also syntactically creative, addressing God directly and intimately at first – 'you are' – then shifting to reaffirm a pledge to Him through the pronoun *hu* (He), which requires a forceful physical release of breath. This and many similar phrases typical of Sufi *dhikr* poignantly express the convergence and interaction between an outer, verbalised veneration of God and His internalisation through the act of breathing. Although this is a relatively common liturgical phrase in rituals of many Sufi orders, Hamid Algar noted, while doing research on Bosnian Naqshbandis in the mid-1970s, that it was not used during the formal session of *dhikr* but recited afterwards, along with locally composed devotional songs (*ilahiyat*), prayers and utterances.[119] Still, its Sufi origins seem quite clear as its deeply spiritual and devotional elements are integrated into the commemorative process.

Like other commemorative rituals and practices of mourning in Bosnian Islam, the *tevhid* acknowledges the feelings of loss and mortality, while simultaneously affirming faith and hope that the loved one is not ultimately lost in death but continues to be protected and anchored through divine mercy. Importantly, however, the *tevhid* modulates the gendered practices of mourning by bringing both women and men into the same ritual and liturgical mindset, if not space. Like God, the dead are both here and elsewhere and the role of the community is to keep the channel between the two modes open

---

[118] H. Algar, 'Some Notes on the Naqshbandi Tariqat in Bosnia', *Die Welt des Islams*, 13: 3–4 (1971), 183.
[119] H. Algar, 'Some Notes', 187.

and meaningful for all. Both mainstream and Sufi rituals provide venues for such interactivities to continue.

In a milieu historically impregnated with different forms of beliefs and practices concerning death, Islamic commemorative culture has carved and maintained a meaningful niche through a dynamic and intimate interaction with the religious cultures it encountered, both by integrating some features thereof and imparting on them a number of its own. Islamic commemorative culture in Bosnia and Herzegovina has from the start negotiated the existing and dominant practices, conditions, values and beliefs of the region in circumstances demanding that it shape itself by refracting historically separate traditions. In what follows, the practices and beliefs surrounding death and memorialisation will be explored in reference to ritual and material culture, specifically gravestones and funerary inscriptions. We will delve into how memorial stones unlock the cultural history of Bosnia by creating an intricate connective web between memory, space and identity.

Figure 1.5 Dobrun, eastern Bosnia. One of the earliest Ottoman Muslim cemeteries in Bosnia and Herzegovina. Photo by Velibor Božović

Chapter 2

Remembering the Dead and Marking the Deathscape

> Do not interfere with the dead,
> for they shall reap what they sow.
>
> Hadith

Having discussed from a broader historical perspective Bosnian Islamic attitudes and cultural practices towards death and dying, it seems necessary to investigate, in diachronic and synchronic ways, the continuity and changeability of Bosnian Islamic death culture in relation to the typologies of memory and commemoration. Despite its focus on Islamic practices, this chapter does not assume that Islam in Bosnia and Herzegovina exists detached from other religious and secular views on the issue, or from the wider Balkan region. The dead often mix and interact across religious and ethnocultural lines, just as the living do. In sharing the cultural and physical landscape, the dead engage the living into a number of shared practices. Therefore, the idea that Bosnian Islamic teachings and customs may have remained unaffected by other religious and cultural traditions in the region has little historical or cultural validity.

This is not to say that, over the centuries, efforts have not been made to seal the porous boundaries of different groups, or that theological and political attempts have not been made to differentiate 'true' from 'false', 'pure' from 'imported', 'ours' from 'theirs'. One look at the atmosphere of distrust in the aftermath of the 1992–1995 war demonstrates how fertile the ground for such efforts has become: today most Bosnians, Muslim and non-Muslim alike, caught between their own traumas and the discourse of their political and religious leaders, seek to assert authenticity and difference as a way of self-preservation. Paradoxically, in their efforts to demarcate and solidify internal boundaries, they also borrow from each other's styles, vocabulary and practices. While this dialectic ignites and increases desire for mutual demarcation it also intimates how intertwined these communities are and have been over the centuries. Alas, 'narcissism of small differences' is at work in the nationalist hold over public and political life. This creates a convincing framework for mutual differentiation and it suffuses many cultural practices, including those surrounding death.

Understandably, the relationship between trauma and memory and the general crisis of identity brought about by recent political upheavals have set in motion a more intimate and pressing relationship between death, identity and memory. The ongoing discoveries of forensic evidence – primary and secondary mass graves, mortuaries holding the remains of unidentified victims, architectural ruins, minefields, scars on bodies and the landscape – act as mementos of violence and represent new locations around which Bosnian Islamic modes of remembrance are being shaped. The role of the dead is not just to tell about the past, but also to retell the present and the future. Though dead, they live on in everyday public domains ushering new commemorative ethics in a close connection to political self-affirmation. As such, spaces of death act as new sites of identity formation, often orchestrated by religious officials who, by playing a political as much as a spiritual role, distil, orchestrate and control the process of commemoration and, in turn, influence the narratives of belonging.

The relationship with the dead, as discussed in the previous chapter, operates at several levels of ritual action and is intimately tied to the formation and renewal of the cultural landscape shared between the living and the dead. This chapter, in turn, focuses on the multiple trajectories, especially commemorative ones, that enable the living to interact with and give meaning to the deceased, but also facilitate and enable the reverse. More than just the material remains, the dead animate cultural and religious life and repeatedly feature in stories, rituals and commemorative objects and practices across Bosnia and Herzegovina. Earlier we tried to account for both intimacy and estrangement present in Bosnian Islamic responses to death: the ritual of nurturing the dying, ensuring their passage to the other world and severing ties of life in a way that allows them to meet the Creator and His celestial deputies in the grave. The intimacy is enhanced by communal participation that is both culturally and scripturally encouraged, while estrangement is occasioned by the Qur'anic injunction whereby each of us will face death on our own accord at our individually and unalterably appointed moment in time. Still, as suggested earlier, the hope of a continued relationship exists, and this hope is enacted in both ritual and private practices that unite liturgical, cultural and environmental aspects of mourning and commemoration. In an effort to highlight the complex strands of commemorative culture, this chapter aims to recover some of the lost subjectivity of the dead. It will first and foremost trace the presence and participation of the dead in the development of Bosnian culture – especially Bosnian Islamic culture – and then assess their representation in memorial practices and related cultural expressions.

The dead, in memory, are always dually experienced, personally and publically; cultural memory folds them into a collective, abstract category of ancestors. Their remembrance is mediated. In the course of time, as first-hand memories become lost to future generations the feeling of loss is diffused. Individual memories become filtered and recast through group narratives of belonging, continuity and heritage, all of which are deeply intertwined with various discourses such as religion, identity, nationalism and now globalisation. At the same time, the presence of the dead around the living community, made visible by graves, cemeteries and memorials, leaves an important imprint on the organisation of everyday life. Our proclivity to dichotomise life and death is challenged by the way we integrate the dead in our cultural system. The necropolis, Michel Ragon once suggested, is the reverse of the metropolis.[1] Of course, this reflection is hardly a clean mirror image but rather one inundated with distortions and refractions resulting from historically shaped practices of everyday life.

Memory and Its Workings

While not new to cognitive sciences, memory and memory practices have started to permeate almost all aspects of the social sciences and humanities, resulting in new theoretical, empirical and methodological questions of what, why, how and when individuals and societies remember. Memory is investigated as both an art and a tool, and its role in retrieving and retaining the past is examined in a variety of narrative, visual, tactile, textual and other forms of expression. As a formative field, memory studies postulates that remembering is rarely spontaneous but is continuously shaped through social and cultural domains, retained in narratives, communicated through different media and commonly tied to questions of agency, authority and identity. It is intimately relevant to the issue of forgetting, which is subject, along with memory, to particular ethics.[2] Partly individual and partly social, memory may have different facets, so the numerous questions, such as whose memory is most relevant in understanding the past, how memories corroborate or cancel each other, whether memory influences truth, and many others, all demonstrate that the keen interest in memory studies is driven by the need to move away from hegemonic historiographies which favour dominant accounts of the past and treat all others as marginal. Moreover, there is an attempt to reduce the distance between master-narratives and micro-narratives, the official public and unofficial individual accounts, and explore the ways in which the two interact in reference to things remembered and things forgotten. As the founding father of memory studies Maurice Halbwach suggests, people acquire their memories in societies and it is in societies that they recall and localise them: the separation between the two is meaningless so they must be examined instead as part of the same continuum.[3]

---

[1] M. Ragon, *The Space of Death* (Charlottesville: University Press of Virginia, 1988).

[2] Works by P. Ricoeur, *Memory, History, Forgetting* (Chicago: Chicago University Press, 2004) and A. Margalit, *The Ethics of Memory* (Cambridge, MA: Harvard University Press, 2002) are especially insightful regarding the issue of ethics.

[3] As cited in P. Connerton, *How Societies Remember* (Cambridge: Cambridge University Press, 1998), 36–8.

Thus, the idea of a stable collective memory that neatly folds into its fabric individual and even group memories has been increasingly discredited. As most societies consist of plural forms of self-identification, memories are inevitably fragmented and frequently contested. The question of how societies negotiate the challenge of plural memories often concerns the matter of power and authority: for example, in his study on the Holocaust memorials, James Young persuasively shows that there are multiple ways of remembering this catastrophic event despite the general consensus on its historical facts, clearly suggesting that memory is subject to specific historical and cultural resonances.[4] In a related way, a recent study focusing on the German cultural scene after the unification advocates for the term 'memory contests' to account for the differences in interpretation and commemoration of historically related events.[5] Acknowledging fissures in cultural memory and differences in interpretation of one and the same set of events compromises the stability and integrity of any group identity. By extension, heavy-handed official narratives that tend to dominate a society's memory at the expense of its minorities and marginalised groups are likely to get caught up in 'memory contests' that require the normative model to be redacted and reinscribed.

Bosnia and Herzegovina is no exception in that respect, although its challenges are quite specific to the historical circumstances that have evolved since the collapse of Yugoslavia in 1991 and the bloody conflict between 1992 and 1995. In the aftermath of genocide and destruction, Bosnia's postwar nation building has been set up by the 1995 Dayton Accords on the premise that the three constituent peoples – Serb, Croat and Bosniak – must not only nurture a common goal of a unified state – Bosnia and Herzegovina – but are also encouraged to enshrine their differences and memories in discrete terms. The realities of war gains and losses are thus channelled into postwar commemorative narratives and practices. One village's memory of destruction coexists with the same village's memory of triumph. The push and pull between two normative value systems, one state-centred and geared towards postwar rebuilding of a unified Bosnia and Herzegovina and the other nation-centred and divisive, has further fragmented the uneven map of collective memory and created disputes over whose memory of victimisation is more objective. Within such an atmosphere, the aforementioned questions of how individual memories become cultural, how memories of a society are sustained, how remembering is reciprocal to forgetting and how the ethics of memory is shaped by political culture, all closely impact the production of new historiographies across the country.[6] As the focal concern of the present study is memory of

---

[4] J. Young, *The Texture of Memory: Holocaust Memorials and Meaning* (New Haven, CT: Yale University Press, 1993).

[5] A. Fusch et al. (eds), *German Memory Contests: The Quest for Identity in German Literature, Film, And Discourse Since 1990* (Camden: Camden House, 2006).

[6] For useful reference collections amidst numerous books on the subject, in addition to P. Connerton, *How Societies Remember*, check J. Olick, et al. (eds), *Collective Memory Reader*

the dead, the issues of plural memory and memory contests bear on how we understand new forms of commemoration and assess the new criteria of accountability towards collective memory in Bosnia and Herzegovina.

Remembering the Dead and Life in Death

In Jan Assmann's formulation, remembering the dead is a primary formation of cultural memory because death is the key experience that differentiates the past from the present. Death, he submits, is 'both the origin and the centre of memory culture'.[7] Assmann differentiates between retrospective and prospective dimensions of memory in this process: the former is a universal practice of keeping the dead close and remembering them as full members of the community. Through remembrance of previous generations, a society maintains the link between past and present. The intensity and character of that practice may vary, but its fundamental principles are universal. The latter or prospective type of memory is the ability of the dead to assert their own presence and relevance in the future by performing deeds and enacting virtues in life and leaving a legacy to be remembered across generations.[8] In both cases, the dynamic of inter-dependence between the dead and the living is secured and the bond of continuity affirmed. In a related way, Jon Davies postulates that death creates the most important covenant that transcends and envelops all other social bonds, adding that 'a community without a properly incorporated relationship with its dead ancestors can be destroyed'.[9] In order to be successful, we could add, this covenant must be multifaceted, utilising both secular and religious vocabulary and exploiting multiple genres of material and immaterial culture – arts, narratives, customs, rituals, theology and so on. Only then can there be a durable connective fabric between the dead and the living. Individual or unregulated memory is not enough to sustain this connection; rather, any personal experience of loss and bereavement ought to be collectively mitigated through what Assmann refers to as a 'symbolic universe' whereby memory, identity and cultural tradition come together in a stable and meaningful continuum.[10]

If remembering the dead is important for a society's reproductive cycle, does that mean that the dead have agency or are they simple mirrors through which individuals or societies observe, shape and authenticate themselves?

(Oxford: Oxford University Press, 2011) and M. Rossington and A. Whitehead (eds), *Theories of Memory* (Baltimore: John Hopkins University Press, 2006).

[7] J. Assmann, *Cultural Memory and Early Civilization* (Cambridge: Cambridge University Press, 2011), 45.

[8] J. Assmann, *Cultural Memory and Early Civilization*, 46–8.

[9] J. Davies (ed.), *Ritual and Remembrance: Response to Death in Human Societies* (Sheffield: Sheffield Academic Press, 1994), 14.

[10] J. Assmann, *Cultural Memory and Early Civilization*, 2.

In most writings about the dead the latter is more often the case: the dead are objects of our attention and memory and channels for our self-reflection. We remember them, commemorate them or forget them. We mourn them, attend to them or disown them. We take for granted the conventional knower/known paradigm and approach the dead as the *other* among us, absent and invisible, but present and heard at our convenience, through the representation of our choice. Challenging this common distinction between the living and the dead as subjects and objects, Howard Williams proposes a more complex interrelationship where the dead are neither acquiescent nor mute but where their corporeal presence 'provides an agency to affect the experience and actions of mourners and evoke memories of the past, rather than serving as a static and passive set of substances manipulated and disposed of by the mourners to serve their sociopolitical ends'.[11] The dead, in other words, have the potential to participate in and not just receive favours after the onset of biological death. Simple examples of such a function include setting out, in the lifetime, specific instructions as to how to conduct the burial, organise the grave and manage visits, or incorporating some clauses into the last will that may reorganise the life of the family or community.[12] Because such instructions take effect after the person dies, his or her agency changes in death and redefines the nature of any relationship with the living.

The idea of the dead as having agency partly resonates with the aforementioned notion of prospective memory defined by Assmann whereby the subject, before death, sets the stage for his/her own memory to endure. As a typical example of prospective memory Assmann cites ancient Egypt's practice of erecting one's own tomb to ascertain enduring remembrance: one such tombstone that belongs to a high priest explicitly reads, 'I have completed this tomb and created its inscription in person, while I was still alive'.[13] While this practice may have been compelled by the fear of being forgotten, it also inspired the common etiquette of reciprocity among the living subjects to show respect and in turn expect respect from future generations. However, unlike retrospective memory that works as legacy rather than agency, Williams's argument suggests the possibility of preserving subjectivity and personhood in death. Rather than persisting only as 'a static set of substances' through a symbolic function bestowed on them, or by choreographing their own memory through testimonial instructions, the dead potentially maintain an affective social presence that can leave a lasting impact on the way they are remembered.

While it is not entirely clear how enduring the agency of the dead may be and how it is expressed, it may be worthwhile to consider it as a function of memory. In personal recollections, memory returns the dead to history, to

---

[11] H. Williams, 'Death Warmed Up: The Agency of Body and Bones in Early Anglo-Saxon Cremation Rites', *Journal of Material Culture* 9:3 (2004), 265–7.
[12] H. Williams, 'Death Warmed Up', 266.
[13] J. Assmann, *Cultural Memory and Early Civilization*, 46.

the way they once were rather than the way they may be now. The paradox of that return is that it familiarises cultural connections to the dead, but in a relationally altered way: the dead are now claimed as our possession thanks to familial, ethnic, cultural, social or other ties we may have had with them. Such claims, perhaps inadvertently, turn the dead into objects submitted to the mercy of our will to remember them. We talk to them in our dreams, visit their graves, recall them in specific situations in their lives; we keep their mementos and memory as if these were an item of possession, to be handled as we see fit – which, in the case of urns, may literally be the case. Our memory keeps our dead in the shape and form they had when we knew them. It is difficult to recreate their memory as anything else, especially when the dead are invoked in the material condition as 'remains'.

In addition to being a mental conundrum (for we are unlikely to remember something of which we have no mental representation), there is also a theological side to the paradox found at the heart of Islamic and other monotheistic traditions: can we imagine the corporeality of a dead person after the decay has occurred? While some form of bodily reconstitution appropriate for the Hereafter seems to be Qur'anic reassurance to the believers, not everybody has been equally assured: in the Avicennian philosophical tradition, for example, bodily resurrection is understood in a metaphoric sense. It is logically impossible, many Islamic philosophers argue, for the corruptible body to regain its original form after decay (or cremation, one may add), in contrast to the soul, which is incorruptible and therefore enduring. The body, in other words, once dissolved, has dissolved beyond recovery. Ibn Qayyim, on the other hand, basing his opinion in the sacred traditions, submits that the martyrs will be given better bodies than the bodies they once had, and through such new bodies their enjoyment of divine provisions will be more intense than the enjoyment of all other spirits who have no bodies.[14] Life that continues in death is likely to continue in immaterial fashion or in a different corporeal manifestation. To the access of such memory, it is safe to say, we are not privy.

Memory of the dead thus gets entangled with transcendental considerations of death's inaccessible and incomprehensible workings to which most religious and secular teachings respond with hesitance, ambiguity, even silence. This perhaps is the key difference between memory of the dead and other forms of cultural memory, in that memory of the dead – and by extension of death – contains gaps resistant to interpretation and vacuous pockets that cannot be cognitively breached. In contrast to memory of events or places, which we can preserve in 'factual' ways, as having existence outside of us but one to which we are entitled by virtue of remembering them, our memory of the dead tends to challenge our sense of entitlement. Whichever way it is

---

[14] R. Eklund, *Life between Death and Resurrection*, 102.

approached, death remains the unknown, a cul-de-sac that becomes the sole and esoteric property of the dead. Our creative imagination, of course, remains busy with attempts to fill in this cognitive vacuum and give the dead a fair representational value. The inaccessibility of death serves frequently inspires fantasies about life in death. But the opposite is also true: the acceptance of death's esoteric otherness is also a way of adjusting cultural perceptions and behaviour. Consider, for example, the warning of Muhasibi, the ninth-century Sufi author from Baghdad, for whom the all too common egoistic impulse to deny our intellectual limitations must be replaced by a humility before death, the memory of the dead and acknowledgement of death's absolute unpredictability: 'The godservant remembers death by emptying the heart of everything except for his consciousness that death has no specific known time or cause or stage of life and his awareness of what death will bring to the human being. This awareness continues as he takes into account those who went before him.'[15] To know death is to accept its unknowability. To die is to learn it. Approximately a century later, another Sufi master, Qushayri, would poetically ponder that 'no one truly dies/who finds rest in dying/To truly die/is to live your death'.[16] Both Muhasibi and Qushayri seem to imply that death expands knowledge and that this new knowledge happens as a moral, conscious act *as* death happens, not before or after.

But except for the devotees who use Sufi moral psychology as everyday standard, approaching death and remembering the dead in this fashion is not easy. In fact, most of the time private and collective memory of the dead operates through ephemeral connections during intimate personal recollections or public ritual evocations, *in situ* or on specific occasions in their sacred calendar. Whether ritualised as Day of the Dead or its many vernacular versions, memory of the loss of life which commonly leaves an isolating effect on the mourner is partly dissipated through culturally framed expressions of bereavement and memorialisation whereby the mourner is able to attach their memory to a shared symbolic and eschatological vocabulary or material memento. While commemorative expressions are ritually and spiritually gratifying, however, the infinity, solitude and inaccessibility of death prolong the sense of isolation. It is within these distant boundaries, which fail to offer comfort for loss, that memories of the dead cease, incising a gap between those we once knew in their living condition and their condition in death which lacks any referent. This vacuous dimension of memory nevertheless adds to the 'connective tissue' that Jan Assmann considers integral to cultural unity. In this empty realm of memory, of vacuous abstraction, where representation is not possible and the distance between *us* and *them* expands, our dead are often elevated with all other dead, that is, beyond their projected

---

[15] Cited in M. Sells, *Early Islamic Mysticism* (New York: Paulist Press, 1996), 184.
[16] M. Sells, *Early Islamic Mysticism,* 101.

eschatological locations – Islamic, Christian, Jewish, agnostic or any other. This memory-of-no-memory is no longer individual and personal, nor is it collective and cultural. Here they are no longer the objects of our memory but rather persist as subjects in death, pushing the boundaries of our comfort zones established by our symbols, values and norms.

It is from this location of freedom from the contours of our memory that the dead may gain agency and acquire a proactive function in shaping, rather than being shaped by, our social bonds and cultural practices. This is especially the case with the dead whose glory, deeds and stature elevate them above average human beings. In life, they stand apart from the rest of us because they triumph over forces with which we cannot reckon. In death, as they continue to subsist beyond our cognitive, spiritual and experiential boundaries, our expectations of their out-of-the-ordinary powers increases. At best, such individuals are venerated as martyrs and saints, and their grace extends above and beyond the limits drawn by worldly institutions, social norms and common expectations. Contrarily, others can appear as bad spirits, in the Balkans also as vampires, werewolves and witches, to feed our fears and fantasies yet command simultaneous awe. In both accounts, these exceptional dead live on hagiographically, in collective and cultural memory as individuals who are able to defy greater powers, rise above everyday conditions and regulate our memories.

In the vernacular religious imagination in particular, these exceptional individuals are often released from the simulacrum of our eschatological projection and placed into the highest realm of the unknown, where they are in close proximity to the divine and worldly realms. From there, they can interact with us, assist us, heal us and occasionally hurt us. They do not merely exist as foci or targets of our commemorative attention but persist as subjects whose agency can take on different forms. In so doing, they participate in cultural transactions at levels that enhance and cement, or challenge and subvert, moral values and cultural meanings, but also surpass narrow boundaries drawn by individual communities, religions or ethnicities.

The Balkans serves as the prime example of such productive transactions. Throughout the region, the exceptional dead traverse the malleable boundaries between this world and the next to participate in the life of the community, temper its curiosity and expectations and engage in its affairs in benevolently or potentially threatening ways. As they negotiate the space between worlds they also affect the way people respond and behave, fuelling a vast pool of beliefs and practices that defy simple categories of official and unofficial religiosity. Their presence is also tied to social functions as they appear to assist their communities in times of crises. Across the Balkans, for example, there is a general distrust, historically formed and ideologically fuelled, in the ability and willingness of political and religious institutions to deliver the 'true and real story' at most levels of action. In contrast, the invisible space where the dead can make connections with both this and divine domains can offer alternative ways of establishing truth, resolving problems, unravelling secrets and assuaging loss, while at once grounding the communities with the help of ancestral bonds. Ambiguous in their absence, these dead emanate expansive and spectacular powers, often becoming venerated as healers or saints, respected as untimely heroic martyrs or dreaded as angry and dangerous spirits. The powers they exercise often defy official truths, with which the living are required to contend because of the demands imposed on them by religious, ethnic, or political affiliations. The diversity of the repertoire and transactions the dead offer – when they are remembered in appropriate times and ways – opens up space for knowledge and empowerment that institutional or political membership fails to provide. This is a more stimulating cultural form of remembrance of the dead because it carves new spaces of interaction that can often neutralise the dysfunctions of the real world or mitigate problems and tensions that occur among individuals and groups in real life.

Memories of the Better Times to Come

In the fluid spectrum that envelops mainstream commemorative rituals and highly localised vernacular beliefs in the region, the closest approximation of normative religiosity is the interaction with the dead whose powers of healing and divination preserve through memory across different generations and communities. This form of memorialisation is often associated with shrine culture, the local sacred and harvest calendar and various forms of ancestral and hagiographic memorialisation. In Bosnia and Herzegovina, remembrance of the fallen martyrs from earlier times and other righteous members of the community is facilitated by both cyclical and occasional visitations to their places of burial. The power of the dead inheres in the area where they rest, even though the resting ground can be both evoked and transcended thanks to their extraordinary spiritual powers of engagement beyond specific geographic or temporal parameters. The dead can also be visited in impromptu sacred journeys that provide an opportunity to retell their story and renew its relevance at any given time. The following are some examples of commemorative practices which preserve and reproduce the subjectivity of the dead and enhance their role in the shaping of cultural memory, values and internal and external boundaries of ritual life.

Waqf Endowments and Bequeathed Memories

Assmann's prospective memory, or memory where the dead choreograph their own commemoration, is most readily exemplified by the *waqf*, the Islamic charitable trust foundation through which its founder sets aside a portion of his or her property to be used for public or private benefits. Set up in both urban and rural areas in the Ottoman times and covering a range of assets, from agricultural, static, movable, commercial, residential and so on, the *waqf* trusts were a comprehensive mechanism for managing and circulating family assets and generating revenue for the beneficiaries through various modes of contract (rent, commerce, agriculture, etc.) and securing their wellbeing during the life and after the death of its founder. Most founders in this 'prospective' sense ascertained their active participation in the permanent affairs of their immediate and distant communities. The establishment of the *waqf* was mandated by the Prophetic *hadith*, commonly quoted at the front of the *waqf* contracts, that states, 'when a man dies, only three deeds will survive him: ongoing charity, profitable knowledge and a child praying for him', and under the Ottomans in particular this dictum reached expansive applications.[17] In one sense, then, a *waqf*'s aspiration is commemorative: to facilitate remembrance of the dead through bequeathed deeds, continued intellectual engagement and prayer, as stipulated by divine command and executed by the contractual nature of the trust. For example, in the 1582 *waqf* trust of the affluent Ottoman administrator Sinan Beg, complex mechanisms are set in place for the flow of profit, knowledge and remembrance. This last section is particularly pertinent to the idea of prospective memory and it includes detailed stipulations about the kind of gravestone/shrine (*turbe*) to be built for him, the appointment of four permanent guards (*turbedar*) who will work in two-by-two shifts and will offer daily blessings for the Prophet Muhammad, for which they will receive a daily salary; to appoint 10 skilful Qur'anic reciters who will recite a daily *juz'* [one-thirtieth part of the Qur'an] after the morning prayer and perform, every three days, a ritual of remembrance that will include prayers and the saying of the *Fātiḥa*. Moreover, the shrine should be adorned with a prayer rug, quilt, candles and candlesticks, a thyme-scented dispenser to be lit on Friday and other blessed eves and to hire a cleaner (*farrāsh*) to look after the shrine.[18]

Ostentatious though it seems, none of this is unusual. The cycle of righteous action, beneficial economy and commemorative appreciation of the founder of the trust within a long lineage of good-doers, beginning with the Prophet Muhammad, is achieved by integrating all elements of the endowment into a series of inter-connected transactions. Because the validity of the trust can only be legally terminated under very specific circumstances, the conditions set within are meant to last into perpetuity. The commemorative diagram of *waqf* trusts is thus set within a broader economy of gifts, responsibilities and benefits that, rather than imposing a demand on the act of remembrance, require connecting the dots in time and space and establishing an open channel

---

[17] For more on the subject see 'Wakf', in *Encyclopaedia of Islam*, 2nd edn, BrillOnline Reference Works, http://referenceworks.brillonline.com/browse/encyclopaedia-of-islam-2.

[18] *Vakufname iz Bosne i Herzegovine*, 209–10.

of communication between the deceased founders and their beneficiaries. In such a scheme, the immediate beneficiaries of the trust are equally responsible to ascertain that the purpose of the trust is respected, along with the founder. In this particular trust, Lady Shams, the wife of the founder, who herself is of a notable family background as the sister of the great vizier Sokollu Mehmet Pasha (Mehmed Paša Sokolović), is the beneficiary of a handsome daily allowance of 30 *akçe*, but is assigned with the responsibility to

> Deliver one hundred blessings a day for the soul of the best of the humankind [Muhammad]. As long as she is alive, let her enjoy this allowance. When by the decree of Lord she passes from this to eternal life, may five sections (*juz'*) of the Qur'an be recited at her shrine (*turbe*). Have the righteous and knowledgeable people skilled at reciting the Qur'an gather at her shrine after morning prayers, let them also say a prayer and recite the *Fātiḥa* and let them present that prayer to God for the soul of the greatest among the prophets of God. Let them complete the prayers of supplication every six days. For that, they shall receive the daily salary of two *akçe*.[19]

Understandably, each stipulation of the endowment was not necessarily followed to the letter, nor was it spelled out in such minute detail by every founder. The conditions and requirements of any trust reflected the power and ambitions of its endower and it required a certain social cachet in order to be implemented. Although the *waqf* was a remarkably well-represented and durable mode of investiture, ordinary folk who had no means to endow trusts pursued other forms of religious expression and engagement so as to nurture their hope of being remembered.

Petitionary Memories: Dova and Dovište

In addition to shrine visitations and recitations of prayers planned out by specific endowments, commemorative connections are also established at designated locations and at particular times, and are submitted to the dead as a plea to intervene. One such type of location is known as *dovište*, the place where the supplication plea, *dova*, is said (from Arabic *duʿā*). During such rituals these locations are activated as sacred sites imbued with spiritual and mnemonic significance, but they do not retain such status at other times. Here too, commemorative evocations are usually accompanied by petitionary pleas on behalf of the self or others. Prayers are asked for forgiveness or mercy in worldly matters and afterlife and hopes are expressed that the dead will transmit fragments of divine mercy to those who remember them. The dead are therefore not themselves the beneficiaries of such invocations, nor are they objects of worship. Rather they are at once spiritual conduits through whom the worlds are brought closer together and individuals and communities

---

[19] *Vakufname iz Bosne i Herzegovine*, 211.

provided with a safe commemorative depository. The worship is directed to God's mercy, but the pleas for its delivery are commonly – though not exclusively – issued to the dead. Because the *dovište* is only implicitly connected with a particular individual but more so with his or her deeds, the ritual focus is not anthropocentric, or cult oriented and as such tends to receive more acceptance in normative Islam despite its historical and ritual association with popular practices.

While many such commemorative events are held in honour of specific occasions to celebrate accomplishments and show support for the community and its living members, also common are *dovište* gatherings offered for favourable weather conditions to aid the harvest of healthy crops (*kišna dova*, or rain prayer).[20] Rain prayers, as attested by the Prophetic traditions, are said to have been recited by the Prophet himself (*istisqā'*), but these are clearly related to the local harvest season as well. Environmental considerations, economic prosperity and religious benefits work side by side. Many such events connect communities across religious and other divides and their administration fuses official and unofficial dimensions of belief. For example, some events are held on Fridays in or around the mosques to reflect Islamic ritual patterns while others are performed in the fields away from mosques and settlements and scheduled on days necessitated by agriculture and husbandry which lie at the core of the local economy, not only for Muslims but local Christians as well. The benefit of such commemorative prayers commonly extends to all. Local Christians, while not attending the prayer, enter the ritual frame by contributing with food and good wishes for the town feast that follows the ritual.

Historically, this form of communal intimacy may carry only local resonance, but internal to it is an exchange of goodwill mediated through the commemorative act. In the aftermath of the recent war, however, many such events have been cancelled, some because of the success of the ethnic cleansing campaigns that dispersed local Muslim populations and others because of the shift in public religiosity occasioned by a more assertive presence of normative Islamic injunctions in everyday life.

On the other hand, some other local practices have in fact been canonised by the Islamic leadership and transformed into instruments of religious and political affirmation. The most relevant example is the Ajvatovica *dovište* located in central Bosnia, which fuses several elements: ritual remembrance and supplication prayers, commemorative visitations, beliefs and practices and postwar identity formation. In fact, since the early 2000s, Ajvatovica has become the most visible and widespread example of commemorative pilgrimage in Bosnia and Herzegovina, having entered the official religious calendar and narrative as emblematically Bosnian Islamic and as such fully

---

[20] E. Mulahalilović, *Vjerski običaji Muslimana u Bosni i Hercegovini* [Religious customs among the Muslims of Bosnia and Herzegovina] (Tuzla: Hamidović, 2005), 166–91.

supported by Islamic clerical leadership and its followers. Historically performed in both Ottoman and post-Ottoman times on a smaller scale, the ritual was abandoned in 1947 after the establishment of Titoist Yugoslavia. After the end of the 1992–95 war, Ajvatovica was revived and became vital for postwar rebuilding of Bosniak identity on both religious and political grounds.

Located in central Bosnia, Ajvatovica is named after a local benefactor and the patron of arts and education in the region, Ajvaz Dede. The legend has it that around the time of Ajvaz Dede's arrival in the town of Prusac in the early Ottoman times, the water supplies had been low and unreliable because of a large rock that had landed on the spring, cutting off water flow and causing drought and indigence. To make things worse, the local government showed no regard for the town's predicament, leaving it in complete destitution, neglect and disgrace. Then Ajvaz Dede came along: for 40 mornings on end he prayed to God to split open the rock. On the fortieth night he had a dream that two rams butted into the rock and crushed it apart. Indeed, on the fortieth morning, when he went to resume his prayer, Ajvaz Dede saw the rock had split into two and the water had begun its free and life-giving flow towards the town, bringing back prosperity and health before too long.

Although its origins are unknown, the legend is clearly related to festivities surrounding fertility and renewal and is likely extricated from a pre-Ottoman context. This is especially relevant as the commemoration of Ajvaz Dede's triumph is allocated to spring time in the sacred calendar, though notably not the Islamic Hijri but local Slavic calendar, as it is said to fall on the seventh Monday after Jurjev, or the day of St George, the patron saint who had defeated a dragon and saved his community from destruction. Protective and regenerative action is associated with the rites of spring and is celebrated among Balkan Christian and Muslims alike in a variety of rituals despite the fact that St George is primarily associated with the Orthodox Christian hagiography. The aforementioned ritual prayers for rain and bountiful crops at other *dovište* sites are also counted in relation to Jurjev, clearly pointing to plural origins of this ritual performance. In the case of Ajvatovica pilgrimage, on the seventh Monday after Jurjev, a large procession of pilgrims leaves the neighbouring towns towards the town of Prusac, in whose precincts Ajvatovica is located. Another perspective likens the legend to the Hajj pilgrimage, to the point that it is at times referred to, albeit contentiously, as the minor Hajj, or *mali hadž*. Here, similarities are drawn with Abraham and Hagar's story of the gushing of the Zamzam water near the Ka'ba, and the visitations of the grave of Ajvaz Dede is compared to the period the pilgrims spend in Medina.[21]

When the procession departs, at its head march the *muftis*, followed by horses decorated to match their riders, then the bearers of different religious

---

[21] N. Clayer and A. Popovic, 'Le culte d'Ajvatovica et son pèlerinage annuel', in H. Cambert-Loir and C. Guillot, *Le Culte des Saints dans le Monde Musulman* (Paris: École française d'Extreme Orient, 1995), 353–65.

Figure 2.1 Ajvaz Dede's rock.
Photo by Velibor Božović

and political banners and finally all other pilgrims, male and female. The dramatic flow of the procession is interspersed with relaxing moments of communal intimacy, which includes drinking coffee, sharing food, performing prayers and singing spiritual songs. Prayers are also said along the way at the shrines of Bosnian Muslim martyrs, recent and ancient, whose sacrifice is remembered in a festive fashion, until the final destination of the procession is reached at the site of the portentous rock. There the main prayer follows, headed by the spiritual and religious leader of Bosnian Muslims, Reis ul-Ulema, who concludes the pilgrimage with a speech in remembrance of Ajvaz Dede followed by the praise of his community and its historical unity.

In 2012, the speech delivered by the former Reis, Dr Mustafa Cerić, clearly integrated multiple symbols into the narrative of communal unity and national self-preservation. In Dr Cerić's words, the highly spiritual message that nature can be subjugated to the power of prayer can also be understood as a call to political mobilisation and awareness, especially in the aftermath of the genocidal war against Bosnian Muslims. 'Ajvatovica,' he hailed, 'is a clear *feth* [opening; conquest] because it is here that Heaven opens so that the Earth may inhale pristine air to purify the soul from the sins that taint with corruption the land and the sea ... Ajvatovica then is a great *nasr* [victory] because it is here that Good Bosniaks gather in freedom and joy to rejoice their land and their faith.'[22] Cultural memory functions as a frame through which different moments and individuals in the history of Bosnian Islam are drawn into the present narrative of Bosniak national identity. Here Cerić clearly evokes the memory of Ajvaz Dede, in the role of the founding father of the community's ethos and commitment to God, as well as the prosperity of his community, and affirms belief in an ultimate triumph against all worldly challenges. Many different Bosniak martyrs, disconnected in historical time, are associated as symbols of cumulative sacrifice and willingness to give up life for the good of all: the famous sixteenth-century Bosnian scholar from Prusac, Hasan Kafi Pruščak, who left a lasting mark on the Ottoman intellectual history; Bosniak victims of genocide and atrocities in the recent war; Bosniak past and current political leaders and religious guides and so on. Building thus on both the transcendental message by integrating the Qur'anic text into the commemorative narrative and historical references through which Bosnian Islam has been configured, Dr Cerić infuses Ajvatovica with decisive ethico-political demands for group unity and identity. The appeal to the memory of the dead – Ajvaz Dede and the subsequent martyrs in defence of Bosnian Islam – solidifies this group identity and is paramount for the sense of togetherness and connection. 'The notion of identity,' John Gillis writes,

---

[22] 'Farewell Speech of Reis ul-Ulema Dr Mustafa Cerić at Ajvatovica, Shaban/June, 1433/2012', http://www.rijaset.ba/index.php?option=com_content&view=article&id=14642:govor-reisu-l-uleme-na-ajvatovici-2&catid=40:minine-vijesti.

'depends on the idea of memory and vice versa ... [and] a sense of sameness over time and space is sustained by remembering.'[23]

Ajvatovica is of course one of many *dovište* locations in Bosnia and Herzegovina but it has become the most popular and significant one for the normative value given to the memory of Ajvaz Dede. He facilitates the link among different strands of cultural memory: in remembering Ajvaz Dede, unsettled historical problems are explained and contemporary challenges are addressed. He is therefore not just an object of memory but a participant in historical developments beyond his lifetime. New historical experiences are integrated into the meaning of this old legend, giving it dynamic relevance in the restorative link between the dead and the living. Other such rituals, activated by commemorations of a more localised type, also point to the importance of cultural sedimentation which allows the memory of historically isolated individuals and events to be filtered through a similar commemorative continuum. The dead become a spiritual family actively overseeing the wellbeing of the community and not just mute ancestors held captive by a distant cultural heritage or valuable only as a symbolic cultural inventory. Active and engaged, they demand committed acts of remembrance so as to make their presence favourable and their legacy relevant.

Turbe Visitations and Saintly Commemorations

While *dovište* may not always be associated with the resting ground of someone's remains, it nevertheless draws strong parallels with the workings of divine grace through specific saintly individuals for whom death has brought higher levels of spiritual authority and capacity for intercession thanks to their deeds and virtues in life. In this latter case, a visit to the shrine is more directly focused on the memory of individuals who, in death, activate spiritual blessings, evoke trust and perform good deeds for those who remember them in this life. Such shrines appear either in the form of mausoleums known as *turbe* (from Turkish *türbe*) or martyr's graves (*šehitski nišan*), although they occasionally overlap in terms of spiritual meaning and ritual function. In the case of *turbes* the shrines are architecturally designed as simple rectangle, house-like structures or, if dedicated to more affluent individuals, octagonal and/or hexagonal stone mausoleums capped with a dome that signifies a protective firmament for the wooden or stone sarcophagus and often, although not always, open on the sides in a birdcage exposure.[24] While most *turbes* are erected within precincts of mosques as part of the deceased's notable endowment, across the Balkans in general and Bosnia and Herzegovina in

---

[23] J. Gillis (ed.), *Commemorations: The Politics of National Identity* (Princeton: Princeton University Press, 1994), 4.

[24] J. Dickie (Y. Zaki), 'Allah and Eternity: Mosques, Madrasas and Tombs', in G. Michell (ed.), *Architecture of the Islamic World* (London: Thames and Hudson, 1995), 44–5.

particular they are also found within or outside larger cemeteries and are sites of popular piety and remembrance. They exist as spiritual lampposts for local and foreign travellers to consult in dire times, to remember the virtues of the person lying in it in hope of favourable resonance in one's own lifetime and to bring small offerings in times of prosperity. In the common jargon, these individuals are collectively referred to as '*dobri*', the good one(s), a term carried over from pre-Ottoman times when the dead, according to the local tradition, returned in dreams to grant favours and fulfil wishes of those who remembered them. As discussed earlier, the overlap between the concept of *dobri* and the Islamic notion of the 'friends of God', or *awliya/evliya*, is striking, in that both are mediums through which divine grace is manifested and both require virtuous hosts to transmit that grace from the divine to the human realm. Across Bosnia and Herzegovina, such shrines stand between official and vernacular modes of memory of the dead and renegotiate the question of dead as subject/objects. A nineteenth-century 'roster' of saints of Sarajevo includes over 80 such locations in this city alone. Most of them are identified by name – the great majority of which is male except for three female shrines – but there are also several anonymous ones. They range professionally from Sufi masters, dervishes, religious scholars, military martyrs and others, all of which are remembered as '*dobri*' and '*evliya*'. The shrines, the roster states, are pilgrimage locations where candles are lit and *murad* (wish) is made.[25]

Some of the popular *turbes* include the Seven Brothers, also known as the Yediler, in Sarajevo, a shrine visited both ritually and casually because of its downtown location. The Yediler legend has it that each of the seven tombs side by side in the *turbe* belongs to a martyr, not fallen in war but as innocent victims of crime. Wronged and killed in different ways and moments in time, the seven are not brothers in blood but in injustice, and are united in death through a condition that allows their life to continue altruistically, by bestowing favours on those who remember them through visitations and prayers. Placed side by side in seven sarcophagi, they are vested with a single symbolic charge distributed within each in equal measure. When paying a visit, one ought to remember and offer prayer to each brother so that kindness can flow from all.

Other famous *turbes*, some of which have not been fully dated or documented, include that of the Malkoč and Skenderbeg family in Kopčić; Mustafa Gaibi in Nova Gradiška; the Filipović family in Glamoč; Šejh Jujo in Mostar; Kadri Alaybeg's *turbe* in Ustikolina; poet Hasan Kaimi's *turbe* in Zvornik; Hazret Ali near Prijedor; The Young Woman's *turbe* near Tuzla and

---

[25] A. Bejtić, 'Jedno vidjenje sarajevskih evlija i njihovih grobova kao kultnih mjesta [One perspective on the saints of Sarajevo and their graves as veneration sites]', *POF* 31 (1981), 111–22.

many more.[26] Also worthy of note are the tombstones believed to contain the remains of the aforementioned Sisters of Rum. They too are referred to as *dobri/dobre*. Like in many other examples, some of their gravestones are topped with a cup-like cavity. It is believed that the rainwater collected in these stone cups acquires healing benefits and is ritually consumed so as to help ease labour pains, chronic aches, infections and other physical ailments.[27] The curative action of such rituals is thus caught up in a dialectical relationship between memory of the dead and prosperity of the living. Without it the wellbeing of both the dead and the living would be put to risk.

Judaism and Christianity in the region participate in similar beliefs and practices. In fact, as suggested above, these sacred memorials are often shared despite their grounding in one specific religious tradition. The porous and open character of these restorative connections transcends politically or religiously drawn boundaries allowing symbolic meaning to arch above the language of religious or ethnic exclusivity. An example of such commemorative locations associated with Judaism is the shrine of Moshe Danon, the nineteenth-century Jewish rabbi of Sarajevo who died in Stolac, Herzegovina, on the way to the Holy Land. His story begins with his arrest along with many other influential Jewish merchants of Sarajevo by an infamous Ottoman governor of Bosnia after an assumed murder of a Jewish convert to Islam by a group of displeased Jews. Such collective punishment after the perpetrators could not be found was met with discontent by the Muslim neighbours who staged a protest demanding the release of Rabbi Danon and the other wrongfully arrested and accused Jews. Refusing to take no for an answer, they stormed the prison and released the prisoners, while the governor fled the city, never to come back. Rabbi Danon, saved from imminent execution, spent the rest of his life in meditation and doing good deeds until he decided to make his pilgrimage. Dying on the sacred journey placed him among the righteous martyrs and saints. He was remembered annually through ritual visitations until the Second World War, twice a year by Jewish pilgrims, and at other times less formally by local Muslims and Christians in search of good fortune.[28]

Another relevant example with pan-traditional commemorative value is the tombstone of a fallen young woman in Ostružnica near Fojnica. The legend has her as secretly commanding a unit of the Ottoman army during the conquests of Bosnia while impersonating a male officer; victory in many battles is attributed to her. Her furtive self-representation had gone unnoticed throughout her deployment until a fatal shot from a Christian

---

[26] E. Kujundžić, *Bošnjacka tradicijska kultura: uspomenar* [Bosnian traditional culture: memoir] (Sarajevo: LAPIS, 2009), 259.

[27] M. Hadžijahić, 'Badžijanije u "Sarajevu"', 116; A. Bejtić, 'Jedno vidjenje sarajevskih evlija', 116–17.

[28] S. Schwartz, *Sarajevo Rose: A Balkan Jewish Notebook* (London: Saqi Books, 2005), 52–4.

canon ended her life. When her body was taken to wash and prepare for burial, her transvestite secret was shockingly disclosed to all. Despite the initial confusion, she received full military honours and a recognition that her female identity had never stood in the way of her military heroism. In fact, her deviance from 'normalcy' ultimately proliferated into many stories of her heroic martyrdom and contributed to the motif of gender-free chivalry that pushed the boundaries of social mores and values. Her tombstone, stylistically adjusted by the masons to reflect her female identity without compromising military prowess, became a visitation site for non-Muslim and Muslim women alike. Muslim women hold Friday liturgies at her grave, but at other times both Muslim and non-Muslim women pray at its side for healing purposes, specifically if they cannot lactate as new mothers. It also became customary for unmarried young women to chip a piece of the tombstone and carry it as talisman against infertility and bad spirits.

In a similar vein, a cluster of martyrs' cemeteries near the village of Baskije in central Bosnia attracts local farmers who take their horses for circumambulation of the tombstones in hope that the martyrs, the fallen cavalrymen, would help cure the horses' bladder problems. In these three

Figure 2.2 *Turbe* in Ustikolina.
Photo by Velibor Božović

Figure 2.3 Ajvaz Dede's *turbe* in Prusac.
    Photo by Amila Buturović

examples, as in many others, healing is not restricted to one community but open for shared benefits of all those who seek it. The dead, long past their biological demise, manifest their presence and engage the living, jointly affecting social and cultural practices and norms. Moreover, the ethical dimension of these transactions is not dispensed in exceptional times or switched on at specific days of the sacred calendar but is the condition of everyday life. As such, it is part of a continuum where the renewal of memory of the dead, re-affirmation of their exceptional personhood and prosperity of the living are interdependent and necessary for a regenerative bond between the graves and the community in which they reside.

Figure 2.4 Ostružnica shrine with 1171 AH/1758 CE etched in the stone. Visible in the middle are the traces of stone scrapings used for curative powers.
Photo by Amila Buturović

Figure 2.5 Inside ruins of the *turbe* in Glamoč.
Photo by Velibor Božović

The Double Life of Beheaded Martyrs

Of related interest in memory workings is the type of martyr remembered primarily as a cephalophore: a head-bearing hero. In both Christian and Muslim lore of the Balkans this topos pertains to an instance of heroic sacrifice where a warrior is decapitated but continues to struggle valiantly while carrying his head under his armpit.[29]

The severed head seems to be a wider motif in the literary and religious imagination around the world. From the Celtic cult of the heads to Chhinnamasta, one of the 10 Tantric goddesses, the motif of the decapitated body and its head spans many different cultures, and occasions a variety of interpretations. In the European context, Beatrice White contends that the ancient Greek and Latin authors, including Homer and Virgil, who used this motif to dramatise violent encounters between heroes and anti-heroes and to shock the audience, provided ample material for later writers to produce dramatic and magic effects with the same motif.[30] Often, disembodied heads speak, telling of things of which embodied heads do not know. Disembodied heads may be confusing and frightening to the ordinary eye but they are commonly truth telling and life giving. In the religious imagination across

---

[29] V. Yankova, 'Светци-воини. Балкански легенди за светци кефалофори. [Martyrs-Warriors: Balkan legends of saints kefalofori]', *Ethnocultural Interactions* (2005), 39–55.

[30] B. White, 'A Persistent Paradox', *Folklore*, 83:2 (1972), 121–3.

Christian hagiography, examples of decapitated martyrs who live on and miraculously carry their severed heads with purpose abound. St Denis, the patron saint of Paris, is perhaps the most famous example of the rich cephalophoric repertoire in Western Christianity. In Islam, decapitation is a subject of various literary and mystical writings, as well as theological and legal discussion of praying over mutilated and beheaded bodies, even heads alone.[31] However, the motif of cephalophory is rare but there are several important examples such as the story of King Yunan and his doctor Duban in the *Arabian Nights*, al-Hallāj in the rendering of Farīd al-Dīn 'Attār's *Bīsar-nāmeh*, the tragic seventeenth-century poet martyr, Sarmad of Sindh, and others.

Bosnian beheaded martyrs seem to draw neither directly from the Islamic tradition nor from the Catholic lore, but from Byzantine Christianity into which they weave strands of the Qur'anic and Sufi ideas of martyrdom. In Byzantine Christianity, cephalophory is most commonly integrated into the culture of warrior saints. Drawing on the broader Biblical and non-Biblical lore, the concept of the warrior saint evolved around the idea of spreading the word and laws of Christ, defending the land and destroying enemies. Warrior saints functioned both as the army engaged in a divine mission and as police monitoring the outer and inner borders of the Empire. As Christopher Walter suggests, Christ's teaching that one should turn the other cheek did not particularly inspire the Byzantines. Rather, they focused on Christ's revelation that the world is the dominion of Satan and those who occupy it without committing to Christ's word had to be fought.[32] Combating the enemy was a spiritual mission as much as worldly. Dying in it constituted martyrdom and enabled recruitment into the celestial army. Thanks to divine guidance, warrior saints possessed special protective powers that enabled them to intervene in Byzantine battles. Their representation in iconographic art and hagiographic literature reveals a diverse typology within which cephalophoric types occupy a prominent role. In most cases, after the enemy beheads them they pick up their head and walk some distance carrying it in their hand until they arrive at a desired site, which they transform into sacred ground by leaving their relics to be venerated.[33] Unlike severed heads in Western or Middle and Far Eastern folklore and literature, Byzantine severed heads are rarely, if ever, talking heads. Rather, they reveal that our somatic perception of life and death is limited and skewed: the sacrificed head and its detached body continue to be metaphysically/psychologically connected, promising a new beginning despite the brutality of decapitation.

In the Bosnian Islamic tradition, cephalophore martyrs, like their Byzantine counterparts, are most commonly associated with military hagiography. They

---

[31] L. Halevi, *Muhammad's Grave*, 163–4.
[32] C. Walter, *The Warrior Saints in Byzantine Art and Tradition* (Aldershot: Ashgate, 2003), 141.
[33] C. Walter, *The Warrior Saints*, 142–3.

stagger through battlefields, sometimes even continuing to wreak damage on enemy soldiers, taking control over their own death. Though dead, they are given a chance to live another life. The broader Islamic tradition holds that martyrs to not actually die, 'nay, they live on', the Qur'an tells us, 'but you do not perceive them' (Q2:154). In the dramatic unfolding of their death they witness the truth of the world beyond while still engaged in this one. Such double agency is spellbinding. Martyrdom is a gift of knowledge inaccessible to ordinary human beings. Cephalophores are alive and dead at the same time; they are visible *here* in life and present *there* in death. They alter our mundane understanding of the lines that separate the two realms, diminishing the savagery of violence, making it more meaningful and less frightening.

While commonly associated with military and, by extension, male virtues, cephalophory is also associated with other experiences of violence. One shrine near the north-eastern city of Tuzla, for example, is said to belong to a young Muslim woman who stood up to defend her honour against inappropriate advances by an Austro-Hungarian soldier. Enraged by her resistance, the soldier cut off her head. The defiant girl martyr lifted her severed head and walked back to the village where she fell to the ground, clutching her head all the way. The shrine was promptly erected at the very spot where she fell, becoming holy ground. Like other martyrs, the young woman in this legend did not require the conventional burial that includes ritual washing and an orderly interment in the grave. Violence had ennobled her and given her a new purpose while freeing her of the requirements associated with ordinary death.

Two other examples of 'lay', non-military cephalophory are worthy of note as well: the first one, recorded in 1908 by the Austrian journalist Robert Michel, connects it with the concept of '*dobri*':

> Near a major mosque on the bank of the river in Mostar lies a *dobri*. His story, dated to the eighteenth century, runs as follows: when the news of an Austrian incursion into Bosnia reached Mostar, a man was sitting in his store and shaving. Upon hearing the news he rushed out, his face only half shaved, swinging his walking stick ferociously and summoning his fellow Mohammadans to rise and take a revenge on the Austrians. After that public outburst he disappeared from the face of the earth. At the moment when he was swinging his stick, the Austrians all the way in Banja Luka are said to have experienced intangible pains of the whip. Many years later that same man was spotted at a hill overlooking Mostar. He carried his severed head under his armpit down into the market, walked over the Ćejvan Pasha's mosque and disappeared into the earth. A *turbe* was immediately built on the spot of his disappearance and it became a pilgrimage site for both Muslims and Christians where they burn candles at their holidays.[34]

The second example involves the famous albeit enigmatic figure of Sheikh Gaibi, a seventeenth-century Sufi master remembered for ecstatic utterances,

---

[34] R. Michel, *Mostar 1908, with Photographs by Wilhelm Wiener* (Sarajevo: Dobra knjiga, 2006), 123–4.

prophecies and an open criticism of corrupt Ottoman governors and elite. The earliest written record of Gaibi is found in an eighteenth-century Catholic work on parish priests and religious officials of the town of Gradiška, known as the Berbir Fort, bordering between Bosnia and Croatia. In this Latin source Gaibi is called a great prophet and healer, having cured people of plague. It is also said that foreign travellers in the Balkans would cross the Sava in boats and pray beside Gaibi's grave.[35] Relevant to our discussion is that his death is wrapped in a cephalophoric mystery. In 1936, a Serbian journalist chronicled it as follows:

> Near the town's penitentiary, on the hill overlooking the river Sava, lies a white mausoleum surrounded by flowerbeds and a heavy steel fence. A legend has it that it belongs to the saint Gaibi. People believe his predictions all came true. An unusual incidence is also told about his death. One quiet evening after the prayer, the sheikh walked across to the Slavonian (Croatian) side of the river Sava to relax in a nearby park. An earlier prophecy of his had stated: *Sava medja – Gaibina ledja* [Sava the boundary – Gaibi's back] came true on that eve, because as he was sitting quietly a bunch of drunk Janissaries decided to beat up and behead 'the filthy dervish with much pleasure', as they later boasted to the judge. The next morning, the commander of the Berbir fort sent an order to fetch the body of the poor man and bury him in the Berbir cemetery on this side of the river.
> In the late hours after the burial, when only the stars make flickering sound, the guard of the northern gate spotted an apparition walking slowly in his direction over the surface of the river, as if floating. The poor guard felt shivers all over his body, his hair stood on end, his eyes bulged open. He saw a ghost, a man, carrying his severed head under his armpit. This surreal creature walked on the water as if it was dry land. As the moon rose, the guard took a good look at the severed head: its complexion was pale like wax, its eyes wide open and lit by the moonlight, looking at once threatening and saintly. This ghastly apparition walked calmly towards the spot where a couple of days earlier the old dervish was beaten and beheaded. The apparition was Gaibi's ghost. The following Friday, as per the commander's orders and under the pressure of the saint's keen followers and general populace, his remains were transported to the location of his death and, with the approval of the Austrian authorities, a shrine was erected over his grave.[36]

In all three stories, martyrdom is rewarded in both divine and social terms: divinely, because an act of injustice suffered by the martyrs lead to their ability to bear witness to the highest truth, and socially, because their cephalophory occasions a sacred journey from the place of violence to the place of rest and peace, recognised and venerated by the living. Cephalophores' insight

---

[35] M. Huković, 'Gaibija, šejh Mustafa – mistik i buntovnik [Sheikh Mustafa Gaibi, mystic and rebel]', *POF* 41 (1991), 401–8; F. Hadžibajrić, 'Risala Šejha Mustafe Gaibije [Treatise of sheikh Mustafa Gaibi]', *Anali Gazi Husrev-begove Biblioteke* 4 (1976); M. Kostić, 'Gaibijino Turbe kod Stare Gradiške [Gaibi's *turbe* near Stara Gradiška]', *Narodna Starina* 13 (1934).

[36] R. Radić, 'Bosanska Gradiška – nekadašnji Berbir [Bosanska Gradiška – previously Berbir]'. *Politika [Daily]*. 1 September 1936.

enacted as the last journey is thus doubly acknowledged and commemorated. In the Bosnian Islamic tradition, regardless of whether they are military cephalophores or ordinary ones, the relics are not venerated the way they are in Orthodox Christianity. Rather, the shrine erected on these chosen locations assumes a similar function of channelling divine grace. Like the previously mentioned examples of shrine culture, cephalophory too is spatially memorialised. The spot where decapitated heads fall has, on occasion, purportedly been consecrated on impact, resulting in a miraculous geological event: a spring bursting from dry soil, a creek turning into a torrential waterfall, a barren spot transforming into a lush shrub. The transformative power of these events affirms martyrdom and embeds its memory in the landscape. The landscape becomes holy ground, naturalised through death and commemorated subsequently through ritual visitations to the site and retelling of the legend. These different strands contribute to a sense of continuity of popular religion but also to the consolidation of learned religion as well, allowing both Muslim and Christian populations to develop a sense of shared lore, values and rituals.

Because the majority of cephalophore martyrs are associated with early military expeditions, most are built in the early Ottoman style: an oversized upright slab topped with a large turban. They are commonly folded into the category of *šehitski nišan* in case of a single grave and *šehitluk* in the case of a cluster of graves. Slabs are not usually inscribed although they may include an image or relief common among pre-Ottoman tombstones, such as sword, hatchet, semi-sphere, rosette or shield. The story is thus simultaneously tethered to a specific tombstone and set free through fluid and versatile folklore that releases it from fixed narrative detail. The martyr's death gives the story a sense of textual finality and completeness but its repetitions open it up to an extended narration, to a post-scriptum that can render new details to the hero's story of double life and death. Because the tombstones do not include biographical data, individuality is lost in collectivity. Even the aforementioned roster of saints from Sarajevo never mentions this particular type of martyrdom. As a result, the anonymity places cephalophores into the common pool of heroes so it is not unusual to encounter variances in names and religious affiliation. In fact, only one tombstone found in Kozarac near the town of Prijedor narrates the legend in the epigraphic text. The inscription reads:

> Lord, this is a martyr's shrine. God has made him into the manifestation of His Glory. He fought for some time heroically, then came to this spot carrying his own head. May Muhammad pray for him. Lord, receive this as our gift on behalf of all martyrs and in the name of our Prophet Muhammad. We thank the Lord, the Creator of the world. This tombstone was erected by the noble captain of Kozarac, Mehmed Bey. Year 1125 (1713 CE).[37]

---

[37] M. Mujezinović, *Islamska epigrafika Bosne i Hercegovine* [Islamic Epigraphy of Bosnia and Herzegovina] (Sarajevo: Sarajevo Publishing, 1998), 3:43.

Figure 2.6 Cephalophore martyr, Turovi.
Photo by Amila Buturović

Figure 2.7 Cephalophore martyr, Lukavac.
Photo by Amila Buturović

Thus, although born out of violence and strife, the cephalophores have entered cultural memory as heroes whose self-sacrifice for the greater good became a shared lore among Muslims and Christians. Communities that live near these shrines partake in commemoration by reproducing their stories as common heritage and cherishing their benevolent presence as they are believed to provide assistance in times of crisis and resolve seemingly impossible conflicts, tasks and demands. Because cephalophore martyrs highlight the ethics of just strife and the capacity to receive divine grace in the moment of ultimate duress, it is arbitrary whose battles they fight. They are elevated from the historical moment. The individualism of their sacrifice stimulates a collective responsibility to remember the martyr and immortalise the ethical effects of their deeds. In the case of the cephalophoric and indeed all martyrs, remembrance is thus not urged in order to procure their salvation; it is to facilitate ours. To forget these slain dead is to forsake the grace freely bestowed upon us through the act of commemoration.

Bad Spirits, Dangerous Memories

In contrast to such affirmative and productive participation of the dead in community life, some forms of post-mortem activity, such as those associated with foul spirits, witches and vampires, can negatively possess the dead and persuade them to haunt the living. This type of presence is not amicable and must be shunned.[38] The qualitative difference results from the liminal period of the soul's vulnerability as it enters the space of death. Protecting the corpse from negative forces during this transition by giving it proper burial rites is an obligation initially bequeathed to those who are caring for the corpse, preparing it and laying it to rest, and is then entrusted to a wider community of mourners.

Although some scholars of local Balkan folklore suggest that the arrival of Islam uprooted many rituals associated with bad spirits, witches and vampires,[39] one can nevertheless observe a series of post-mortem beliefs and practices of Muslims across the region that are reminiscent of ancient folk traditions in combination with local Christian and Islamic teachings. In fact, by the time Islam spread in the region, the belief in the powers of the undead had taken root among various religious cultures in the region, and it was often projected as a sign of undesired and dangerous otherness by the Christian establishment.[40] With the advent of Islam, the belief was further incorporated into the aforementioned Islamic concerns for the wellbeing of the dead as they ease their way into the hereafter. Geared to prevent the torment of the soul and its abduction by foul spirits, which may lead to the fracturing and displacement of the deceased's identity, these concerns reflect an unease with the body and soul being placed beyond the reach shortly after death happens. While the Islamic understanding of the passage into death promotes the idea that bones keep some form of identity and subjectivity, the Qur'an also conveys that the souls of the dead are retained by His side until the Judgement Day (Q39:42) and only then reunited with the material remains that lie in the grave.[41] The body, the Qur'an tells us, rests abandoned in the interspace, the *barzakh*, which for the first generations of Muslims presented an intellectual and psychological conundrum. Literally meaning a barrier, the *barzakh* is scripturally introduced as a type of eschatological liminality, a transitional spacetime that shuts the dead out of this world while intimating to them their predicament in the life to come. However, the Qur'an is silent about the experiential processes in the *barzakh*, giving no insight into the state of physical remains. Early Islamic tradition, guided by the Prophetic *hadith*, responded to this absence by mitigating a sharp separation of the body and soul and expatiating on the interconnection between the spirit (*rūḥ*), with

---

[38] T. P. Vukanović, 'Witchcraft in the Central Balkans II: Protection against the Witches', *Folklore*, 100: 2 (1989), 221–36.
[39] T. R. Georgevitch, 'Serbian Habits and Customs', *Folklore*, 28:1 (1917), 38.
[40] B. McClelland, *Slayers and their Vampires: A Cultural History of Killing the Dead* (Ann Arbor: The University of Michigan Press, 2006), 47–8.
[41] J. Smith and Y. Haddad, *The Islamic Understanding of Death and Resurrection*, 40–41, 55–6; L. Halevi, *Muhammad's Grave*, 210–12; also, A. Buturovic, 'Death', in J. Elias, *Key Themes for the Study of Islam* (Oxford: Oneworld, 2010), 123–40.

which God awakens to life each and every animate creation (Q32:7–11), the soul (*nafs*), which He shelters until the Judgement and the corporeal remains (*jasad*) that rest buried in the soil, also until the Judgement. In this elaboration, the *rūḥ* returns to the body after its deposition into the soil and the two regain a semblance of identity and self-awareness. As Leor Halevi suggests, 'whereas in the Qur'ânic system, the self becomes fragmented at the moment of death, in the post-Qur'ânic system, personal identity continues to reside in the body beyond death until the resurrection, at which time finally a metamorphosis will take place rendering the dead body incorruptible'.[42]

Although not shared by all learned (and non-learned) Muslims in the early period, the idea of an ongoing relationship between the remains and the spirit in the liminal space of the grave has captured the imagination of most Muslims as they have tried to come to grips with the hiatus, in theory and practice, between mortality and immortality. The absolute severance of body and soul was offset with the help of *rūḥ*, the spirit. For most devout Muslims, the grave is no longer feared as a place of deadly silence and expiry but one of restrained if unsettling continuation. The living must do their best to safeguard and keep the dignity of the dead in this vulnerable condition. Although death is a painful torment as repeatedly told by the founding fathers of Islamic thought, starting with the Prophet himself, respite is achieved within a period of time, usually reckoned to be 40 days, after which the spirit, *rūḥ*, allows the body a more comforting anticipation of Judgement Day.

In Bosnia this premise fused with the existing local beliefs in the soul's vulnerability towards bad omens after the onset of death. In practice, that meant offering environmental and psychological comfort to the incarcerated and tormented soul: keeping the voices and sounds down in the house of the deceased, which also means avoiding loud wails and laments; covering the mirrors and mirror-like surfaces so the soul may not observe its own torment (in modern times, that also means turning off television sets and computer screens); forgiving the petty wrongdoings the deceased may have committed in life to help the soul transition and perhaps receive a favourable intimation of its eternal life; uttering petitionary prayers for the soul of the deceased; and remembering the dead in generally positive ways. Among other factors, the fear of being neglected and forgotten informs the commemorative practices of Muslims and is premised on the Prophetic *hadith* of recommending a prayer in front of any grave. One old urban legend in Sarajevo tells of a dervish who used to walk daily by the shrine of The Fallen Warriors (*Gaziler turbe*)[43] for over 40 years never failing to say a prayer for the fallen souls. One evening, accompanied by his wife on the way back from a social gathering, he became

---

[42] L. Halevi, *Muhammad's Grave*, 211.
[43] This was a *turbe* in Sarajevo's centre dedicated to Shamsi Dede and Ayni Dede. The *turbe* was torn down in the 1950s and the two tombstones were placed into the graveyard of the Ali Pasha's mosque. See. M. Mujezinović, *Islamska epigrafika*, 1:406.

engrossed in conversation and failed to do so. Farther along the way the couple encountered a tall, dark apparition cloaked in black walking agitatedly in their direction. The apparition approached the dervish and gave him a loud slap on the cheek with a reprimand: 'Shame on you, is this how you should pass by my grave? Is your wife more important than me?'[44]

In contrast, in the popular albeit disappearing Balkan ritual of the exhumation of vampires, the interaction between the dead and the living is very volatile and the power assigned to the vampire much more menacing. Birth and death are closely interrelated as vampirism can be intrinsic rather than incurred during life. In its inception, however, the vampire is a mistreated corpse, subjected to improper handling and exposed to foul forces that prevent the necessary separation of the body and soul. They are not blood-sucking creatures as per their common image in the Western imagination but rather, disembodied souls or wandering corpses.[45] As Mario Kreuter points out, there is a critical historical dimension to the vampire myth associated with cultural otherness, within which gender dimension plays an important role: women, who are commonly assigned the task of preparing the dead for burial, are also responsible for ensuring that the body bears no signs of 'difference', including vampirism and, if it does, to eliminate possible threats thereof. Just as military martyrdom as discussed earlier is necessary for the defence of honour and cohesion against external threats, so is vigilance against otherness found within. Although the belief about the menacing dead among us was more common in pre-modern and early modern history of the Balkans, Kreuter recalls an anecdote as recently as 2003 when an 80-year-old woman in Romania described to him a male corpse she was preparing for burial. Troubled by his unusually fresh look and a protruding short tail, she found it necessary to insert a nail into the corpse's chest so as to pre-empt any possibility of vampiric reanimation. To her satisfaction, the intervention was successful and the body promptly lost the tail and gained the preferred lifeless appearance.[46] Such and similar practices and beliefs in the region further point to the fact that the dead are not just designated objects with a passive role in society; they can occupy a more equivocal position and their reanimation and reintegration into the society may follow different trajectories and manifestations, some benevolent and other maleficent. Although normative Islam, as mentioned earlier, is believed to have uprooted – and persistently uproots – popular religiosity, repeated calls to end 'superstitious' and non-Islamic beliefs and practices by

---

[44] V. Palavestra, *Historijska usmena predanja iz Bosne i Hercegovine* [Oral histories from Bosnia and Herzegovina] (Sarajevo: Buybook, 2004), 495.

[45] Excellent research on vampire belief has been done in the context of Macedonian beliefs and practices. Consulted here is L. Risteski, 'Categories of the "Evil Dead" in Macedonian Folk Religion', in G. Klaniczay and E. Pocs (eds), *Christian Demonology and Popular Mythology* (Budapest: CEU Press, 2006), 202–12.

[46] M. Kreuter, 'Women in Southeast Vampire Belief', in A. Buturovic and I. Schick (eds), *Women in the Ottoman Balkans* (London: IB Tauris, 2007), 236–8.

Islamic clerics point to the fact that a belief in the dead's capacity to interfere in the life of the living has persisted to date. The long list of proscriptions issued in written manuals on handling the dead include removing black cats from the room where the dead wait in preparation for burial so as not to risk vampirisation; not leaving a bowl with water for 40 days to quench the thirst of the dead while their soul is being extracted; not leaving a dish of butter on the window sill for the dead to have some sustenance when they visit their home at night; not insisting that the dead, while still lying at home before the funeral, should be asked to heal animals, resolve marital disputes, make the poor rich, cure alcohol addictions and so on.[47]

The intervallic lists published and disseminated within the Bosnian Islamic community suggest that the twilight zone in which memory of the dead coexists with a belief in their continuous engagement in social and ritual action has never sealed normative religious borders despite proscriptive interventions by scholars and clerics to that effect. Yet precisely because human remains, as Howard Williams suggests, are 'intrinsically situated as being both "person" and "object"',[48] it is important to consider memory of the dead as an attempt to bridge the gap between death and life by creating buffer zones in which the dead gradually transition into the space of the unknown, in which their subjectivity and agency can still manifest, albeit on new terms, before they move on to become the objects of our memory. Overall then, treating them as allies or aliens is not only a matter of cultural memory but an aspect of our broader approach to otherness within. Feeding on our hopes and anxieties of the living, the dead have access to realms of existence and knowledge that transcend our limitations. Thus sharing space with them can be comforting or frightening, depending on our circumstances and conditions. Furthermore, the dead possess the skill to affect our daily lives, our public behaviour and our political culture by being comfortingly or frighteningly close to us. They are 'us' but they are also 'them' and that paradox repeats itself over time along many different trajectories, fuelling and sustaining our memory in discreetly personal but also overtly public measures.

Landscapes of Death, Landscapes of Memory

The aforementioned examples of the porous lines between the dead as subjects/persons and the dead as objects/remains raise the question of mediation not only in cultural and mnemonic but also spatial terms. Temporally, remembrance of the dead may be activated at random moments as well as during specific times in the calendar. In most cases, however, a spatial placement is needed

---

[47] S. Hodžić, 'Odbacujmo štetne običaje i sujevjerja [Let us discard harmful customs and superstitions]', *Glasnik VISa* 8–12 (1952), 220–22; S. Sokolović, *Islamski propisi*, 71–4.
[48] H. Williams, 'Death Warmed Up', 264.

for the interaction to take effect. Spatial framing of death is therefore another important element in the commemorative complex designed to acknowledge and sedate loss. As seen in several examples above, memory of the dead is not exclusively temporal but is also anchored in a recognisable setting that facilitates geographic orientation and reference. This anchoring is key to both religious and secular narratives and those that lie in between.

Space, of course, has been a key theme in the scholarship of identity, and memory has become an increasingly relevant part of the triad. As Gillis points out, the relationship between memory and identity is historical[49] but it is also geographical in that it is enshrined in commemorative practices, landscape and memorial objects. Collective memory within a defined space is also what lies at the core of modern national imaginings as it clarifies national traits by 'sharpening more ambiguous cultural and ethnic markers'.[50] Benedict Anderson argues that the evocation of cultural roots and remembrance of ancestors within space by national projects brings the latter in line with language of the sacred: the land is politically and ideologically colonised so as to give group identity a spatial reference and to an individual a feeling of belonging.[51] In a more philosophical line of analysis, Yi-Fu Tuan differentiates between 'rootedness' and 'a sense of place': the former has a primordial quality and little concern for historical time and is deeply rooted in human psyche. The esoteric overtone of the idea of rootedness is opposed to his other 'sense of place', which requires a more engaged intellectual and more public presence and attitude towards space.[52] Correspondingly, John Agnew underlines that having an active 'sense of place' is necessary for identity formation in both collective and individual terms.[53]

Memory of the dead does not function in a vacuum either, but through a variety of cultural and social mediums. In Bosnia and Herzegovina, landscape is the key setting in which artefacts – graveyards, memorials, shrines – and other material memorabilia tend to be located. They have an evocative function on the one hand and a testimonial function on the other, objectifying memory and affirming the reality of loss. The landscape that hosts artefacts gives a broader grounding to memories and provides a panoramic domain in which to remember many connected and disconnected deaths. To render Jan Assmann's suggestion, spatially marked memories make us more socialised.

That said, the landscape of Bosnia and Herzegovina, enchanting and evocative as it is, also has an abstruse and uncommunicative quality. This is meant neither as a truism about the natural scenery nor as a metaphor so often

---

[49] J. Gillis, *Commemorations*, 6.
[50] G. Herb, 'National Identity and Territory', in G. Herb and D. Kaplan (eds), *Nested Identities: Nationalism, Territory, and Scale* (Lanham: Rowman and Littlefield, 1994), 19.
[51] B. Anderson, *Imagined Communities* (London: Verso, 1991), 196.
[52] Yi-Fu Tuan, 'Rootedness versus Sense of Place', *Landscape* 25 (1980), 3–8.
[53] J.A. Agnew, *Place and Politics: The Geographic Mediation of State and Society* (Boston: Allen and Unwin, 1987), 20.

invoked when discussing the Balkans. Rather, Bosnia's dramatic physical geography, like any other populated space, must also be appreciated for cultural formations that destabilise and dislocate memory. Webs of different claims about past events occasionally clash with the landscape's memorabilia of the dead. In addition, burial grounds are often secluded, isolated and inaccessible, inciting questions of the different experiences, events and meanings that have been expressed within Bosnia's landscape and inscribed into it in the course of history. The cumulative value of such expressions is not easily measured or accessed. Some suggest that landscapes ought to be read as one reads a book,[54] but many landscapes, including the landscape of Bosnia and Herzegovina, hardly possess any narrative coherence. It may be layered but it is hardly possible to think of it as a sum total of components that follow a linear sense of time and place required for any cogent narration or remembrance. The accumulation of 'experience', 'culture', 'history' or 'memory' in any landscape populated over a period of time is a matter of process and relationship: on the one hand, the process entails a focus on some but not all historical moments; the relationship, on the other hand, depends on the social and cultural positioning towards the landscape. In that sense, cultural landscapes are not just books to be read but interactive sites in the formation of broader social and cultural systems, including group identities, in which some elements are subjected to remembrance and others to forgetting.[55]

Here, we are especially interested in this latter issue, namely, what kinds of relationship can be forged with the landscape and mapped out in reference to the dead who occupy it. Needless to say, societies differ not only in their relationships with the dead but in the conditions they create for the preservation and disposal of bodies, so no generalisation can be made about the tripartite relationship between the dead, the living and the landscape. In some societies, as John Chapman points out, the main reason for the existence of permanent burial grounds derives from 'the cultural centrality of the physical remains of the dead, in terms of their representation of reproduction'.[56] In other words, without the dead deposited in the earth, the idea of a cohesive community may be hard to achieve. In societies such as Bosnia and Herzegovina where burial is the most common form of disposal, the landscape is continually recreated as the dead bodies are placed into the earth, often in competition with other bodies over the same burial space. Religious, personal, aesthetic,

---

[54] 'As we read what is written on the land, finding accounts of the past, predictions of the future, and comments on the present, we discover that there are many interwoven strands to each story, offering several possible interpretations'. M. Thielgaards Watts, *Reading the Landscape of America* (New York: Macmillan, 1957), ix.

[55] For useful discussion of landscape as an ideological tool see W.J.T. Mitchell, *Landscape and Power* (Chicago: The University of Chicago Press, 1994).

[56] J. Chapman, 'The Living, the Dead and the Ancestors: Time, Life Cycle and the Mortuary Domain in Later European Prehistory', in J. Davies (ed.), *Ritual and Remembrance: Responses to Death in Human Societies* (Sheffield: Sheffield Academic Press, 1994), 47.

Figure 2.8 Bones upon bones: old and new in competition for space, Sarajevo. Photo by Velibor Božović

political and other issues intermesh, allowing the living to relate the abstract questions of death, memory and continuity to the material condition of the remains. Physical objects placed in the landscape to mark the presence of the dead denote that the landscape acts as a crucial regenerative site of connection between deceased ancestors and the living community, between memory and forgetting and between the subjectivity of death and its objective manifestations. As a result, both secular and religious expressions tend to deploy naturalistic elements.[57] The ecological importance of burial emphasises the intimacy between the landscape and the cycle of life, evidencing that, far from being simply a pictorial, neutral environment and object of contemplation, the landscape possesses a significant cultural force that temporalises and reins in the feeling of infinity and loss associated with death.

Marking Death and Memory: Graveyards and Gravestones

Marking spaces of death in the landscape is a way of directing cultural memory as well as delineating the dead from the living. As discussed earlier, the landscape itself, being a 'contextual horizon of perceptions, providing both a foreground and background in which people feel themselves as living in their world',[58] enables cultural navigation in both spatial and temporal terms: spatial, because the frame is territorial in character which grounds us and gives us a sense of direction, and temporal because the landscape is allowed to travel through time as our attempts to make sense of its different components link the past and the present. Cultural landscape and specifically landscape of the dead is therefore not a static entity but a product of our engagement with its different layers whereby we bridge our subjective/internal knowledge and memory with its objective/external fixtures such as gravestones, shrines and memorials. Moreover, the landscape is a shared space conducive to intimate encounters between the living and the dead, on the one hand and necessary for a community's sense of embodied continuity on the other. Consequently, one of the key questions to be addressed here relates to the visibility and role of material culture embedded in the landscape in the process of making and remaking memory.

Memory Matters

In Bosnia and Herzegovina's deathscape, where memories are fragmented and many historical factors interfere with commemorative practices, not all gravesites bear equal value and purpose at any given time. Rather, their

---

[57] J. Davies, 'One Hundred Billion Dead: A General Theology of Death', *Ritual and Remembrance*, 24.
[58] P.J. Stewart and A. Strathern, *Landscape, Memory and History* (London: Pluto Press, 2003), 4.

pertinence waxes and wanes depending on the function they carry within specific historical moments. Thus, despite their physical grounding and immobility, their value is mobile and transportable and as such is subject to use and abuse in interpretation. The interpretative shifts are most often enhanced in relation to public memorials built to feed and preserve the official politics of memory and to cement group identities. When these identities are endangered or changed, the memorials lose their function and so are demolished, displaced or simply forgotten.

In the former Yugoslavia, for example, including Bosnia and Herzegovina, numerous memorials built after the Second World War to commemorate the socialist revolution and anti-fascist war battles and to glorify the victorious postwar nation building of Titoist Yugoslavia now lie abandoned in the aftermath of the country's dissolution. Their condition and status has not been given equal treatment in all of Yugoslavia as this period has been unevenly re-interpreted in the political and popular imagination of the successor states. In fact, while some parts of the former Yugoslavia simply marginalised them, others introduced active policies of erasing them from collective memory. As one poignant example Jezernik discusses the fate of many monuments to this period in Slovenia which were swiftly removed after the declaration of independence in 1991 as a way of demonising the past and imagining a bright(er) future free of the special treatment afforded Slovenia within Federal Yugoslavia as the economically most prosperous and therefore most entitled of the constituent republics. Once Slovenia seceded in 1991, there was a swift process of historical rewriting and the abolition of ties with the communist ideologues and institutions of the past. However, Slovene public opinion was not anonymous on the issue of memorials: the editorial column introduced in a leading local paper under the title 'Monument Yes, Monument No' showed a considerable polarisation as to the fate of the monuments between those who did not want to see them removed and those who fully supported relieving Slovenia's memory of its antecedent ideological burden.[59]

Similar differences in opinion emerged elsewhere in the former Yugoslavia pointing to two parallel and mutually exclusive models of memorialisation. One such model evoked pre-Yugoslav times, especially the nineteenth century, and fostered national aspirations towards single statehood in the Balkans. The other one, popularly known as Yugo-nostalgia, sought to reinvent former Yugoslavia, the country built in the aftermath of the Second World War amidst the ashes of petty nationalist projects, according to the inclusive supranational (or multinational) principle of 'Brotherhood and Unity', held together by the watchful eye of Tito and his Communist party. Although nostalgia for the vanished communist systems has broadened, sweeping over many post-

---

[59] B. Jezernik, 'No Monuments, No History, No Past: Monuments and Memory', in R. Hudson and G. Bowman (eds), *After Yugoslavia: Identities and Politics Within the Successor States* (New York: Palgrave McMillan, 2011), 190–91.

communist lands and is perhaps a common sentiment in any large-scale upheavals and transitions,[60] it is important to note that in the former Yugoslavia, as Zlata Volčić points out, Yugo-nostalgia emerged primarily in response to the extreme nationalist designs that were the basis for various forms of ethnic cleansing, genocide and culturecide in the early 1990s.[61] Given such mutually exclusive forms and shades of nostalgia within former Yugoslavia in general and Bosnia and Herzegovina in particular, the role of memorials, both old and new, has become indelibly fragmented and volatile. Their meaningful presence in the landscape is closely linked to the questions of identity, power and national self-affirmation, frequently at the expense of other groups who do not share the same sense of belonging. Consequently, when and how these memorials are authenticated, foregrounded and assigned a commemorative role depends largely on who is in charge of collective memory and to what end. What emerges as a pattern, however, in such cases of establishing credibility of some memorials and disavowal of others is that the dead are not all created equal and not equally drawn into the pool of ancestors. Remembering some of the dead and forsaking others is a powerful method of co-opting the past into the struggles and contestations of the living and entangling ancestors into various political, social and economic interests. In turn, refuting their memory, waging a war on their memorial markers and systematically dislocating them from ancestral bonds represents a highly effective way of manipulating, transforming and rewriting group identity and its sense of placement in the past, present and future. Thus, despite the fact that memorials are material witnesses of death that successfully activate memories of the dead, their value is always historically framed and fully related to the value assigned to the episode of the past in which death occurred. This is especially relevant for the dead who did not just live in history but who made it, left a mark on it in some shape or form and as such may symbolically represent the meaning of the past in the memory artefacts of the present. The will to remember them, then, is not induced by cultural or spiritual spontaneity but more often than not is produced by political privilege.

Given such fluctuations and displacements, what can we make out of material representations of death and of cemeteries as sacred sites of cultural memory? If memorials are treated with reverence for the numinosity they carry, it seems pertinent to explore whether the gravesites in question command similar attention, occasion divisive strategies of remembrance or undergo comparable shifts and challenges as regards their social and cultural significance.

---

[60] For a provocative and thorough treatment of nostalgia, especially in the context of national projects, see S. Boym, *The Future of Nostalgia* (New York: Basic Books, 2001), 41–8.

[61] Z. Volčić, 'Yugo-Nostalgia: Cultural Memory and Media in the Former Yugoslavia', *Critical Studies in Media Communication* 24:1 (2007), 27.

Sacred Space, National Space, Memorial Space

According to the famous and original Eliadean bifurcation, space is divided into two main kinds. One constitutes the space of order and consequence thanks to divine manifestations that contribute to its focus and purpose. Such space is deemed sacred. It functions to break the amorphous quality of the other kind of space – profane space – by means of hierophanies, which are signs of supernatural blessings in history that open up connections between the cosmic and earthly realms.[62] In sacred space human beings seek and uncover the source of worldly orientation and meaning, in contrast to everyday profane space that lacks such durable significance. Rituals are important means of rendering sacred orientations possible, repetitive and fulfilling. Without sacred space, Eliade argues, human beings are lost in everyday life in which all things and experiences carry equal or comparable value and provide no answer to metaphysical questions about the meaning of life and death. We traverse profane space without being pulled into any centre or higher meaning. This conceptual division of space has offered explanations for the differences in locations imbued with numinosity and those that lack it: temples, pilgrimage sites, sacred grounds and so on are therefore understood to be fixed and non-transportable; mundane spaces, in turn, are not.

While still evoking these differences introduced by Eliade, recent scholarship is more hesitant to concede as sharp and entrenched a distinction between sacred and profane spaces. Just like memory, sacred space has been increasingly recognised for a plurality of meanings.[63] Whether we speak of religious contestations over Jerusalem, the desecrated burial mounds of Native Canadians, the Buddhas of Bamiyan, or Ground Zero in New York City, it is clear that the meaning of most sacred sites unfold first and foremost through our relation with and interpretation of them. It is possible, then, to look at sacred space as not being esoteric as Eliade proposed, but precisely as being a product of external, situational relations as much as spiritual and religious ones. Moreover, while most religions cultivate a well-defined sacred cartography, many sacred spaces exist outside the easily identifiable parameters, because of theological, denominational, geographic, historical, gender or any other forms of differentiation. Religions, while commonly assumed to be homogenous, are in fact always multivalent and drawn around multiple forms of spatial sacrality. 'Sacred spaces,' Adrian Ivakhiv aptly postulates, 'are those spaces rendered sacred through practices of sacralization … If the sacred is not the domain of the unquestioned then is it anything more than a relic of history in which certain things have been

---

[62] M. Eliade, *The Sacred and the Profane*, trans. W.R Trask (New York: Harcourt Brace Jovanovic, 1961), 20–21.
[63] For an excellent overview of recent scholarly trends in understanding sacred space see aforementioned P. Sheldrake, *Spaces of the Sacred: Place, Memory, Identity*.

designated sacred and others not?'[64] Sacralisation, then, involves a selection, demarcation, orientation and ritualisation of space[65] in an effort to give it religious or spiritual meaning, coherence and relevance. The necessity to engage with space in a way that would 'set it apart' as sacred or meaningful is also present in non-religious realms: take the example of spontaneous shrines at the sites of traffic accidents that undergo transformation from being quite ordinary to becoming hallowed. Through a private act of consecration they provide an opportunity for public marking of a personal tragedy otherwise reducible to statistical import. While most spontaneous shrines are only temporarily elevated to the status of sacred ground, some become institutionally administered and ritualised in more enduring ways, such as Ground Zero in New York City.

In weeding out different elements that contribute to the production and experience of sacred space in our secular times, the role of memory warrants additional consideration. In many respects, the relationship between sacred space and memory is best expressed but also most comparable in relation to war memorials. Because war memorials are commonly the product of political rebuilding and because the preservation of the nation assumes a sacred purpose and meaning for the national project, death is commonly mourned as sacred sacrifice. National war memorials draw heavily on religious language and symbolism, focusing especially on the redemptive message that such sacrifice is never futile. As they identify events and heroes, war memorials simultaneously commemorate, remember and warn. To render Homi Bhabha's terminology of nationhood, memorials can be viewed as being both performative, in that they are engaging public signifiers of war loss and war gains, and pedagogical, in that they are meant to offer lessons on national suffering and defiance. All around Bosnia and Herzegovina, memorials have been erected as raw testimonials to national grandeur. Mortality, experienced in a violent and traumatic way, is translated into the language of immortality, usually with the help of salvific idiom drawn from religion, even if stripped of overt references to God. The space the memorials occupy, which may have previously been nondescript, is now altered by their overbearing presence. Because of the administrative division of Bosnia and Herzegovina, war memorials are propped by contested nationalist narratives of victory rather than a shared narrative (since there is none). Thus, three separate armies – the Croatian HVO, Serbian VRS and the formally inclusive Bosnian ARBiH – have been monumentalised in the territories under corresponding administrative jurisdictions. One exception is the northern town of Brčko where all three monuments exist side by side. In their mute presence, these monuments authenticate the past and fix it in the moral landscape of particular national

---

[64] A. Ivakhiv, 'Toward a Geography of "Religion": Mapping the Distribution of an Unstable Signifier', *Annals of the Association of American Geographers* 96:1 (2006), 171.
[65] A. Ivakhiv, 'Toward a Geography of "Religion"', 171–2.

memories. The sacred in these instances unfolds through the repetition of lessons about trauma, messages of redemption, didactic stories of sacrifice, ritual visitations and other activities that garner the memorials' symbolic importance. Conversely, they inevitably create unease among the survivors of violence, reminding us that monuments, despite their mute presence, can stir intense emotions, rekindle unacknowledged traumas and supress rather than acknowledge the reality of loss. In many of these cases, then, sacrality and profanity coexist in a disquieting tension.

In a somewhat different vein, war cemeteries too acquire a sacred function but here the dead preserve an important degree of subjectivity. In Bosnia and Herzegovina, traditional modes of mourning and commemoration of the dead associated with graveyards have been strained but also enhanced by postwar nation building. Because the 1992–95 war targeted first and foremost civilians, they have become the main conduits for this political process. The war losses were indeed devastating: across Bosnia and Herzegovina, over one million people were displaced, internally and externally, and over 100,000 died.[66] In part because of being a consistent target of atrocities and ethnic cleansing and in part for the aesthetics of their memorial culture, Bosnian Muslim tombstones – tall, white and slender – stand out prominently and hauntingly in the postwar landscape. Significantly, it is the tombstones and graveyards rather than memorials and monuments that have been vested with major force in the commemorative efforts of the Bosniak nation. To that effect, the leadership of the Islamic community designated all Muslim/Bosniak dead as *šehidi* (martyrs). In so doing, the Islamic leadership has erased the lines of differentiation between civilian and military victims, enhancing the suggestion that all Bosnian Muslim victims had died in self-defence rather than through aggressive actions. In a 2008 speech commemorating the civilian victims of atrocities in the eastern town of Bratunac, the Grand Mufti stated: 'It is not same to be a martyr defending his home, stead and family, and be the one attacking and killing other people's home, stead and family', making a clear moral differentiation between death by aggression and death in self-defence.[67] Furthermore, declaring everyone as martyr promised to trigger the gift of divine grace for each war victim, regardless of individual circumstance of death, and it enhanced spiritual support to the families. It also highlighted the importance of keeping the war victims close to memory and ritual attention so that their sacrifice would not be dishonoured or ignored. Whenever possible, then, their white stone markers have been inscribed with the Qur'anic verse

---

[66] Estimates of war-related military and civilian deaths vary from low 100,000s to 150,000s. A team of experts appointed by ICTY puts the figures at 104,732. See J. Zwierzchowski and E. Tabeau, 'The 1992–95 War in Bosnia and Herzegovina: Census-Based Multiple System Estimation Of Casualties' Undercount', 16. Online: http://www.icty.org/x/file/About/OTP/War_Demographics/en/bih_casualty_undercount_conf_paper_100201.pdf.

[67] Online: http://www.rijaset.ba/index.php?option=com_content&view=article&id=3264:cehidi-bratunca-vjei-svjedoci-sistematskog-zatiranja-bocnjaka&catid=41&Itemid=220.

that the martyrs are still alive despite our limited perception: 'And do not say for those who died in the name of God that they are dead; nay, they are alive but you do not see' (Q2:154).

Shifting the focus on the cemeteries where the war dead rest has also left an important effect on the way landscape is inscribed and redeemed in the Bosniak narrative. In the ongoing battle for numbers, the landscape filled with haunting white tombstones speaks for itself. It also counteracts the trope of the Bosnian space being historically populated only by Croats and Serbs, which has prominently featured in the territorial claims of the two national mythologies. Finally, it creates connections between the war dead and many ancestral gravestones scattered randomly across the landscape. Not only are these too referred to as 'martyr's tombstone' (*šehitski nišan*) in popular idiom, but also they have become the aesthetic blueprint for the postwar funerary style.

Encounters with the dead across urban and rural areas thus give a sense of continuity and closure but there is an unsettling side to this impression. The ongoing discoveries of mass graves and the awareness of unresolved mysteries of wartime victims' physical location infuses the landscape with a disquieting sense of continued trauma of displacement and undelivered justice. Many dispersed dead wait to be returned home. Until a proper burial, they cannot be fully integrated into the ritual life of their immediate community. The management of their repatriation, however, is not only the matter of closure, spiritual and physical, for the bereaved families and community. It is the subject of postwar reconciliation, administration of justice, forensic investigation and a host of other civic, religious and international engagements. In the city of Tuzla in northeastern Bosnia, mortuary facilities of the International Commission on Missing Persons (ICMP), whose mandate includes locating and identifying victims of war and which contains thousands of remains in body bags, have assisted in making thus far over 14,000 identifications of different individuals who perished in the 1992–95 war. One particularly stark example of the difficulties associated with this process relates to the victims of the Srebrenica genocide where the bodies were buried and reburied in order to conceal the evidence. As a result, 'body parts are found disarticulated in numerous primary and secondary mass gravesites. Identifying these mortal remains is labor intensive and requires an integrated approach in which DNA is used to guide forensic anthropologists in re-associating disarticulated body parts'.[68] Under such complex circumstances of bodily and spiritual discord the process of commemoration is equally discordant. Finding, exhuming, composing, and reburying the dead is fraught with moral and practical challenges. Conventional places of burial and remembrance are insufficient and inadequate in the face of these ongoing processes. Standard methods of closure run into the problem

---

[68] ICMP website, http://www.ic-mp.org/press-releases/over-7000-srebrenica-victims-recovered/.

of simultaneous absence and presence of so many scattered remains. The earth typically contains the bodies after burial, but in this case without the prelude of socially and culturally meaningful rituals. Conventions of mourning and remembrance cannot be properly observed. Instead, an alternative repertoire of marking and commemorating the dead has evolved around spontaneous shrines, new forms of ritual visitations and auxiliary modes of memorial practice so as to grieve for and comfort the dead until the aim of securing their appropriate burial and social placement can be fulfilled.

These and many related factors evoke dilemmas associated with the conflicting role and function of cemeteries dedicated to the victims of war. In Srebrenica, for example, burials are done annually and collectively for the remains that have been identified and sufficiently 're-associated': in July of 2013, on the eighteenth anniversary of the mass killing, 409 dead were buried.[69] One year earlier, 520. This and similar collective burials represent a bittersweet success of reaching deeply personal closure in a public act choreographed by state officials and carried out among political dignitaries, religious clerics, humanitarian groups, activists and the general public. Funeral processions are performed as a form of pilgrimage, occasioning collective bereavement and search for meaning, albeit not in the transcendental divine but through an intense group validation of torturous memories. The organisers try to reach out to a wide audience, local and international, to draw attention to the unspeakable trauma that still haunts the survivors and make pleas to bring to justice many perpetrators still at large. The otherwise intimate experience of burying the remains is exposed to mass media and political and legal speeches. Although women do not traditionally participate in ritual burials, the surviving female relatives of the dominantly male victims attend, expressing grief with intense emotional charge and further spectacularising the tragic events. In January 2009, the European Parliament had passed the resolution to officiate 11 July as Remembrance Day for the Srebrenica genocide. The date is recognised in locales as distant as Canada as well, having been passed as a motion in the House of Commons. The Ontario MP Brian Masse, who introduced the motion, made a pledge: 'I hope that justice will prevail and healing can begin for these victims and their families. We will always remember.'[70] All the while, the spectacle of the war crimes tribunal at The Hague to bring the perpetrators to justice continues, as does the reluctance of the Serbian government and Serbian political elites to recognise the genocide, meagrely expressing instead 'regrets over the deaths'.[71]

---

[69] R. Weschke, 'Bosnia: 409 dead after Srebrenica massacre buried', http://www.missingblog.net/409-dead-after-srebrenica-massacre-reburried-in-bosnia/.

[70] 'Masse Remembers Srebrenica Genocide', 16 July 2012, http://www.rijaset.ba/english/index.php/template/latest-news/268-masse-remembers-srebrenica-on-the-17th-anniversary-of-the-genocide.

[71] 'Serb President Tomislav Nikolic "Sorry" for Srebrenica Massacre', *The Australian* (26 April 2013). http://www.theaustralian.com.au/news/world/serb-president-tomislav-

Pierre Nora's theory of change in relation to the function of memorial sites may be of relevance given that the cemeteries can be at once solemn places of quiet comfort and sites of highly public exchange and activism. Pondering the difference between memory and history Nora suggests that, unlike history, memory

> remains in permanent evolution, open to the dialectic of remembering and forgetting, unconscious of its successive deformations, vulnerable to manipulation and appropriation ... History, on the other hand, is the reconstruction, always problematic and incomplete, of what is no longer. Memory is a perpetually actual phenomenon, a bond tying us to the eternal present; history is a representation of the past.[72]

For Nora, the most significant, or perhaps the only, time the two unify is in the context of national memory. Here, nation building requires the two to complement and support each other so as to create a framework for what Benedict Anderson terms 'subjective antiquity' of a nation,[73] namely, a trajectory into the past where memories are sufficiently distilled and aligned so as to seal any lacunae in national self-realisation. They are shared and sustained publicly. Environments where individual memory is spontaneously formed and experienced, *milieux de memoire*, Nora pessimistically contends, are no longer available. National historiography has reconstituted them through its archival, material and condensed lens. We have lost access to these environments and, instead, for the lack of any other option we resort to the sites of memory, *lieux de memoire*, to anchor the past but they artificially epitomise what may have happened. One reason for this change, Nora postulates, relates to the de-ritualisation of social life. Secularism and modernity have removed the traditional sacred quality from memorial practices and places. Practices have been reorganised to extract the most meaning out of any given repertoire of memory and then represent it in a functional, 'objective' way. To Nora, this shift accompanied nineteenth-century nation building, specifically in France.

Persuasive as regards the permutations in memory practices occasioned by the rise of modern museums, memorials and archives to safeguard collective memory at the expense of numinous environments of lived memories, Nora is perhaps too quick to ignore the possibility of their simultaneous working. Jay Winter has meticulously and insightfully demonstrated this interweaving while examining memories of the Great War. Analysing a set of case studies across Europe, he shows that, contrary to mainstream analysis of the Great War as a radical breakaway with the tradition, the sites of memory were at once expressions of grief and traditional sites of mourning using old models. The

---

nikolic-sorry-for-srebrenica-massacre/story-e6frg6so-1226629769906.
 [72] P. Nora, 'Between Memory and History: Les Lieux de Mémoire', *Representations* 26 (1989), 7–24.
 [73] B. Anderson, *Imagined Communities*, 5.

sacred returned in both form and content.[74] Nearly a century after the Great War, in Bosnia and Herzegovina, the dead, honoured at numerous cemeteries across the country, are also remembered and summoned in both 'traditional' and 'modern' ways, in a simultaneous process that resonates with modernity while remaining fully infused with traditional practices. The sacred has been restored, at least in this case, so as to give more representational force to war losses and trauma, despite the predictions of many theorists, including Nora, that it was no longer needed.

As mass graves across Bosnia and Herzegovina keep emerging in the painstaking process of creating a comprehensive inventory of loss,[75] the necessity to remember and memorialise reflects the dialectic between expressing the sanctity of personal grief and articulating political ethics. Other forms of sacralisation are thus in the making. Religious organisations and groups play a vital role in this process, combining traditional religious language about worldly injustice with transcendental retribution and final rewards. Moreover, as religion has taken a more centre-stage position across the political spectrum, its rhetorical force is revived and its patterns of sacrality reintroduced into public discourse. Ironically, as far as Islamic regulations are concerned, such efforts are not necessary: because of their special status, martyrs are exempted from prescribed funerary rituals. They can be buried on the spot, with their clothes on, and, like the exemplary Uhud martyrs of the Prophet's time, they can even be buried in one and the same grave. The condition and placement of their corpses is not a prerequisite for propitious afterlife and generous divine provision. They no longer require the living to assist them on their path to God because the nature of their death ensures God's immediate favours. However, the value of the efforts to unite and repatriate the bodies resulting from war atrocities in Bosnia and Herzegovina is not vested in religious gratification alone despite the customary supervision of funerary rituals by Islamic officials. The matter is as much psychological, pursued for the benefit of the victims' families to achieve closure, as it is political, motivated to usher public sympathy and outcry beyond the grieving community. In the 2013 sermon delivered at the memorial site, the Grand Mufti of Bosnia Dr Mustafa Cerić offered a moving moral exhortation to the grieving families and the general audience on the significance of the event of laying the dead to rest, combining persuasive evocations of scriptural norms of conduct, salvific reassurances and ritual responsibilities towards the pending month of fasting with a modernist discourse on social ethics, political consciousness, human rights and undelivered justice. Carefully crafted as

---

[74] J. Winter, *Sites of Memory, Sites of Mourning* (Cambridge: Cambridge University Press, 1995).

[75] Just in recent months forensic experts have identified yet another large mass grave in northwest Bosnia near the town of Prijedor, barely a year after they discovered over 400 bodies at Tomašica, another mass grave in the vicinity. Online http://www.reuters.com/article/2014/03/27/us-bosniaherzegovina-grave-idUSBREA2Q1KV20140327.

an appeal on behalf of the martyrs of Srebrenica, the sermon – *khutba* – was poised between intimate emotional experiences of loss with a shared sense of sacrifice among Muslims around the world, calling for a global spiritual re-awakening out of the ashes of Bosnia's tragedy:

> This is the message of the Bosniak Muslim victims of the Srebrenica genocide to the Muslim *Ummah* of Egypt, Syria, Iraq, Yemen, Bahrain, Afghanistan, Pakistan, Bangladesh, Iran, Tunisia, Libya, Mali ... be conscious of Allah and follow the path of the Messenger of Allah who has taught us the lesson of *Hudaybiyya* so that we know that the way out of bloodshed is peace and tolerance. The victims of the Srebrenica genocide call upon all the nations of the Muslim *Ummah* to follow the example of the Messenger's peace of *Hudaybiyya* and to take the best from the wisdom of European Westphalia because a wisdom is lost thing for a Muslim so that wherever he finds it he should take it. And the Westphalia wisdom teaches us that after all the only way for the *Ummah* to succeed here and to be saved in the hereafter is to make peace with itself and to observe tolerance with others. For the sake of peace and security of our *Ummah*, we urge you to heed our appeal for the unity of our *Dīn* and *Ummah* for the sake of our children who should never suffer genocide again.[76]

As a good example of Nora's alignment of collective memory and national historiography, this speech clearly requires traditional heritage to be effective, but it permeates the language of heritage with appeals to political action. It stirs up as much as it calms. It comforts the mourners but it also cautions them against abandoning their dead. The living and the dead are called into a joint action of political resistance through remembrance. Little, if any, space is left for private loss, on one's own terms and at one's own pace, because all loss has now become a matter of public and collective responsibility.

As Nora rightfully contends, in parallel to such habitual fusion of the personal with the political, our age has introduced yet another cycle, in which national history, its structures and claims are no longer afforded reverence. History is allowed to write critically about itself rather than be aligned with national imaginary. Other channels and repositories of memory have emerged in the process. In Bosnia, the mourners hold on to various memorabilia, participate in individual and group therapy and create a variety of interpersonal and social networks to find solace and counteract forgetting. They also engage in activist work to raise awareness and mobilise public consciousness and instil a sense of shared responsibility towards the dead. 'Women of Srebrenica', 'Mothers of Srebrenica', a number of country-wide associations of camp survivors, non-governmental agencies and many online social networks committed to memory and justice act as intermediaries between individual and collective grief, framing, within their space and

---

[76] 'Srebrenica Khutba by Ef. Mustafa Cerić', (11 July 2013), http://www.rijaset.ba/english/index.php/template/latest-news/278-srebrenica-khutba-by-mustafa-ef-ceric. Westphalia is referring to the treaty signed in 1648 to end the Thirty Years' War.

expression, the sacred memory of war victims. Remembering and reminding go hand in hand across different media. Personal memories are sheltered in multiple locations, no longer only in national war memorials.

As loci of memory shift, then, so does the function of memorials, real and virtual. Postwar Bosnia and Herzegovina thus reflects a convergence of different ways in which war dead are remembered. While graveyards emerge as prime sacred sites transmitting message of grand national loss, alternative spaces are also fashioned where personal grief, dialogue and reflection can help come to terms with the horrors of the past and unresolved issues of the present. Many such spaces exist in vernacular, activist and artistic expressions, often in more localised and inclusive terms. Here, remembrance may be experiences in more uneven, personalised ways, at times emotional and lyrical and at others contested and divisive. A sense of sacrality is thus not the sole prerogative of grand national narratives but precisely of more intimate evocations and affective responses that often challenge the feeling of sameness typical of national monuments and war memorials. One example which poignantly demonstrates this varied commemorative experience is associated with the so-called 'Sarajevo Roses', which are traces of bomb blasts etched in the pavement, like wounds in the asphalt, found all around the city. Having a distinct floral pattern, some of these 'roses' were filled with red resin to create street memorials as reminders of loss and trauma. As they do not name

Figure 2.9 Sarajevo Roses, two blasts side by side.
Photo by Velibor Božović

names or add recognisable symbols, they resist distillation into overarching nationalist narratives or standard forms of closure and exist on a different plane of sacred geography. Despite being authentic locations of atrocities, the Roses persist as quiet shrines that transcend conventional language and sites of remembrance by appealing to all victims of the aggression rather than a specific ethno-religious community. They add to the web of material and immaterial referents to the war that haunt the memory of the living and complicate their responses to the war dead. Assuming, therefore, that neither space nor memory ought to be inherently profane or sacred but can become consecrated or desecrated because of historical, ethical, political or other processes, the next chapter will explore the formative historical relationship between memory of the dead, its grave markers and space through which Bosnian Islamic funerary culture has been shaped.

Figure 2.10 A typical tombstone of a fallen Bosniak soldier, depicting fleur-de-lis as the State insignia (bottom), the *Fātiḥa* (top) and the Qur'anic quote affirming martyrdom: 'And do not say for those who are killed for the cause of God they are dead; nay, they are alive, but you do not perceive them' (2:154). Photo by Amila Buturović

Figure 2.11 Kovači 1992–95 war cemetery in Sarajevo in the background; an old Ottoman cemetery in the foreground.
Photo by Velibor Božović.

Figure 2.12 Srebrenica Potočari memorial to civilian casualties, with inscriptions stating the same martyrdom verse from the Qur'an (Q2:154).
Photo by Amila Buturović

Chapter 3

Converting the Stone: Text and Images in Early Ottoman Bosnia

The previous chapters situated various forms of Bosnian Muslims' commemoration of the dead – ritual, official and non-official, public and private – into the expansive field of memory studies and questions around spatial representation of death. Rather than existing as an abstract faculty, an object, or an esoteric mental reality to be summoned when needed, memory of the dead is recognised for its attachment to complex modes of signification associated with material and immaterial culture alike. Among different forms of memory, memory of the dead is particularly intricate because it is poised between the emotive expressions of bereavement, loss and remembrance and the ethical quandary regarding the transformation of the subject/ person into the material object/remains with whom a personal and social relationship may continue. Furthermore, the dead who inhabit our space are assigned material and symbolic signification to help us reflect on continuity in the past, present and future. There is physical proximity between us and the dead, but also distance occasioned by new ontological configurations. Although the speaking, living subject is absent, materialised into remains and silenced by the burial act, s/he can be re-animated through cultural and political interactions. Private memories and public ritual acts, official and unofficial, play an important role in connecting visual markers of death and memory and activating the imaginative and narrative processes to make the relationship with the dead meaningful and unbroken in some situations, and dysfunctional and severed in others. Memorial markers can occasion contact, usher debates, generate conflict, lead to reinterpretation of history, and erase many dimensions of memory. In this sense, although memorial markers – gravesites, plaques, shrines, monuments – appear to be stable and impervious physical structures encouraging connection and remembrance, they also function as precarious and contentious arenas which are mapped symbolically as much as geographically. As such, they are important to examine in depth as primary cultural sources in which the dead come closest to self-identification and self-affirmation.

In light of these intersections between death and its material markings, this chapter will further explore the relationship between death and memory, focusing less on embodied ritual practice and more on the textual basis for the communication enshrined in the stone as image and word. The historical framework of this chapter is early Ottoman Bosnia, between the late fifteenth and late seventeenth centuries, during which the nascent Islamic community developed funerary literacy in reference to both local and imperial norms. The process of transition between the pre-Ottoman, dominantly Christian, cultural system into the Ottoman-Islamic one occasioned a confluence between different funerary styles, reflecting the broader issues of conversion and new eschatological sensibilities. How did early Muslims of Bosnia memorialise their ancestors, Christian and Muslim? What change in the commemorative culture did the conversion occasion? What do funerary data tell us in the absence of the speaking subjects?

In answering these questions, several observations are worthy of note: first, the physical geography of funerary texts is somewhat inconsistent. Some texts are chiselled in the gravestones close to focal religious structures such as mosques and churches, some others are found on sprawling tombstones in town and city graveyards, and yet others lie scattered in inaccessible remote areas. This unevenness has inevitably impacted upon the practice of mourning and memorialisation due to the multiple nodes of commemorative contact. Second, there is a dynamic interplay between the personal nature of funerary inscriptions detailing intimate biographical data and the condensed iconographic and epigraphic references reaching out to a general audience. The repetitive nature of such references creates a nexus around which cultural meaning is formed and memory regenerated and expanded. Third, the choice of language demarcates a particular direction of cultural communication. In the case of Ottoman Bosnian tombstones, language and script enshrine religious identity as well: Arabic script (Ottoman Turkish, Arabic, Persian, and *Arebica* (Slavic in Arabic script)) is commonly used for Muslims, and Church Slavonic and Cyrillic, and later Latin, for Christians. Although pre-modern literacy levels were generally low, the visual effect of the script was often a sufficient trigger for a communal recognition of the dead and invocation of appropriate petitionary prayers and other ritual responses. Fourth, while the relationship between language/script and religious identity is both historical and theological, visual images play an important function in breaking down any stringent lines separating the identity of the dead. Here, the relationship between oral and textual domains, shared visual symbols, and a general tension between local and totalising, official imperial and religious standards steer cultural and identity formations into dynamic, fluid and intimate categories of cultural communication. As observed in other studies of Islamic funerary material, the common scholarly prejudice that privileges the text as the most relevant source is also noticeable in the study of Ottoman tombstones, inadvertently leading to a sharper differentiation between Christian and Muslim converts' gravestones.[1] Prioritising the written word downplays not only the related fields of inquiry but also assumes a fully literate audience capable of engaging in textually conditioned modes of communication and commemoration. In contrast, the main argument here is that these different domains of funerary expression belong to the same commemorative culture and ought to be considered as interdependent rather than mutually unrelated sources of knowledge.

These and a number of other observations will need to be considered to understand better the role played by funerary texts in the formation and regeneration of commemorative culture among Bosnian Muslims. Bosnian tombstones, Islamic and non-Islamic, generally reflect intimate data about everyday life rather than abstract theological or social norms. While they contain a shared religious and secular vocabulary, they express different forms of literacy that break apart a sense of unified sensibility towards the dead and their memory. Consequently, Bosnian Islamic funerary texts can be best assessed in reference to the Ottoman imperial obituary legacy on the one hand and, on the other, intimate local relations that have encouraged a collective and enduring participation across the deathscape of Bosnia and Herzegovina. Ottoman Bosnian funerary praxis came about at the confluence of vernacular epigraphic and/or iconographic customs and the imperial lexicon of death.

Locating Memorial Texts

A fundamental similarity between Christian and Islamic beliefs that an omnipotent creator oversees the passage to eternity on unswerving ethical grounds facilitated the persistence of the existing funerary forms across Bosnia and Herzegovina as the new Ottoman styles began to spread. In a similar vein, a shared environmental and ritual tradition of disposing of the body through burial, most commonly in a single-person grave, and of marking the graves in a way to promote their visibility, averted any conspicuous clash of customs and norms in the treatment of the dead. While the orientation of graves may be at odds in that the Muslims headstones are commonly positioned to enable the dead to face the direction of Mecca (and Eastern Orthodox to face Jerusalem), there is no predictable differentiating pattern in the sacred topography of either type of graveyards. As such, the visual characteristic of Muslim and Christian graves in early Ottoman Bosnia reveal

---

[1] E. Lambourn aptly points out this bias in reference to South East Asia, in 'Tombstones, Texts, and Typologies: Seeing Sources for the Early History of Islam in Southeast Asia', *Journal of the Economic and Social History of the Orient* 51:2 (2008), 252–86.

minor typological differences especially when one considers all aspects of this funerary culture – location, type of burial, general masonry, environment, visual and textual clues. In maintaining important commonalities that allowed the overall transition to be gradual, multilayered, and inclusive, it is not unusual to find many early Muslim tombstones in close vicinity to the medieval Bosnian burial sites where they visually belong to the same frame of reference. To elucidate better the significance of funerary texts and the change they underwent as the Ottomans consolidated power in Bosnia, let us consider some specific examples of continuity and discontinuity and the shifts that accompanied the process of conversion.

In terms of historical continuity, pre-Ottoman burial practices in Bosnia commonly involved disposing of the dead under monumental monoliths that came in a number of different shapes: upright stelae, rectangular prisms, sarcophagi, slabs, cubes, or in related combinations. Although these monoliths can be found clustered in the form of graveyards as well as in solitary placements in and around towns and villages, most often they lie scattered in remote mountainous regions inaccessible by regular roads. It is unclear why the dead were often buried so far away from human settlements, but the practice was pervasive and indicative of the tendency to clearly mark, in spatial terms, a physical discontinuity between the living and the dead. Speculations have been made that this was done for reasons of safety and protection, especially among those who argue that medieval Bosnia was the home of the persecuted Bogomil heretics,[2] but it is hardly likely that anyone who strove for invisibility would choose such gigantic monumental stones to mark their resting place. Rather, remote burials prompt us to consider the possibility that the deceased members of a community need not benefit from a physical proximity to the living, but, to the contrary, from a commemorative connection to the land rather than people. This tripartite relationship of life–land–death frames the sense of a community and connects many strands of cultural production and action – myths, spirituality, history, and politics – in an embodied and continuous way. Thanks to that relationship we can best observe from a synchronic perspective the shifts in funerary rituals and commemorative styles, and engage long stretches of history, pre-modern and modern, with contemporary concerns about territorial integrity and belonging that inform the discourse about Bosnia and Herzegovina.

---

[2] A long-standing debate about the nature of Bosnian medieval Christianity, the Bosnian Church, Bosnian Bogomilism and its assumed heretical characteristics have been thoroughly addressed in N. Malcolm, *Bosnia: A Short History* (London: Macmillan, 1994), 13–42; B. Nilević, 'Slika religioznosti srednjovjekovne Bosne pred osmanski dolazak [Religious composition of medieval Bosnia prior to the Ottoman arrival]', *POF* 41 (1991).

CONVERTING THE STONE: TEXT AND IMAGES IN EARLY OTTOMAN BOSNIA 113

Figure 3.1 Medieval *stećak* necropolis, Kupres.
Photo by Velibor Božović

Figure 3.2 *Stećaks* under a blanket of moss. Ladjevina, Rogatica.
Photo by Velibor Božović

Commonly known as the *stećak* (pl. *stećci*) in contemporary idiom, pre-Ottoman burial stones of Bosnia and Herzegovina have been given many different names, indicating the unevenness of cultural memory and the modes of self-identification of the people who have inhabited these lands. In fact, while common in urban argot, the term *stećak* (literally, a 'tall, standing stone') is quite uncommon in regional dialects. Bearing no etiological value, the term has nevertheless taken root among city elites, paradoxically highlighting its somewhat imprecise connotations.[3] In contrast, the communities living around and in close vicinity to the medieval graveyards refer to these stones in a number of different ways: for example, in some areas of Herzegovina the *stećak* is called *mašet*, a word deriving from either the Italian *massetto* (rock), or the Turkish *meşhet* (tombstone to a fallen hero).[4] In central and western Bosnia, they are frequently referred to as *mramor/mramorje* (marble), while in Serbia and Montenegro as *usadjenik* (implantation).[5] In some instances, especially in reference to smaller clusters of graves, local legends associate their origins with feuds and violence, especially in wedding processions, remembering them as a result as *svatovska* (wedding rites). Because of their large size, they have also been known as *džinovska* (giants). Conversely, the stone's textual self-references, consisting mainly of carved epigraphs and signatures between the twelfth and sixteenth centuries, include terms such as *kam/kamen* (stone), *bilig/biljeg* (mark, imprint), *hram* (shrine), *raka* (pit), *greb/grob* (grave).[6] Furthermore, as various cultures spread within the broader region leaving an imprint of their commemorative lexicon and practice on the local population, these monoliths have been variably – at times alternately and at others simultaneously – named in ethnic terms as Greek graves, Roman graves, Hungarian graves, Turkish graves, Serbian graves and *kaurinska* (foreign, or non-Muslim) graves. Despite its manifest association with specific ethnic origins, it would be misleading to treat such a typology as a mode of ethnic appropriation or alienation. These labels point more to the stones' antiquity, less than their ethnicity. The dead belong to the land in which they rest, and the stones are awe-inspiring for their size, durability, and continuity in space and time, indicating a level of authenticity and a possibility that someone more powerful and grand than 'us' may have constructed them. In fact, the popular lore often connects the legends of giants living in these lands

---

[3] M. Wenzel, *Ukrasni motivi na stećcima* [*Stećak* decorative motifs] (Sarajevo: n.p., 1965), 15; D. Vidovic, 'Simbolična predstava na stećcima [Stećaks' symbolic representations]', *Naše starine* 2 (1954).

[4] S. Bešlagić, *Stećci*, 15–25. Notably, in the Ottoman sources *meşetlik* seems to have been used in reference to non-Muslim gravesites.

[5] A. Buturović, *Stone Speaker* (New York: Palgrave, 2002), 50–58.

[6] Referenced in M. Vego, *Zbornik srednjovjekovnih natpisa u Bosni i Hercegovini* [Anthology of Medieval Inscriptions in Bosnia and Herzegovina] (Sarajevo: Zemaljski muzej, 1962–64), vols 1–3; V. Ćorović, 'Prilog proučavanju načina sahranjivanja i podizanja nadgrobnih spomenika u našim krajevima u srednjem vijeku [Contribution to the study of burial practices and erection of tombstones in medieval times]', *Naše starine* 3 (1955).

with such ethnic markers, creating a cultural and biological link between this world and the world of fantastic beings. It is deeply linked to the notion of spatial belonging and the fact that the ancestors who had settled here may have mixed with mythical figures in this region, leaving the *stećak* as an enduring remnant.[7] Monumental people bequeath monumental artefacts. Folk tradition has it that these mysterious trolls often played fetch in the open fields with the monoliths, tossing them around among each other and letting them fall freely on the ground, creating the clustered formations still visible in the landscape. Some of them, they say, had already been used as graves and the epigraphs' warnings against vandalism were directed against this playful negligence of the giant ancestors.[8] The fact that the *stećak* has retained ritual and cultural attention is a testimony to its ongoing integration into social relations.

However, in contrast to such loose and non-binding pre-modern modes of classification, the *stećak* has also been subjected to modern ideological appropriations by exclusivist ethno-national myths of cultural antiquity and grandeur. Given its monumentality, uniqueness and ubiquity, the *stećak* became an icon of ethno-national ownership, and its historical recovery emerged as a recurrent motif in nationalist historiographies and topographies. The debate that began in the late nineteenth century has continued to date. This is perhaps an inevitable side effect of the fact that Bosnia does not exist as a national category but only as a territorial and political unit, so its constituent national groups – Serbs, Croats and Bosniaks – when exercising their exclusive modernist notions of belonging, advance claims that the *stećak* ought to be segregated within preconceived trajectories of national self-formation and claims to territorial continuity. Scholarship, alas, has not only succumbed to but has in turn promoted such segregations. The lack of recognition of these graves' proximity to all other constituent religious groups of Bosnia – Catholic, Muslim, Orthodox and even Jewish – speaks to the general shortsightedness of nationalist historiographies, which is usually linked to the anachronistic questions about the pre-Ottoman identity of the Bosnian people and their spiritual and ritual loyalties. Identity, that reductive concept that has become probably the most discussed topic of social scientists in recent decades, is pregnant with modernist projections of political self-affirmation, agency, psychology, myths of belonging and others, most of which are not applicable to pre-modern patterns of individual and group behaviour.

However, the appropriations are at some level inevitable. In any collective necrographic endeavour, grave markers not only mark a dead person's resting place, but a community's territorial point of reference, defining its spatial belonging in much the same way, if not even more potently, as a house, church, school, or any other public edifice and institution. The line

---

[7] A number of such stories are recorded by V. Palavestra, *Historijska usmena predanja* [Oral histories from Bosnia and Herzegovina] (Sarajevo: Buybook, 2004), 33–8.

[8] V. Palavestra, *Historijska usmena predanja*, 34–5.

separating a necropolis from metropolis is often only superficial, drawing attention more to their mutual inclusion and less to exclusion. In some cases, such as Cairo's City of the Dead, the line is practically erased. Following Jon Davies's aforementioned suggestion that every death is dually constituted as a personal and collective experience involving a social administration of emotions, practices, and rituals, we are urged to wonder how individual death is narrated, integrated and remembered by the collective and channelled into a regenerative process of its cultural complex. The administration of death is intimately tied with the representation and naturalisation of death through texts and contexts that allow it to be part of a group's narrative, especially when those narratives absorb the issues of religion, memory, and geographic location. Individual graves and gravestones are forensic and archaeological artefacts, but they are also sites on which larger issues of commemorative, ritual, eschatological, and related meanings are inscribed. The relationship generated and sustained between a community and its ancestors is significant not only for the study of social action and group identity, but also for the understanding of religious and cultural meanings that are assigned to the dead, their memory, and the landscape in which they rest.

In the case of *stećak* necropoleis, the lack of scholarly insight regarding their historical and cultural origins yet their physical ubiquity and proximity to more identifiable tombstones and cemeteries associated with later periods, including those which are still active, are all suggestive of a continued and interactive cultural intimacy and mixing of the dead against the general reluctance now to do so. It is within that framework of reference that their relevance can best be assessed, including their enduring role in the cultural memory and imagination of the Bosnian people of different religious persuasions.

To Write or Not to Write: Funerary Text in Image and Word

Laying a body into the earth and marking it with a stone is an act of affirmation. The body may now belong to the earth, but its memory and its physicality are socially delineated, and are either individually or communally sustained. The memory thus gains at once a spiritual quality and material manifestation. As in most ritual enactments, visual or textual clues are included as mnemonic devices to facilitate the regenerative bond between the living and the dead. In the majority of cases, however, the *stećak* is a simplified object containing no such clues, that is, it bears no inscriptions or images. Of the roughly 60,000 *stećaks* that have been recorded in Bosnia and Herzegovina, the great majority – some 50,000 – consist of plain, undecorated and non-representational stones.[9]

---

[9] M. Wenzel, *Ukrasni motivi na stećcima* [Stećaks' decorative motifs] (Sarajevo: n.p., 1965), 13.

Barren and silent, such *stećaks* activate the elegiac memory without consoling us, enlightening us, or guiding us farther into the ritual or informal space of commemoration and interpretation. They give out no hint of what death is like. Actually, in failing to conjure up any representation of death, a symbol of afterlife, divinity or benediction, they are not only unassuming but also unassumable. Death, they seem to imply, cannot be represented. Frustrating as this may be for those who expect disclosure and clues for historical recovery, and too mundane for those interested in the secrets of infinity, such reticent *stećaks* in fact entrust us with the memories of life in this world, not with possible variations of death. Like tabula rasa, these *stećaks* impose nothing that may subject death to the anxieties and constraints of theology or ritual imagination. The identity of the dead is undisclosed, and their historical or religious circumstances hide under such nondescript, austere and mute stone blocks. As the stone blocks are unlikely to be removed, death cannot be ignored, but no name binds the grave, no symbol reveals the dead's religious or cultural belonging, no date situates death in time. Only a massive stone, inwardly with its forensic secret subject and outwardly with nothing to betray it, signals a person's final resting place. If viewed in such transhistorical terms, the term *biljeg* – marker – generically given to such gravestones can be appreciated for opening up rather than restricting the modes of remembrance and motivates us to form our own relationship with death, in our own way, from our own experience of life.

In contrast, around 10,000 *stećaks* bear figural and scriptural motifs, albeit all derived from a relatively limited repertoire. Despite this limitedness, *stećak* symbolism must be approached without a predetermined, static lexicon. Symbols can suggest a plurality of meaning and their specific contexts can reveal a variety of concerns and subjectivities. Though one would expect certain fixed patterns in lapidary language, it seems that the safest route to decoding this language is in combining the questions of 'how' visual symbols are formed with 'what' they suggest. This approach is necessitated by the fact that the visual text moves through history and is at once a method of alienation and familiarisation: whereas the images are scooped from a shared brew of values, they visualise stories about an individual's rite of passage from this life into the next, which makes the symbols at once worldly and eschatological, individual and collective, real and imaginary. That there is a relatively small repertoire of *stećak* motifs should not concern us in light of the fact that there is an infinitely larger pool of visual combinations that mediate between what is experienced in this life and what can be assumed about the next. This is especially relevant in view of the argument that all Bosnians, irrespective of religious persuasion or ethnic background, used the same sepulchral language. The existing decorations therefore ignore religious, ethnic, even class differentiation, and draw attention to a shared burial praxis despite differences in belief about the relationship between this world and the hereafter. Moreover, it seems that the visual vocabulary expanded in response to major historical upheavals in the region may have left important imprints on the social practices of commemoration. A turning point is associated with the wake of the Ottoman conquest. Wenzel concludes:

> The decorated *stećci* appear as a phenomenon within a relatively narrow range of time. This was a crucial historical period. It began after the battle of Kosovo in 1389 and the fall of Serbia to the Turks, spanned the short emergence of Bosnia as an independent kingdom, and finished in the earlier years after the Turkish conquest of Bosnia. Only a few shapes of tombstones, such as crosses and steles, carry on well into the Turkish times. It would seem that the earliest decorated tombstones were erected by feudal aristocracy, and that the custom was later adopted and the decoration much elaborated by certain groups known as Vlachs who were organized on a tribal, non-feudal basis. The Vlachs, having been economically strengthened as a consequence of their dealings with the Dubrovnik traders, adopted this custom in imitation of the upper classes. It is quite likely that other, non-Vlach inhabitants of Bosnia and Hercegovina adopted the same custom for the same reason.[10]

In that sense, the visual evidence as read by Marion Wenzel reinforces the theory of the *stećak*'s polyvalent aesthetics in several ways: first, it locates the practice of decorating the *stećak* at a crucial phase in Bosnian history –

Figure 3.3 *Stećak* at Gornje Ravno. Human representation.
Photo by Velibor Božović

---

[10] M. Wenzel, *Ukrasni motivi*, 15.

Figure 3.4 Zoomorphic representation, detail. Bitunja.
Photo by Velibor Božović

Figure 3.5 Human representation, detail, Bitunja.
Photo by Velibor Božović

the eve of the Ottoman arrival; second, it traces a re-configuration of class and economy in medieval Bosnia on the basis of the *stećaks'* decorative detail; and third, it points to the fact that the practice of constructing *stećaks* did not recede with the Ottoman consolidation in Bosnia and Herzegovina. These arguments certainly renew the appreciation of the *stećak* as a distinctly Bosnian phenomenon shared by all confessional communities. Furthermore, they present us with the *stećak* inside rather than outside of history insofar as they offer insights into its subjection to social and cultural flux rather than representational paralysis. Connotations of imperviousness to historical change are challenged by the very act of carving.

In the necro-lexicon of pre-Ottoman Bosnian tombstones, however, the discord between history and memory is stark. While the general tendency has long been to link the *stećak*'s visual and written text with the dualist Bogomil teaching, the scholars now agree that Bosnians of other religious beliefs and persuasions also buried their dead under the *stećaks* and must have therefore participated in the making of its lexicon. In other words, although some components of this lexicon may be suggestive of dualist Bogomilism, it would be misleading to associate any such image with a single teaching.

Over the course of time, the *stećaks* were decorated and inscribed with both figurative and abstract representations, with or without the text. The visual motifs include geometric shapes (circle, square, crescent, polygons, quatrefoil, hemisphere); floral and vegetal images (rose/rosette, vine, lily, herbs, grapes); decorative borders; animal representations (lion, deer, snake, horse, lamb, birds of prey); scenes from everyday life but also hunting, festive, and heraldic captions; anthropomorphic representations; objects (wand, shield, spear, book, working tools); and occasionally, facial close-ups. These are either carved or done in relief, appearing randomly positioned, rarely concerned with margins, and not subjected to a pre-set string of associations or a linear visual narrative characteristic of monumental architecture.

A fraction of the decorated *stećaks* bear inscriptions, mostly in the old Bosnian Cyrillic alphabet, *Bosančica*, some in Church Slavonic or *Glagoljica* (Glagolitic), and the remaining few in Latin script. Their number, by the count of historian Marko Vego in 1970, was 277, and 323 by the historian Šefik Bešlagić.[11] It is significant to note that a crucial shift in our understanding of pre-Ottoman and early Ottoman landscapes of death is occasioned by the scholarly focus on inscriptions. In contrast to the mute, anonymous gravestones, the inscribed tombs – be they useful for biographical detail, epitaphic note or benediction – change our perception of the subject by invoking a real name in real spacetime, and by giving the landscape a new meaning in the study of cultural history and memory. While the inscriptions

---

[11] S. Bešlagić, *Stećci, katološko-topografski pregled* [The *stećaks*: a topographic catalogue] (Sarajevo: Veselin Masleša, 1975), 54.

CONVERTING THE STONE: TEXT AND IMAGES IN EARLY OTTOMAN BOSNIA 121

Figure 3.6 Detail from a *stećak* in Fatnica. A man and a woman.
Photo by Velibor Božović

in question are often terse, broken and incomplete, or are written in an uneven and obtuse way, they nevertheless draw attention to the culture of writing and communication and the spread of literacy across the region. They draw into conversation the visitors who stop at the grave. In addition, the common references to the mason (*kovač, klesar*) and scribe (*dijak, pisar*) in the epitaph itself indicates the importance of acknowledging the value of the literate class in a sporadically literate society.[12] The landscape, like the gravestone, is culturally moulded and marked for posterity, securing its continuity against amnesia and the general passage of time.

Content wise, there is little that is lyrical or comforting about these inscriptions. For the most part, they read as brazen reminders of mortality and relay a dread of death. The medieval Bosnian dead seem to be resting in a state of anxiety, not peace. Death as articulated in the funerary text does not bring respite from finitude and doom; it actually amplifies it. The dead are not freed from their own history or materiality but forever entrapped in it and therefore eager to be visited, protected, and remembered: 'I have for long lain here, and for much longer shall I lie'; 'May he who topples this stone be cursed'; 'Have pity on the one who once was like you'; 'I was born into a great joy and I died into a great sorrow'; 'Be cursed if you come near me but are not my kin'; 'I

---

[12] V. Bogićević, *Pismenost u BiH* [Literacy in Bosnia and Herzegovina] (Sarajevo: Veselin Masleša, 1975), 47–50.

was nothing then, I am nothing now'; 'Here lies a servant who feels no joy', and so on. In contrast to later funerary texts, especially the Islamic ones which downplay any somatic experience of and after death, the inscriptions such as these intimate that the deceased not only retain the ability to feel but experience a heightened sense of vulnerability, agony, torment, and disconnect.

In contrast to this personal, inner landscape of doom caused by death, the outer, physical landscape is most often referred to with pride and comfort – the land in which the dead lie is referred to as sacral, fair and noble (*zemlja plemenita*) on the tombstones of feudal landlords, and as ancestral (*baština*) in more general terms. This opposition between the feeling of inner anguish and of positive affirmation assigned to the land introduces a psychological and social tension into the lexicon of remembrance. The dead are not glorified, their death is not celebrated, and they seem to harbour continuous nostalgia for life above ground rather than below. The land, on the other hand, offers comfort and a continued sense of self-affirmation. The recognition that the people are taken away from their kin, community and land evokes an urgency to stay close to the local soil, community, and culture. This is further amplified by the fact that many inscriptions mention, by name, specific landowners, nobility, and rulers who were directly or indirectly in charge of the local or state affairs. Not only can this data be useful for reconstructing some aspects of social history but it also offers a more complex perspective on spatial belonging as it frames the dead within a broader topography which, to put it in Pamela Stewart's terms, serves as 'a contextual horizon of perceptions, providing both a foreground and background in which people feel themselves as living in their world'.[13]

Given this parallel practice of either not marking tombstones at all or inscribing them with highly localised historical, ritual and symbolic texts, the process of transition occasioned by conversion in early Ottoman times and the introduction of new funerary practices and styles must have signalled an important shift in the vitality and continuity of social relations among the living and the dead in early Ottoman Bosnia. As mentioned above, when present, the funerary text, of both an epigraphic and iconographic kind, reflects personal beliefs, offers information and intimates shared symbols and expressions between the dead and the living. It is both a public register and a commemorative site that harbours deeply personal concerns. In its absence, the stones belong to all, generalising death and making it everyone's business. In this sense, while the remains in the grave may be lifeless, the records on the grave markers make the dead very much alive, serving as culturally and spiritually intimate signifiers about the role of death in the most immediate environment.

---

[13] P.J. Stewart and A. Strathern, *Landscape, Memory and History* (London: Pluto Press, 2003), 4.

Bosnian Deathscape and Ottoman Islamic Influences

In order to consider further the transition from pre-Ottoman to Ottoman eschatological sensibilities, we need to address again the process of conversion. How were the new Muslims of Bosnia to mark their own death in a way that would not sever the link with either close or distant ancestors? How did they accommodate newly acquired beliefs about the afterlife and the related practices of burial and commemoration? In broader terms, what was the identity of the new converts – was it well defined and resolute or was it hybrid and flexible? From a comparative perspective of the two religious systems, both Christianity and Islam share the monotheistic belief in life after death, designed by the omniscient God as either eternal reward or eternal punishment in accordance with the deeds committed during one's lifetime. On the other hand, the two religions differ in their ritual, scriptural and commemorative vocabulary that frames the afterlife, and those differences are key to their doctrinal self-identification and promulgation. In a context simultaneously rich with individual markers of death and communal consolidation around medieval necropoleis, the task of adapting the existing funerary sensibilities to a new system must have been formidable. Furthermore, as seen above, Christian funerary culture in pre-Ottoman Bosnia was well established if somewhat idiosyncratic in relation to normative Christian practices in the broader region. The Ottoman Islamic system brought into it not only a different kind of burial tradition but also a different vocabulary, idiom and script of articulation. Like in other non-Arabic speaking lands, the adoption of Arabic was intimately tied with the acquisition of religious knowledge and sacred symbols and as such possessed an irreplaceable and untranslatable quality. But does this mean that the local vocabulary and styles readily disappeared with the arrival of Arabic and other Ottoman linguistic cultures? The answer is no. On the contrary, what emerged out of these historical conditions was a polyvalent environment, consolidating around religious status, social position, intellectual, regional and other criteria, indicating an important level of cultural pliability in this small region during the transmission and exchange of resources and knowledge. This means that the adoption of new styles, which included the form, language, and imagery, inevitably led to a simultaneous and often unpredictable continuation and rejection of the old ones.[14] While such lengthy and uneven processes of transition may be at work in all societies caught up in religious conversion, what makes Bosnia an interesting case is that it not only followed a synchronic trajectory of moving the past into the present, but it also resulted, diachronically, in the shifts in funerary culture among the Orthodox and Catholic Christians, as well as the Jewish Sephardic

---

[14] For a general overview of the material objects dating from the early Ottoman period, see A. Nametak, *Islamski kulturni spomenici Turskog perioda* [Islamic cultural monuments of the Turkish period] (Sarajevo: Državna štamparija, 1939).

settlers in Bosnia. This buzzing, multidirectional change and exchange in funerary literacy left profound effects on the cultural landscape of the region.

Changing Funerary Idiom: Issues of Language, Challenges of Translation

While traditional Islam may have discouraged the erection of visible lasting tombstones, history shows that this has been neither consistently followed nor preferred. Throughout the Islamic world, the magnitude and opulence of monumental architecture demonstrates that this legal and theological position is often but a vague guideline, and one that is frequently mitigated by cultural preferences. Already during the earliest period of Arabo-Islamic military expansions into North Africa and the Middle East, the rise in monumental architecture began to reflect a growing preference for tangible modes of remembrance along with those that possessed more intangible and unobtrusive qualities. As a result, all around the Muslim world simple gravestones with little or no inscription coexist with grand shrines meticulously embellished with visual and textual motifs. By the time of Islam's arrival in Bosnia and the Balkans at large, Islamic monumental architecture had evolved along different styles and forms. The Ottomans themselves had already begun to develop a distinct funerary material culture with composite origins in Turkic, Arabo-Islamic and Byzantine traditions. Stylistically, the Ottoman tombstone is an upright stela, consisting of a headstone and a footstone: the headstone is turned towards Mecca and bears an inscription that records at the very least the name, the date of death and a liturgical invocation or benediction. The male headstone contains a turban or another type of headgear on top of the stela, which, because of its uniqueness in the Islamic world, some scholars trace to an ancient Turkic tradition.[15] The female headstone does not contain a turban but is stylised and, like male stones, often visually decorated in addition to being inscribed. The footstone, on the other hand, is commonly neither decorated nor inscribed.

Despite regional variances that melded into it over time, this imperial style became the marker of the majority of Ottoman burial grounds. According to Edhem Eldem, it was fully developed by the sixteenth century, especially as regards epigraphy (biographical detail, benediction), language preferences, and the typology of headgear. In this context, Eldem establishes a strong relationship between the evolution of funerary styles and the rise of urban centres in the Ottoman Empire. As Ottoman cities expanded, the cemeteries became better organised and were either developed *extra muros*, namely, as suburban cemeteries – *kabrıstan* – outside city limits, or as *hazire*, small graveyard enclosures next to town mosques. To this end, Sultan Bayezid II (d. 1512) established pious endowments for the management of funerary

---

[15] H.P. Laqueur, 'Dervish Gravestones,' in R. Lifchez (ed.), *The Dervish Lodge: Architecture, Art, and Sufism in Ottoman Turkey* (Berkley: University of California Press, 1992), 284.

practice in and around the imperial capital, Istanbul, solidifying the standards under the imperial aegis.[16] However, other criteria need to be considered in this process. While focusing their analysis primarily on Istanbul cemeteries – because they contain not only some of the most flamboyant examples of funerary forms but also expansive and diverse subcultures – Eldem and Vatin also engage in a systematic comparison between the imperial capital and provincial cities, tracing the contrasts between trends and establishing common elements.[17] Their findings demonstrate that the provinces follow suit in almost all aspects of funerary culture: from funerary style to formulaic references, religious invocations, and even epitaphic poetry, but they do so with a temporal delay. In the process, as the authors rightfully point out, the trends popular in the centre spread to the provincial urban centres with a lag of some 50 years, and they also acquired some new ingredients in the process.

By extension, then, Bosnian urban centres adopted and partook in the development of Ottoman funerary culture by following its rather standardised model and injecting it with its own elements. Both city cemeteries and especially the graveyards of major city mosques (in Bosnia referred to as *harem* rather than *hazire*) reflect predictable trends in funerary style associated with Ottoman urban culture. Indeed, the most outstanding examples of high-quality marble headstones erected in mosque graveyards are perhaps less flamboyant than their Istanbul counterparts but are as finely ornate. The city of Travnik, which became the administrative capital of the province of Bosnia and the seat of the viziers after Sarajevo was burned to the ground by Prince Eugene of Savoy in 1699, contains some of the finest artefacts of this imperial style. Here, as in much of Bosnia, the majority of these and similar decorous examples of urban tombstones are made of the so-called *uśćupski mramor*, a particular type of crystal marble imported from Macedonia for the Bosnian elite. In the popular jargon, they are also known as 'Istanbul stones', in recognition of their calligraphic and decorative finesse, more so than their origins.[18] What is not entirely clear is under what circumstances this crystal marble arrived in Bosnia: were these tombstones custom carved in Macedonia, then inscribed in accordance with the imperial standard and shipped to Bosnia, or was the marble imported untreated and carved by Bosnian masons and scribes? Given their stylistic uniformity it is likely that such fine gravestones represent both materially and textually imported objects, rather than objects of the Bosnian domestic production, affirming the

---

[16] E. Eldem, 'Urban Voices from Beyond: Identity, Status and Social Strategies in Ottoman Muslim Funerary Epitaphs of Istanbul (1700–1850) in V. Aksan and D. Goffman, *The Early Modern Ottomans: Remapping the Empire* (Cambridge: Cambridge University Press), 207.

[17] E. Eldem and N. Vatin, *L'épitaphe otomane musulmane, XVIe-XXe siècles* (Paris: Peeters, 2007).

[18] S. Traljić, 'Muslimanski nadgrobni spomenici [Muslim folk monuments]', *Narodna uzdanica* 8 (1940), 197. Another hypothesis suggests that *uśćupski* is the adjectival reference to the town of Uskoplje in Bosnia and Herzegovina, rather than Macedonia.

Figure 3.7 Man's tombstone with a turban.
Photo by Velibor Božović

Figure 3.8 Woman's tombstone.
　　　　　Photo by Amila Buturović

argument about the spread of funerary text into the peripheries, albeit in this case by means of economic networks and transmission of goods rather than through ideas and skilled labour.

Other Bosnian tombstones are certainly more modest and less uniform in their stylistic outlook. The material used is not as fine, normally mined from local limestone although some tombstones, popularly referred to as *ugarski* (Hungarian) – because the stone was used for the graves of Muslims fleeing from Hungarian provinces – were made of green granite stone. Of course, a general picture of all the tombstones across Bosnia and Herzegovina with an architectural or textual consistency is hard to establish. Based on this research, not all Bosnian gravestones reflect a neat centre/periphery dichotomy as established by Eldem and Vatin. Rather, one can more readily speak of a foreign/local dichotomy within the periphery because the tombstones reflecting imperial standards were intended first and foremost for the urban elite who could partake more normatively in the new commemorative culture. In the first few centuries, specifically until the mid-eighteenth century, there is no consistency in the Islamic deathscapes of Bosnia. In the course of the eighteenth century the imperial trend was consolidated all across it, along with some local additions, standardising funerary material culture across the region. Until then, vernacular customs common in rural cemeteries vigorously contributed to a complex and longer-lasting negotiation of stylistic, linguistic, and religious exchange. This negotiation was not one directional, namely, between local Christian and Ottoman Islamic norms, but also intra-Christian as well, resulting in much richer layers of funerary exchange. Moreover, we hope to show that local norms displaced the imperial standard in several important ways. Thus, although the Ottoman imperial funerary style may have crystallised by the end of the sixteenth century in the capital Istanbul and its environs, it seems that the standard never fully reached its limits before the eighteenth century in Bosnia, and perhaps in the Balkans at large, as accommodations were made for local interventions in both form and content, namely, text and image.

Perhaps a major factor destabilising the theory of the centre/periphery dichotomy in funerary architecture and epigraphy is the question of historical meaning attributed to gravestones. As suggested earlier, many studies dealing with funerary epigraphy, including the work by Edhem and Vatin, exhibit a textual bias that inevitably favours an urban point of view at the expense of rural areas where literacy was much more limited. Moreover, in evoking the literary value of the funerary material such studies dislodge the tombstone from the landscape and inadvertently diminish, if not sever, the link between religion/culture and space, especially in the areas where numerous anonymous tombstones partake in various spiritual and ritual practices. While the study of funerary texts of Ottoman Bosnia from a literary perspective still demonstrates that local knowledge and culture are never fully displaced in favour of imperial norms, such a perspective disengages from analysis any holistic cultural and religious engagement in commemoration. Why did the vernacular modes of remembrance of the dead persist? What was the significance of preserving some local epigraphic practices instead of adopting fully the imperial norms? The answer is not only literary, but one that takes us back to the interconnection between deathscapes and commemorative culture. Because the body is buried in the land and the tombstone is embedded in it as a marker, the tombstone is not merely a tablet on which biographical data and memorial notes are recorded and literary qualities conveyed. Rather, it is a ritual location where connections with the living can be expressed, meaning after loss regained and commemorative contact enhanced.

Therefore, the contention here is that the understanding of funerary material must transcend the focus on funerary architecture and writing only, and merge them with the ritual and spiritual import of the tombstone. Here we can look to Jonathan Z. Smith's formulation in his study of religious geography, which indicates that the dichotomy usually deployed to differentiate the religious/sacred centre from profane periphery should in fact be understood as 'a locative as opposed to a utopian vision of the world'. In other words, Smith argues that the discourse on a normative, transcendental centre tends to de-spatialise the sacred while local experiences place the sacred into a specific time and place. Although his critique is mainly formulated against Eliade's mystification of sacred space as the centre of cosmic meaning rather than a product of local ritual participation and understanding,[19] Smith's observations shed light on the necessary tension between sacred centre and periphery by positioning religious experience within the push and pull of the two domains. Moreover, it elevates the discussion of periphery from being just a reflection of, or a challenge to, canonical/normative/transcendental demands and permits it to exercise agency in the formation of ritual and spiritual meaning. In referring to their interaction as a tension between the locative and the utopian, Smith places value on the broader context of participation. Therefore, if exploited simply as biographical or literary records which align with or deviate from the homogenising practices of the imperial centre, the tombstones cannot be appreciated for their full religious and cultural value as contexts saturated with spiritual, emotional, political and ritual meaning for both central/imperial and peripheral/local forms. It is this canopy of spiritual, ritual and other engagements that the discussion of the early Ottoman Islamic tombstones in Bosnia and Herzegovina must address in order to elucidate the complexity related to funerary culture.

Lost and Found in Translation: Kabur, Nišan, Mezar

According to important funerary evidence from the early sixteenth century, Muslim converts in Bosnia maintained the usage of the local script, *Bosančica*, along with a gradual infiltration of Arabic language and script. As suggested earlier, funerary epigraphy was not a highly developed and practised craft. In fact, the most recognisable Ottoman tombstones of the earliest period,

---

[19] J.Z. Smith, *Map is Not Territory: Studies in the History of Religion* (Leiden: E.J. Brill, 1978), 101–13.

commonly referred to as the period of *feth*, or conquest, contain no writings. The only clue to their Muslim identity is reflected in the upright architecture of a square or octagonal stela that is commonly topped by a large turban. These tombstones are scattered across the Bosnian countryside, often in small clusters, sometimes alone, but commonly adjacent to *stećak* cemeteries. And, like many a *stećak*, they too are plain, containing repetitive visual symbols: hemisphere, wand, sword, bow and arrow, and occasional human and animal representations. Like the *stećaks*, they too tend to be disproportionately large, marking the landscape, even when solitary, with an unmistaken commemorative presence. The embeddedness of such visual objects within the local cultural landscape is stark. The turban represents a historical addition, a permutation which, along with the architecturally upright form of the tombstone, accommodates the new reality and at once maintains a sense of cultural continuity and historical depth. Unfortunately, rarely does any kind of writing advertise such artefacts. As a result, their meaning is mainly developed in local stories and memories, and is occasionally embodied in rituals, such as the ones discussed earlier in reference to the *dobri*, the good ones, the cephalophoric martyrs, female martyrs and other characters in the hagio-mythic repertoire that allows the community to form and sustain a connection with these old tombstones beyond any historical explanation. The tombstones remain veiled in mystery but the vacuum in historical knowledge is expiated by cultural memory.

Figure 3.9 Solitary tombstone from the period of Ottoman conquest, Trnovo. Photo by Velibor Božović.

Figure 3.10   Tombstone from the period of Ottoman conquest, with a crescent and hemispheres, Sokolac.
Photo by Amila Buturović

One popular local legend that merges history and myth has it that the sultan Mehmed the Conqueror was accompanied by 12,000 masons on his conquests of this province so they might erect tombstones for the fallen Ottoman soldiers. The presence of the large tombstones at odd and unpredictable locations, seemingly without rhyme or reason, is explained by the Islamic tenet that those killed at war are to be buried on the spot, so it is in memory of their outstanding heroism and martyrdom that large tombstones are placed. Despite its popularity, the veracity of this legend has not been historically proven. On the one hand, it would be hard to sustain an army of stonemasons during such military expeditions, not to mention creating adequate conditions to engage in the labour of stone cutting, crafting and chiselling in an impromptu fashion. On the other, the legend does suggest that the tombstones across Bosnia that share similar characteristics must have been crafted on someone's design and by some new standard. Some Bosnian historians suggest the possibility of the Ottoman stonemasons working side by side with local Christian counterparts and fine-tuning the craft. The converts were also an important labour force in this regard: a 1528 document from Sarajevo mentions a stonemason (*taşçı*), by the name of Mahmut, the son of Vukman: a first-generation Muslim. Mahmut must have taken the shop over from his father and expanded his skill to include new forms of funerary literacy while preserving the old ones.[20] Hamdija Kreševljaković points out, for example, that the guild of stonemasons, *taşçı/taščije*, in most Bosnian towns consisted of both Muslims and Christians, and that Muslims gradually abandoned this art in the wake of the Austro-Hungarian annexation of Bosnia and Herzegovina in the late nineteenth century.[21] Of course, Kreševljaković's argument is important as it helps us understand better the structure and function of guild networks for inter-*millet* relations. Because the guilds were conventionally associated with urban trends and developments, it sheds light on the movements within urban demography and economy by identifying the connections among groups and guilds across Bosnian territory. In contrast, rural cemeteries reveal enough inconsistency in terms of their production, epigraphic practices and usage so as to be easily explained through the same theory about guild activities and structures. Yet there is no doubt that some form of interaction between local and foreign masons must have existed because, as illustrated below, even the most remote rural areas reveal the traces of stylistic borrowing and contact in the early years of the Ottoman expansion.

In the Bosnian Islamic tradition, the tombstone ceases to be referred to as a *stećak*, *kam*, or *bilig/biljeg*, as it was habitual in pre-Ottoman times. The most common Arabic word for grave, *qabr*, infiltrated the Bosnian Islamic lexicon through its Ottoman Turkish usage and became a generic religious reference for 'grave'. In the Bosnian Muslim pronunciation *qabr* becomes *kabur* and the word still survives, especially in religious literature, although it has never been fully acculturated into everyday vocabulary. Epigraphically, like in much of the Islamic world, the formulaic Arabic expression 'this is the grave of' (*hādha qabr* and *hādha al-qabr li XY*) is also inscribed on many Bosnian graves. Outside of Bosnia, it is found recorded on what is considered to be the oldest Muslim epitaph dating from the first century of the Islamic era, in 31 AH/652 CE.[22] Throughout the Arab-speaking and Arabic-influenced Islamic societies, this remained a common, although not exclusive epigraphic designation for the resting place of common folk.[23] In some cases, including in Bosnia, the phrase is expanded to 'the resident of this grave' (*ṣāḥib hādha al-qabr*). This is not a specifically Bosnian phrase, as some have assumed, although it fits well in light of the pre-Ottoman practice of not always burying the body where its grave marker is.

Synonyms for *qabr* are rarely deployed in epigraphic references to the grave. The term *marqad*, for example, in the meaning of 'resting place', is not used in Bosnia although it is mentioned elsewhere in the Ottoman lands.[24] Likewise,

---

[20] Š. Bešlagić, *Nišani XV i XVI vijeka u Bosni i Hercegovini* [The *nišans* of the 15th and 16th centuries in Bosnia and Herzegovina] (Sarajevo: ANU, 1978), 77.

[21] H. Kreševljaković, *Esnafi i obrti u Bosni i Hercegovini, 1463–1878* [Guilds and crafts in Bosnia and Herzegovina, 1946–1878] (Sarajevo: Veselin Masleša, 1958), 1: 150–52.

[22] L. Halevi, *Muhammad's Grave*, 14; n.1. 253.

[23] As surveyed in L. Kalus (ed.), *Thesaurus d'épigraphie islamique* (Geneve: Fondation Max van Berchem, 2013). Online edition: http://www.epigraphie-islamique.org.

[24] E.g. in Diyarbakir; see E. Eldem and N. Vatin, *L'épitaphe otomane*, 327.

the term *bayt*, house, found in some Arab lands, is absent. Occasionally one encounters the word *maqām* in the meaning 'place' and 'abode', which in the Sufi context tends to refer to the tomb of the saint, but this is not the case in Bosnia. Another term used to denote a Muslim grave but which the funerary epigraphy avoids is *mezar*, a word otherwise ubiquitous in everyday idiom. Originally an Arabic word for shrine or place of visitation (*mazār*), the term entered Ottoman Turkish in a less technical sense than its original Arabic where it was reserved primarily for the graves of Sufi saints or other holy men visited in a non-canonical pilgrimage, *ziyāra*, for the purposes of obtaining a blessing, *baraka*. In the broader Ottoman context, *mezar* became a commonplace term for the tomb. As seen in the previous chapter, in Bosnia, like elsewhere in the Ottoman lands, the term *turbe* is used in reference to the shrines of notable individuals. Perhaps it was its softer inflection than *kabur* that made *mezar* stick better to everyday idiom. In addition, to visit a grave, *'obići mezar'*, is a standard phrase that also implies an act of intercession, which *kabur* does not. At the *mezar* one prays for the deceased and connects with their memories; at the *kabur*, most closely meaning 'pit', one faces the irrevocable weight of death. In line with that lexical differentiation, the traditional Bosnian lyric and ballad usually contain commonplace references to *mezar*, especially when telling tragic stories of death from unrequited love, passionate but forbidden relationships, premature illness, and other personal misfortunes.[25] In terms of related words, the Slavic word *raka* and *kabur* are intermittently used, and at times in different versions of the same poetic text, suggesting they may be synonymous. The term *kabur*, however, appears to be preferred in religious writings as the canonical Islamic term for the grave. In contrast, the Christians of Bosnia and Herzegovina use the Slavic words *raka*, *grob* (grave) and *spomenik* (memorial stone).

Derivative compound words such as *mezaristan* and *mezartaşı* in the meaning of graveyard and gravestone respectively, are common Ottoman Turkish renderings of the Arabic word. In Bosnia, while the word *mezarlık* and its synonym *kabristan* do exist in the local idiom, the word *mezartaşı* is absent despite the fact that the importation of religious vocabulary from the three Ottoman languages (Turkish, Arabic and Persian) was usually straightforward. Here, by contrast, the most common word is *nišan*. Originally a Persian word, it entered Arabic through Ottoman Turkish (*nishān*), and also Bosnian from Ottoman Turkish. In the original Persian, the word *nishān* means sign and marker. In Ottoman Turkish, it retained that meaning, but also expanded to mean aim, blemish, sign or post. It is common in the Ottoman military lexicon. Its Slavicised verbal form, *nanišaniti*, means to pick out a mark or target. *Nišantaşı*, the target stone, is the mark used in the Ottoman archery for range records. In

---

[25] A. Buturović, 'Love and/or Death: Conflict Resolution in Traditional Bosnian Ballad', in A. Buturovic and I. Schick (eds), *Women in the Ottoman Balkans* (London: IB Tauris, 2007), 73–99.

Arabic, it has retained the target/marker too, as evidenced also by the phrase on the Bosnian tombstones, but in contemporary Arabic lexicon it also means bridal decoration or gift. The word appears in traditional Bosnian poetry in the same fashion and, in addition, it also means skin blemish or blotch.[26]

Why, then, this discrepancy between the Bosnian idiom and this common Ottoman word denoting tombstone? Why did a word with a fully established semantic value in the three Ottoman languages settle into Bosnian with an additional, idiosyncratic meaning? This is not a common term in the Islamic world: other than, fascinatingly, appearing in Malay and Bahasa Indonesia as a generic word for gravestone, it is not otherwise common in Islamic funerary vocabulary. In the Bosnian case the word *nišan* denotes a specifically Islamic tombstone. As early as the 1700s, a number of tombstones contain epigraphic self-references that parallel the phrase *hādha al-qabr* and *ṣāḥib hādha al-qabr* ('this is the grave of') but read *hādha al-nishān* and *ṣāḥib hādha al-nishān*, suggesting that the word *nišan* had been fully incorporated into the local lexicon by this time. The answers may lie in the process of translation.

As suggested earlier, some of the earliest inscribed funerary artefacts from the Ottoman period display independent usages of Arabic and *Bosančica*. Such a parallel is evidenced by the funerary stones found in eastern Bosnia near the town of Rogatica. Rare that they are, they provide an important glimpse into the interweaving of different memorial sensibilities and the configuration of new modes of cultural exchange. Absorbed into the Ottoman rule as of the mid-fifteenth century, Rogatica's urban growth in the Ottoman sources is dated to 1527 with a thriving market life and a number of important guilds, some of which were evidently run by Ottoman settlers and others by local craftsmen. Although stonemasons do not appear in the record of the existing guilds, historical evidence does indicate that local production of various commodities relied on both foreign and native labour, Muslim and Christian, testifying to a socio-economic growth of Rogatica and its environs in a way comparable to other nascent urban centres of Ottoman Bosnia. As in other parts of the province, here too the converts to Islam, following the Ottoman model, gradually discarded the usage of the horizontal tombstone in favour of upright stone slabs. Moreover, this preference started to be general rather than confined only to Muslims. The upright stone became more common, shaped sometimes to resemble an embryonic crucifix but more often amorphously, and were employed to designate Christian graves as well. The lack of a turban capping the stone post is usually what betrays their non-Muslim identity. In many cases of the early period of the Ottoman rule, however, local Muslim tombstones also lacked a turban. They stand upright but have no recognisable Ottoman characteristics. Like Christian stones, they too are inscribed in the

---

[26] A. Škaljić, *Turcizmi u srpskohrvatskom jeziku* [Turkish loan words in Serbo-Croatian] (Sarajevo: Svjetlost, 1985), 493.

Bosnian language, *Bosančica*. Based on textual references and circumstantial evidence, most of these transitional gravestones date from the late fifteenth and early sixteenth centuries, roughly during the urban metamorphosis of Rogatica into an Ottoman town.

One of the simplest and most important of such transitional examples is the tombstone of Suleiman Oškopica, from the village of Dumanjići located in close proximity to Rogatica: built as an upright stela, the headstone contains several conventional decorative symbols – hemispheres, including one on the stela's pyramidal top giving it a less sharp, oblique shape, and another one on one of the sides, which are common on other *nišans* in the same cemetery as well as on the neighbouring medieval *stećak* tombstones; a solar symbol; a carved flag; and a plain inscription that formulaically reads, '*A se biljeg* (here is the marker of) Sulimana Oškopice'. Located a few hundred metres away from a medieval *stećak* necropolis, the *nišan* of Suleiman Oškopica is most likely transcribed as Suliman due to the lack of familiarity with the proper spelling of Muslim names. To Bešlagić, this is clearly the evidence that graves for the Muslim converts were still crafted by the local Christian masons.[27]

In the villages of Brankovići and Oprašići, barely several kilometres away from Suleiman Oškopica's site, stood two remarkable specimens of complete stylistic and epigraphic overlap. Deposited now in the permanent courtyard collection of the National Museum in Sarajevo, one tombstone marks the name of Mahmut Branković, a Muslim, and the other of Radoje Oprašić, an (Orthodox) Christian. Both are indubitably done by the same craftsman as the stones are almost identically chiselled, designed and decorated with visual symbols including the hemisphere and wand. The former reads, 'And he perished in a despot's battle. Here is the marker of Mahmut Branković, on his native land in Petrovo Polje. Blessed be the hand that chisels and writes'.[28] The latter one, of Radoje Oprašić, says, 'Here is the marker of the honourable knight Duke Radoje Oprašić. While I lived, I lived righteously and in high repute. I lie in a foreign land and my marker/tombstone stands in my native land'.[29] There is no question that the connection among the three gravestones, and some others in the area, demonstrate funerary architecture in transition. As Marko Vego suggests, all of these tombstones take on the shape of a *nišan*.[30]

---

[27] Š. Bešlagić, *Nišani XV i XVI vijeka u Bosni i Herzegovini* (Sarajevo: ANU, 1978), 70.

[28] '*I pogibe na boju despotovu. A se bileg Mahmuta Brankovića, na svojoj baštini na Petrovu Polju. Da je blagoslovena ruka koja siječe i pisa*'. For a precise orthographic transcription see M. Vego, *Zbornik zapisa*, 4: 36–7. Š. Bešlagić and other scholars interested in the biography of this Mahmut conclude that he was probably killed in the battle defending Sarajevo against Vuk Grgurević-Branković who led Hungarian troops against the city, attacking and pillaging it in 1480. Mahmut is said to belong to the Branković pedigree of local landowners who became Muslims and retained aristocratic privileges. The heraldic representation of the lion on the tombstone supports that theory too.

[29] '*A se bileg počtenoga viteza vojevode Radivoja Oprašića. Dokle bih pošteno i glasovito živjeh. I legoh u tuđoj zemlji a bileg mi stoji na baštini*'. For a more precise transcription see M. Vego, *Zbornik zapisa*, 4: 36–7.

[30] M. Vego, *Zbornik zapisa*, 4: 37.

Figure 3.11 The *biljeg* of Suleiman Oškopica, Dumanjići, with inscription in Bosančica. Photo by Amila Buturović

They all take on West–East orientation typical of Orthodox Christian graves. What identifies the tombstones as Muslim are the first names – Suleiman and Mahmut – while the surnames continue to carry toponymic references to native villages.

Remarkably, then, the fact that the mason did not hesitate to craft the tombstones in a way that both exhibits a transition into the Ottoman style – an upright stela – and also maintains the vernacular forms of inscribing and marking the dead, speaks to several points at once: an awareness of the new funerary practices, a lack of pressure to embrace the foreign style and a will to recognise the new converts without desecrating or diminishing their memory among the old Christian neighbours. The graves remained compatible despite religious differentiation, regardless of the likelihood that those with the most decorated symbols of nobility, such as the two mentioned above, may have fought in the same battles but on the opposite sides. Like the living, the dead continued to mingle, unified in the appearance of their funerary markers. Neither Islam nor Christianity dominated funerary memory and set the dead apart. Cultural intimacy endured, as if dying in the new order was not seen as anomalous to the ancestral faith and land. It is hard to imagine why otherwise the old referents, both visual and written, would persist. Thus, in the realm of funerary culture, the first century of the Ottoman rule witnessed a slow learning curve about the Islamic worldview and the recognition of the new signifier but not necessarily the new signified. Conversion evolved as conversation rather than segregation. Likewise, this transition from one eschatological sensibility to another seemed superficial. It was not aimed at redefining the identities of the dead but transferring them into a familiar environment to which the living could relate and where they could still find solace and establish connections. In addition to epigraphic texts displayed on the tombstones, this amalgamation is evidenced in the very word. If translation and conversion are two intertwined aspects of the same complex process in which the old meanings and values are not abandoned but reconfigured, then what better way of translating the original *bilig/biljeg*, 'marker', than by turning it into its Persian/Turkish/Arabic equivalent, *nishān/nišan*? The link between what once was and what now is, both in religion and language, has been maintained through commemorative culture.

This, of course, is not to say that the isolated rural conditions were looser and less prone to acculturation into the Ottoman system because of their distance from urban epicentres and ignorance of the Ottoman norms. On the contrary, the gradual infiltration of Arabic script and language in epigraphic texts is almost coeval to the aforementioned examples. In the small abandoned cemetery of Šetići, only a few kilometres away from the village where Suleiman Oškopica is buried, a tall solitary *nišan* marks a burial ground. This *nišan* bears a number of typical Ottoman characteristics – it consists of two upright slabs, a headstone and footstone, with an elegant turban marking the former and bearing an Arabic inscription. The text begins with the same formulaic rendering in Arabic of the common *a se leži* phrase, saying that 'the resident of this' (*ṣāḥibuhu*) is Mustafa Aga, a landlord, and specifying the year of his passing as 962 AH/1555 CE. What makes the tombstone untypical of the Ottoman standard but reflective of the Bosnian vernacular is its colossal size – it stands over four metres tall, although the distance between the headstone and footstone is proportionate to the size of an adult male (see Figure A.9). Below the inscription there is an engraving of a large dagger revealing Mustafa Aga's military import and prowess. Despite the important stature of the deceased, however, his name is wrongly spelled and so is the name of the month of his death. Probably done by a local and still untrained hand, the epigraph is poorly executed and clearly wanting in Arabic language proficiency. Moreover, the tombstone communicates the basic data but does not extend the invitation to pray as is by now common on mainstream Ottoman tombstones. Instead, it stands tall among other graves, testifying to the beginnings of a new practice that conflates the imperial religion and translation into the same process of reorientation of identity, but still without overt appeals to specific types of ritual or spiritual behaviour and response. Besides, it is hardly possible that a common passer-by would understand its message: Arabic was limited to the religious elite which, by and large, hardly ventured into the woods of Bosnia to seek ritual reward. Like many a *stećak*, then, this tombstone was not intended for textually guided ritual engagement but for visual recognition – the turban and Arabic script reveal the identity of the grave's resident but lack any prescriptive ambition to cement group identity or promote religious orthodoxy.

This is perhaps not unusual but it is understudied as regards its scope and consequence. To that end, the astute analysis of Islamisation in South and South East Asia by Ronit Ricci postulates the formation of the Arabic cosmopolis as a 'translocal Islamic sphere constituted and defined by language, literature and religion'.[31] Tracing the primary sources produced in local languages, Ricci investigates the interactive processes of conversion to Islam and translation efforts to disseminate religious knowledge towards the formation of a local Islamic ethos. Her main argument is that Arabic served as 'a generative cultural node',[32] namely, as an axis around which a multilingual and interactive environment was formed, facilitating the consolidation of Arabic within local societies, yet in a way that allowed these societies to expand their cultural vocabulary and advance their own interpretations of what was being brought with (and in) Arabic. This significance of literary texts – by which Ricci means a wide corpus of primary sources of different genres in local languages – must be measured by the production of texts, their circulation, reception and the ensuing networks, as they all point to the importance of culture – not only commerce, politics and social institutions – in the shaping and the prompt expansion of the Arabic cosmopolis.

---

[31] R. Ricci, *Islam Translated* (Chicago: The University of Chicago Press, 2011), 4.
[32] R. Ricci, *Islam Translated*, 14.

Perhaps Ricci's contention can provide a helpful analytical framework for understanding the comparable complexity of the Ottomanisation and Islamisation processes in the Balkans. Can we speak in similar measure about an Ottoman cosmopolis? The parallel process of the shaping of an imperial standard on the one hand and the permutations of local forms on the other allowed Ottoman texts to seep into each other, creating hybrid forms and enhancing production in different cultural arenas. Translation is key in such processes and it is, as in the case of South Asia, facilitated by conversion in that the two produce a symbolic zone to which different imperial subjects add meaning. It also facilitated shifts in the vernacular production at large, of converts and non-converts. It seems helpful, however, to expand the term Ottoman cosmopolis to also include, in addition to written texts and oral sources, visual and material culture. In the case of the Balkans, as a number of scholars have argued, this form of interconnectivity which includes language and other nodes of connection – food, music, architecture, idiom, and so on – is most often described as the Ottoman legacy. Ideologically, however, the term Ottoman legacy was impregnated with negative associations in the process of nineteenth-century nation building, greatly affecting the way in which such inter- and intra-cultural connections have been evaluated in the national historiographies of the region.[33] While a more integrated study of the transformation of Balkan vernacular cultures under the imperial legacy ought to be done, it is important to recognise that common threads of such transformation can be discerned in a narrower regional study on Islamisation and Ottomanisation as well, especially by including cultural practices of non-converts. In the case of Bosnia and Herzegovina in general, some of the local epic and lyric genres, while remaining distinctly local in themes, topography and characters, became saturated with the motifs and language from Ottoman courtly poetry. The most typical example of such formations is the Bosnian woman's song known as *sevdalinka*, which represents an intricate navigation through highly local and evidently imported poetic choices that were, to boot, adapted to Middle Eastern melodic standards but often performed with native or Western instruments. Translation here transcends the linguistic and religious boundaries and involves musical literacy and adaptations of both vernacular and Ottoman scales, without necessarily compromising the integrity of either. *Sevdalinka*, it can be argued, while intimately linked to the Ottoman ethos, functions as a literary venue conducive to solidifying and refashioning the idea of a shared Bosnian ethos. Among broader regional examples, the legends of the heroic Central Asian dervish Sarı Saltık briefly mentioned in Chapter 1 that were localised through a series of vernacular renderings

---

[33] The literature on the subject is prolific. For a good synopsis and articulation of the ongoing discussions see S. Yilmaz and I. Yosmaoglu, 'Fighting the Spectres of the Past: Dilemmas of Ottoman Legacy in the Balkans and the Middle East', *Middle Eastern Studies* 44:5 (2008), 677–93.

point to the fragmentation of cultural production and its translation along ethno-linguistic and religious lines while at once connoting an overarching narrative stability of relevant textual sources. 'Translated' into a number of local Christian saints, Sarı Saltık is said to have been buried in seven different coffins across the Balkan region, suggesting that the legend has been cast and recast with added narrative richness in semantically fragmenting and unifying ways. Translation is shown to be a function of a broader historical process rather than an act conceived and executed in a single identifiable moment of the transfer of meaning from one language to another, and it relies on the ripple effects of a broader cultural and religious exchange.

In contrast to its Arabic counterpart, however, the Ottoman cosmopolis did not rest on linguistic uniformity; rather, with the Ottoman Turkish, Arabic, and Persian woven into the imperial polyglossia, this cosmopolis led to a fertile and multidirectional cultural exchange. Within it, the local Slavic language also gained a broader relevance especially among the literary and social elites to the point of spreading its influence over the imperial centre, beyond its historical reach. For example, several Western visitors in Istanbul in the sixteenth and seventeenth centuries observed that Slavic was common in the Ottoman capital, and held a prominent place after Turkish and Arabic at the Ottoman Court thanks to its numerous native speakers.[34] Persian too enjoyed important currency as a literary medium and inspiration for wide-ranging Ottoman poetry. Language thus became not only an important venue for Islamisation but also self-affirmation and differentiation under the polyglotic Ottoman aegis. Funerary imagery and texts play an important role as primary evidence of these shifts by both affecting and being affected by the process of Ottomanisation and Islamisation. Remaining as a dialogue between the past and the present, the vernacular and the imperial, Bosnian funerary culture in Ottoman times continued diversifying while at once absorbing the unifying characteristics of the imperial standard. The examples cited above, of the close proximity of new Muslim and Christian markers that display both visual and textual similarities reflect this process of translation and reorientation of commemorative practices.

This process is best understood as an effort to facilitate commemorative culture during the period of transition and exchange between local Christian forms and Ottoman Islam. The dead continued to be remembered but the challenges of their identification, and self-identification, did not disappear. The anonymity of some tombstones had open interpretive prospects. The aforementioned legend of 12,000 masons erecting graves to the Ottoman Muslim martyrs during the military expeditions has a different rendering in the local Christian lore in eastern Bosnia according to which the sultan's masons were also memorialising the local Orthodox soldiers whose chivalry stood on a par with the Ottoman heroes. In this version, then, the turban is not a symbol of Islam but a symbol of military prowess and rank. Because

---

[34] J. Fine lists a number of such reports. See his *When Ethnicity Did Not Matter in the Balkans* (Ann Arbor: University of Michigan Press, 2006), 298–300.

most of these uninscribed tombstones lack biographical data but contain visual symbols, they honour the dead impersonally, with the help of pictorial depiction of power, heroism and skill. The motifs of sword, bow, wand, arm, hand, and zoomorphic representations are all borrowings from the *stećak* tombstones and are incorporated into the new artefact. While this can be viewed as simple syncretism typical of popular religiosity, it is more useful to appreciate it as a form of commemorative continuity necessary to assign meaning to the funerary artefact. Just as the dead beg the reassurance that they will be remembered, so do they comfort the living with a continuous presence through the tombstone anchored in the land. If the connection ceases and the living are disconnected, the landscape, and the memory, becomes threatening rather than reassuring. To prevent that disconnect, narratives about such mysterious funerary artefacts give meaning to the land and nourish cultural memory. In turn, cultural memory facilitates a sense of belonging and grounds identity in space, specifically around funerary markers. Historical changes are woven into these legends but are not their sole focus. Legendary material, such as that related to the sultan's masons, absorbs the discord between the flux of history and the desire for permanence. Legends are thus translated, reinterpreted and retold, whereas identity is kept alive through association with such ambiguous funerary stones.

The previous chapters discussed the rituals and stories of warrior saints. Most of these saints are said to lie under these anonymous, oversized and solitary grave markers. In other renditions, many of these stones mark the burial location of another type of martyrdom, the fatalities of violent wedding brawls, often involving Muslim and Christian wedding parties. In all these cases, the prime objective of such stories is not to establish 'what really happened'. It is to form a relationship with the funerary markers and demystify them, ironically, by encrypting them in another kind of enigma as if to ascertain that the dead are sufficiently ungraspable but still familiar. History is thus not turned into stone but into a more pliable cultural text capable of moving with time to absorb and recreate meaning for those who live around it. Much like the heroic Sarı Saltık who lies in seven different coffins, these warrior saints and wedding martyrs have lived many different but similar lives across Bosnia and Herzegovina, having their stories repeated in many renderings in connection with the tombstones.

Mixing the Dead, Sharing the Memories

The first generations of Bosnian Muslims were rarely segregated from non-Muslims. Outside the urban cemeteries, it is rare to find an exclusively Muslim cemetery that came into existence without a physical connection to a previously used, non-Muslim one. To date, many rural cemeteries that have origins in pre-Ottoman times are still active. This situation gradually changed

Figure 3.12a Cemetery in the village of Žunovi, with the *stećaks*, Orthodox tombstones and an early Ottoman Muslim *nišan*.
Photo by Velibor Božović

CONVERTING THE STONE: TEXT AND IMAGES IN EARLY OTTOMAN BOSNIA 143

Figure 3.12b Žunovi.
　　　　　　Photo by Velibor Božović

and by the eighteenth century the shared cemeteries fostering religious diversity of the dead would give way to the need to separate the dead from those of other groups, affecting cemetery location and administration. Until then, however, there was no stigma against mixing the dead or referring to them in similar terms, which speaks to the fact that the boundaries in death were as crossable as they were in life. The dead were placed in proximity with each other without concern for inimical relations, pollution or tension. Moreover, placed neither within church nor mosque precincts, many of these cemeteries located deep in the countryside were not, in religious terms, designated sacred ground. Rather, as the only evidence of human presence, they functioned as a cultural landscape, which, by disrupting the seeming infinity of the natural horizon, amplified the connection with the land below rather than the heavens above. The identification of the graves with humanity rather than divinity came first. The reason the graves were not yet separated along religious lines at this point seems, then, logical: they mediated the horizontal relationship between the land and human settlements more than the vertical one with the transcendental divine.

While most of the headstones remained unmarked, the existing inscriptions continued to make references to such relations: the Christian ones kept referring to the ancestral soil and they appealed for civility not to be desecrated and unearthed. At least one inscribed Muslim headstone of this period does the same: in the eastern Bosnian village of Čadovina, the epitaph of a turban-topped stela, shaped as a typical, heavy rectangular prism and inscribed, untypically, on all four sides in *Bosančica*, tells the story of two Radilović brothers, Ahmet and Hasan. Hasan, the older one, was a hero and an exemplary man. His brother Ahmet, erected the gravestone in great sorrow, with the message, 'blessed be anyone who comes by, and cursed be anyone who tears it down'. Like Suleiman Oškopica's tombstone that stands in the same general region, the mason seemed literate in *Bosančica* but not yet skilled in the orthography of Muslim names – Ahmet is spelled as Ahmat. This is, to repeat, not uncommon. In fact, the epitaphic mention on another tombstone erected for two Muslim men, Alija and Jusuf Milošević, is followed by the signature of the mason Bogdan. Apparently, the two men, Alija and Jusuf (misspelled as Jusup) were first-generation converts as indicated by their Christian last name and Muslim first names, while a local Christian stonemason, Bogdan, built and inscribed their headstone.[35] The highly personalised inscription, as exemplified by this and similar epitaphs, draws upon culturally established norms of remembrance and intimate social interactions rather than official religious precepts that appropriate the dead into exclusive eschatologies.

---

[35] The headstone is not preserved. It was recorded in 1928 by Pero Slijepčević but was then lost to later generations of archaeologists. Š. Bešlagić, *Nišani XV i XVI vijeka u Bosni i Herzegovini*, 72–3

Figure 3.13 The tombstone of Hasan (and Ahmet) in Čadovina, with inscription in Bosančica.
Photo by Amila Buturović

Because of this close relationship to existing social norms, the spaces of death also serve as sites for making, sharing and shaping collective memory. As norms change, so does the meaning assigned to cemeteries. What seems to be normative in the funerary culture of contemporary Bosnia and Herzegovina may not have been common in its pre-modern history. The practice of maintaining common burial grounds was more than just a matter of habit and continuity because it was also a response, as noted by the epigraphic messages, to the threat of oblivion and desecration that negligence of the dead would entail. Customs proximate to marking and remembrance are thus equally shared as part of the same culturally constituted focus on the meaning and role of the dead within the social space. Even when sequestered in the natural landscape and made anonymous through epigraphic silence, the dead can still intimate their presence through the images on tombstones. In the move from Christianity to Islam, some images and texts were transplanted as well. Important examples of textual mobility and translation were cited above: '*biljeg*' became '*nišan*'; '*a se leži*' became '*ṣāḥib hādha al-nishān/al-qabr*'. A common Roman Catholic phrase, originally found in Roman epitaphs, which reads '*fui quod es, eris quod sum*' or 'I once was what you are, you will be what I am', also found its way onto pre-Ottoman Christian Bosnian tombstones in several versions, the most common resonating the Latin inscription almost ad verbatim, as in the case of a Vukša Dubčević from eastern Herzegovina whose fifteenth-century epitaph reads: '*Bratije, ja sam bio kako vi/a vi ćete biti kako i ja*' ('Brothers, I once was as you are now/and you will be as I am').[36] Messages which relate the inevitability of death to the concern for grave desecrations are especially poignant: 'For this I beg you, fine men/do not step on the grave/for you shall be what he is now/and he no longer can be what you are', is inscribed on a fifteenth-century tombstone near Zenica.[37] Similarly, a fifteenth-century epitaph to a Radojica Bilić, found near the town of Donji Vakuf, pleads with his kin and community with 'visit me and mourn me/but do not stomp on me/for you will be what I am/and I'll no longer be what you are'.[38] Near Donji Vakuf, but among seventeenth-century converts elsewhere in Bosnian towns,[39] this message appears in the Arabic version as a Muslim epitaph as well: '*ya nāẓiran ilā qabrī/mutafakkiran bi amrī/bi-l-amsi kuntu mithlak/ghadan takūn mithlī*', or 'oh you, looking at my grave/do remember what I state/yesterday I was as you are now/tomorrow as me you shall be'. Although not common nowadays among Muslims, the phrase was used by both Christians and Muslims in the Ottoman times, in recognition of death's ultimate otherness and without invoking a specific religious vocabulary. The common idiom was maintained, albeit in translation, even when the demands of different forms of literacy began creating exclusion zones in the recording of memory.

---

[36] M. Vego, *Zbornik*, III: 22–3.
[37] M. Vego, *Zbornik*, IV: 68–9.
[38] M. Vego, *Zbornik* IV: 96–7.
[39] Also found in Prozor/Rama, Mostar, and Travnik. In Travnik, however, there is a variation on an eighteenth-century inscription that reads, 'oh you, standing by my grave' (*ya wāqifan bi qabrī*) rather than 'oh you, looking at my grave', and another one has *taṣīr* for 'you will be', rather than *takūn*.

Funerary forms, like text and imagery, exhibit continuities and discontinuities in the process of transition from Christianity to Islam. It has already been noted that under the influence of the Ottoman standard, funerary architecture in Bosnia became vertical, consisting of upright slabs, rather than remaining horizontal, which was typical of *stećak* tombstones. All shaped as cylindrical solids, some thicker than others, Bosnian Islamic tombstones have either a square or rectangular base, although several quite large headstones have a rare octagonal base. The upright slabs end in semi-circular, triangular, pyramidal or trapezoidal tops. Occasionally, one also encounters trapezoidal tops that are not flat but include an inverted dome. These bowl-like formations, as mentioned earlier, are used to accumulate rainwater. They are referred to as čanak or *kamenica*. In popular healing practices, this water is consumed for curative effects.[40] The footstones do not necessarily follow suit but exhibit more variety in both shape and size, although for the most part they correspond to the headstone's style.

In contrast to the *stećak* tombstones, the Bosnian Islamic tombstones are gendered. Male tombstones commonly display a headgear in the shape of a turban placed on top of the headstone (*bašluk*, from Turkish *başlık*). Used as a method of social differentiation of the dead in the Ottoman structure, the turbans are status symbols. Referred to as *saruk* (from Turkish *sarık*, turban), they indicate profession and rank. While some turbans seem generic, the great majority are intricately sculpted, often leaving an anthropomorphic impression. This is especially the case with tall headstones which match human size, and are often even taller. Big, oversized headgear, whether placed on large tombstones or average ones, usually give more import and affluence to the dead: the extreme example is the eighteenth-century *nišan* of Omer Aga Bašić near the town of Glamoč, which is nearly 5 metres in height and having an equally large circumference of the turban. Although this is a later example of Ottoman funerary architecture than previously described, the *nišan* was modelled on earlier examples, especially the solitary *nišans* of the warrior saints that stand out with imposing stature and firm base against the landscape. In the first two centuries of Ottoman rule, with the exception of the headgear identifying some affluent person or members of the religious elite, the turbans are either inscribed generically to mark the lower social strata and men from everyday life, in which case they are modest and unimposing, or are crafted to reflect membership of a specific administrative or social group: landlords, administrative, military, Sufis, merchants and so on. The typology, however, is not fully consistent, especially outside the main administrative centres and urban cemeteries. The nineteenth century would witness the replacement of the turban with a conical fez, especially for military and civil personnel. In the early centuries, however, the lack of writing on the

---

[40] S. Traljić, 'Muslimanski nadgrobni spomenici', 208.

great majority of headstones places focus on social rather than any private data, suggesting that social affiliation was a more significant marker than religious or personal identity. Ottoman, rather than Islamic signifiers, are the ostensible mode of internal differentiation. It takes one to know one – anyone extraneous to the structure is unlikely to decipher the code of social belonging exemplified by funerary headgear. The landscape was populated with familiar, anthropomorphised symbols of status, power and social placement, and their differentiation presupposed an insider's ability to locate meaning in the typology of the headgear. Enshrined in death by their status in life, the socially identifiable dead are remembered by this visual memento in a way that is as much literal as it is symbolic. In the case of inscribed headstones, the names of the dead render the turban into a secondary point of reference, inducing more subjective and private remembrance. From the contemporary perspective, however, the turban no longer carries the same social relevance and is dislocated from its original purpose. Yet, because of the erosion of soil and the fading of the stone inscriptions over time, many slabs have become either unreadable or have sunk deep into the ground. What remains visible are their turbans, dotting the landscape like bountiful mushrooms, offering an opportunity to examine their historical meaning and significance but hardly carrying the symbolic potency they once had.

The typology of female slabs is less differentiated. For the most part, the turban is missing although some type of headgear may appear, especially after the eighteenth century. Moreover, in the later period affluent women had their gravestones delicately carved and decorated with floral patterns, mainly under the influence of similar gravestones in the Ottoman capital. Female headstones do not reveal affluence and status in the earlier Ottoman period but, if the gravestone is inscribed, they do indicate the name of the deceased. In this period, the common form is a thin stela with a curved top, usually containing plain rosette decorations and a comparably sized footstone. This is not an exclusive female feature and some male stones will look exactly the same as their female counterparts. This happens among members of the same community and family, and it is obvious that they are a product of the same craftsmanship. Graveyards do not adhere to gender segregation, female graves are mixed with male, which indicates that the cemeteries do not observe either normative Islamic notions of public space in which women are separated from men or of privacy and seclusion associated with domestic space. Although there is usually some family connection among adjacent graves among affluent members of the society, this is not a consistent pattern in rural and larger town cemeteries. In relation to this, important to note here is the reference to the mosque graveyards that are in Bosnia known as *harem* rather than in the more standard Ottoman idiom, *hazire*.

Harem is a word that, in its Arabic root *ḥ-r-m*, has two interrelated meanings: one is *ḥaram*, carrying the legal implication of forbidden, taboo, protected, and the other one is *harīm*, which refers to the protected area of the house, to which only the lawful owners have access.[41] The former meaning delineates sacred ground in Islam from all other, implying specific norms of conduct, attire and demeanour from those who enter it. The latter connotes the sanctity of domestic space, and it commonly refers to the quarters where women and children reside, which carries implication for gender relations in both religious and historical terms. The word *harem*, derived from this latter meaning, has been expanded in the Ottoman context at both macro-imperial and micro-domestic levels as a way of spatial gendering. Every Muslim house is normatively partitioned into the space utilised by insiders, both male and female, and outside guests, and the *haremlik* that is reserved for women and children, where male outsiders, other than the close kin, are not welcome. In Ottoman Muslim households in Bosnia, this form of domestic partitioning was respected to varying degrees, more strictly in affluent households, as different kinds of narrative and historical sources attest. Bosnian mosques too have a *harem*, rather than the more common term *hazire*, adding to the idea of sanctity to the mosque yard which is usually absent in normative Islamic vocabulary. In Sunni Islamic tradition, the word *haram* in association with the mosques is reserved to three sacred sanctuaries only: Mecca, Medina and Jerusalem.

Figure 3.14 A mosque with the *harem*, Sarajevo.
Photo by Amila Buturović

---

[41] For a useful and clear analysis of the differences, see I.C. Schick, 'The Harem as Gendered Space and the Spatial Reproduction of Gender', M. Booth (ed.), *Harem Histories: Envisioning Places and Living Spaces* (Durham: Duke University Press, 2010), 69–84.

In Shi'i Islam, the term is also used in reference to the shrines of the Imams in Najaf, Karbala, Kazimayn, Samarra and Mashhad. The legal and moral implication here is that, as holy sanctuaries, they are zones where no violence can be exhibited and strict rules of conduct and reverence must be observed. In contrast to Christianity where the church is spiritually sanctified through divine intervention and as such constitutes sacred space, mosques are places of gathering and prayer but are not, with the exception of the aforementioned sanctuaries, given a holy designation. Moreover, in Christianity most churches contain large crosses outside, intended to consecrate the churchyard and provide a communal memorial to the dead buried within it. Mosque graveyards are not generally consecrated. Notwithstanding other modes of Islamic sanctification of space associated with various symbols and rituals such as pilgrimages and visitations, Sufi spirituality and Shi'i practices as well as a host of regional expressions of reverence, Islamic sacred space is constructed around legal and moral obligations governing its premises and as such follows a different trajectory from Christianity. In Bosnia, however, one discerns an interesting conceptual and semantic hybridity between Christian and Islamic ideas of sacred space: like churchyards where the dead are buried, Ottoman Bosnian mosqueyards are rendered sacred in a way that fuses this Christian principle with the Islamic notion of spatial segregation. Commonly, the harems around mosques in Bosnia are locked, and visitors are allowed into their precincts with the permission from mosque keepers and imams. Mosque harems are thus treated as both holy public and protected domestic space, accessible only via the hospitality of the host but also honoured through spiritual engagement. However, the gender dimension, common to the Ottoman Islamic idea of *haremlik*, is absent in this extension of meaning, as women and men are both permitted entrance and are buried within the grounds without any normative segregation between the sexes.

Images of Life, Metaphors of Death

The semantic blending of terms associated with funerary texts speaks to the fact that translation and conversion from one religious system to another was hardly a linear process. The vocabulary associated with the representation and remembrance of the dead persisted through translation, gaining new attributes but also sustaining inter-generational and inter-communal relations. The new converts were still capable of interacting with their dead ancestors as well as with those who remained Christian. The simultaneous differentiation and blending of texts, meaning and symbols of death enabled the communities to cohere through historical change when the Bosnian spaces of death were no longer just local but became absorbed into the larger imperial framework whose forms needed to be successfully mediated lest the ties between the dead and the living were to be severed.

Metaphors and images followed suit. Far more common than funerary texts, the images on *stećak* slabs provide an array of pictorial expressions. Some exude cryptic and mythic qualities while others seem to portray local and everyday imagery. Some are heraldic and patrician while others appear plain and common. Some point to the celestial realm, others to earthly. The juxtaposition of such opposites has resulted in a lack of consensus over the meaning of lapidary motifs. Neither has there been scholarly agreement about the relationship between funerary image and word in the stones that are both inscribed and visually decorated. Are they, as per Jacobson's contention, metonymic and metaphoric, that is, do they complete each other sequentially and do they translate into each other's medium?[42] It was noted earlier that the medieval epitaphs contain a strong sense of locality as exemplified by their references to specific toponyms, people and situations. The contiguity between the world of the living and that of the dead is reinforced through the epigraphic evocation of familiar names, moments and places. Can one assume a similar relationship between the image placed on the grave and its medieval viewer? While the scholarly tendency has often been to extend the meaning of the images into the cryptic realm of dualist cosmology because of the assumed association of the *stećak* with Bogomilism,[43] attempts have also been made to locate this imagery in the lesser-known early Christian and non-Christian symbolism in European, Near Eastern and Central Asian traditions.[44] An important aspect of that approach, usually associated with art history, emphasises the unchanging and timeless quality of the meaning of these images as vehicles for the divine. Believed to express etiological myths about the world, its creator and creatures, the images travelled across the broader region with minor permutations, in commitment to the same myths. But what if the funerary images in question create a sense of significance and meaning primarily in relation to the funerary text rather than the myths or in addition to the myths? While a connection with the regional religious and folk symbolism is likely to exist, perhaps the funerary images, just like the text, take an empirical point of reference as the starting point, intensely steeping themselves in local geography and sensibilities. After all, floral patterns were derived from the botany of Bosnian and Herzegovinian landscape, zoomorphic images were familiar to the local resident, mythical creatures related to folkloric material and the celestial bodies were observable

---

[42] As cited in W.J.T. Mitchell (ed.), *The Language of Images* (Chicago: University of Chicago Press, 1980), 61.

[43] The early champions of this theory are John Ashbot, Alexander Solovyev, and Ćiro Truhelka, who inspire all its later supporters.

[44] For a good overview and its own contribution, see R. Trako, 'Stećci: božanska igra brojki i slova [Stećak: A divine play of numbers and letters]', *Soc. ekol. Zagreb* 20 (2011), 1: 71–80. Also, a detailed framework and context can be found in D. Lovrenović's study, *Stećci. Bosansko i humsko mramorje srednjeg vijeka* [*Stećaks*: The medieval tombstones of Bosnia and Hum] (Sarajevo: RABIC, 2010).

in the expansive night sky. They all appear in other artefacts and designs and are present otherwise in the local folklore. In a similar way, represented human beings mimic the features, postures and gestures of the living while the chiselled depictions visualise tactile mundane objects. Although all these images may still carry a higher allegorical meaning and symbolic importance, it is their immediacy that enmeshes the living and the dead in an intimate relationship and facilitates the process of memory. As Zelizer suggests in reference to the photographic memories of the Holocaust, images fix collective memory's ephemeral nature, assisting with recollection when disconnect happens with the lived experience. Collective memories, in her view, are ever changing because the mediums through which they are captured and filtered make them unstable and 'vibrating'. Images are there to anchor collective memory. Simplicity is requisite to this aim; visual representations need to be meaningful for an entire group, and to enhance the contemporary pertinence of the past across history.[45] Although Zelizer's focus is on modern photography, funerary imagery too is able to convey visual messages about the deceased and his or her condition, the circumstances of death or any other personal vignette. Thus, recognising and appreciating funerary imagery relates to the realm of cultural practice so the key to its translatability lies not in its timeless quality but in the relationship it can forge with the viewer.

In contrast to Christianity, Islamic art by and large shuns representational images. Funerary art in particular is scarce because priority is given to the word and its transcendental and revelatory value. Except for the decorative floral and geometric patterns, which are also common in architectural design, funerary art and architecture is not inclined to include representational images. In the Ottoman context, however, some of the highly stylised gravestones of Istanbul exhibit both calligraphic/epigraphic and decorative finesse, placing considerable aesthetic emphasis on the sculptural design of the tombstone. The practice of turning the tombstone into a work of art, not only a memorial tablet, has been emulated to an extent by affluent Bosnian Muslims of the late eighteenth and early nineteenth centuries. In the early Ottoman period in Bosnia, however, such elaborate decorative practice is scarce. What is occasionally present are representational reliefs and engravings, most of which are modelled on *stećak* imagery, predating the *nišans*. The majority exhibit crudely chiselled backgrounds, marking them as the work of local masons skilled at basic local practices and forms rather than imported conventions. In addition to reliefs, incisions are also common, appearing at times along with reliefs, and at other times alone. In many a case, the incisions are carved later so they cross over the existing pattern as if adding another layer of history to the tombstone. In most cases the images represent

---

[45] B. Zelizer, *Remembering to Forget: Holocaust Memory Through the Camera's Eye* (Chicago: The University of Chicago Press, 1998), 4–7.

CONVERTING THE STONE: TEXT AND IMAGES IN EARLY OTTOMAN BOSNIA 153

Figure 3.15 Female face, Šišići, Trnovo.
Photo Velibor Božović

Figure 3.16 Raised hand, Džindići.
Photo by Amila Buturović

Figure 3.17 Zoomorphic representations, Vragolovo, Rogatica.
Photo by Velibor Božović

Figure 3.18 Human figure, Turovo.
Photo by Velibor Božović

inanimate objects (wands, swords, hatchets), geometric shapes (circle, disc, hemisphere, crescent) and floral patterns (rose, vine, braids). Occasionally we do encounter zoomorphic representations (lamb, horse, snake, bird, wild boar, lion) and anthropomorphic (portrait, parts of the body, human figure). The only image that seems to postdate the *stećak*, appearing on the early *nišans* of Ottoman warrior saints, is the so-called '*djedovski štap*', which resembles a shepherd or shaman wand with a simple orb. Others belong to the pre-Ottoman visual repertoire and appear to be fully modelled on the images found on *stećak* embellishment.

There is, of course, no perfect continuity. Some images are discarded and not reproduced on the *nišans*, while others seem to have reached a wider application. Whether the images appear by themselves – which is most often the case – or accompany an epitaph, their function is to evoke the same point of reference and thus permit onlookers to recognise ancestors where they rest. Images and text complement each other and establish a link between aspects of culture – visual, written, oral, mythological and historical.

Funerary Hybridity Par Excellence: Christian Crescents and Muslim Crosses

One of the main challenges associated with the taxonomy of Bosnian tombstones in early Ottoman times is the seemingly immutable nature of symbolic and conceptual categories we use in our age, making it difficult to avoid reading them back into other periods. Historical funerary material in question begs a different approach. The recognition and negotiation of religious differences in the transformative moments associated with conversion, migration and resettlement in Bosnia affected the cultural praxis and values of every community. These challenges did not merely pertain to the official imperial norms governing the categories of belonging but also to everyday life to the extent that commemorative culture was impacted. It has already been noted that material funerary forms began to shift not only among the nascent Muslims of Bosnia and Herzegovina but also among its Christian population. The aforementioned examples of the two closely standing *nišans*, one belonging to Mahmut Branković and the other to Radivoje Oprašić, drew on the common literary and visual culture and illustrated the fluidity of cultural differences at this time. In part because of a lack of adequate archaeological research and in part due to the tenacious political neglect of disenfranchised identities rather than appreciation of their commonalities, many funerary symbols and forms have long remained unexamined as building blocks of a common heritage.

Among them is a set of tombstones deemed 'Christian *nišans*',[46] by the historian Đoko Mazalić, which epitomise funerary hybridity associated with

---

[46] Đ. Mazalić, 'Hrišćanski nišani u okolini Travnika [Christian *nišans* near Travnik]', *Naše starine* 4 (1957), 97–118. Also, Š. Bešlagić, *Nišani XV i XVI vijeka u Bosni i Herzegovini*, 78.

the period of historical and religious shifts between Christianity and Islam. There are several key features that both differentiate and unite the tombstones in question. In terms of sculptural form, they are commonly erected as pyramidal-topped tall slabs with, just like Muslim *nišans*, differently shaped tops. However, they also appear as upright trapezoidal stelae with a large, discoidal head, reminiscent of *hilarri*-type Basque gravestones or Irish circular headstones. In Bosnia, this latter form is commonly referred to as *krstača* or *stari križ*, roughly understood as proto-cross, crypto-cross, or amorphous cross, whose transverse arms, if present, do not extend from the trunk but appear as stumps tucked on the sides. These stones exhibit variations but most bear embryonic qualities of a cross and, in some versions, conjure up anthropomorphic impressions. It is believed that the discoid shape draws on non-Christian sculptural artefacts from the late Roman period, and can be found in many parts of Christian Europe throughout the pre-modern period, even into early modern times.[47] In Bosnia and Herzegovina, variants of both sculptural forms appear among both abandoned and active Catholic, Orthodox and Muslim cemeteries, although the latter discoid form is dominant in the Catholic areas. Their upright shape is believed to be the result of changes in funerary architecture in early Ottoman times.

What unifies these stones is their visual adornment, which evokes hybrid meanings and intersecting interpretations. Celestial motifs, especially lunar and solar, typify naturalistic symbolism drawing from a broader cultural context, including pagan, Christian, old Slavic, ancient Mediterranean and Islamic. Solar symbols, common in various mythologies, religions, astronomical and astrological systems, come in several placements and types, from concentric circles, solar wheels, swastika, rosette designs reminiscent of the ancient Slavic solar flower of life and others. They appear as reliefs and engravings, at times isolated and otherwise placed within a visual narrative. They exhibit rich and diverse interpretative potential thanks to their naturalistic and universal associations encompassing a multitude of artistic traditions in ancient agricultural civilisations.

The crescent moon is likewise very common. While we see it also on earlier *stećak* tombstones, its shape and orientation has become more diverse and unpredictable – it can be thin and delicate or thick and imposing in the shape of a horseshoe, turned upward, sideways or downward, engraved or in relief. In modern times, the crescent is most readily understood as the Islamic emblem, especially in connection with a five- or six-pointed star. Although it has been associated with the Islamic lunar calendar and all major religious festivals, it is also a secular symbol appearing in early Islamic history on coins and, since the nineteenth century, on flags and insignia of many Islamic countries. The crescent-star emblem dates back to the Ottoman times as part of the standard

---

[47] G. Thomson, 'Irish Discoid Gravemarkers', *Archaeology Ireland* 20: 3 (2006), 10–14.

official imperial, religious, and state usage.[48] Its original presence on Bosnian Islamic *nišans* and Christian tombstones, however, derives from the *stećak* influence, rather than Ottoman. Only in the eighteenth century do we see it mutate into the Ottoman Islamic version, contiguously with the crescent moon on the Christian tombstones, where it is often placed above the cross, under the cross or the verso.

Because of their frequent inclusion on the Bosnian Muslim and Christian tombstones of this period, the solar-lunar symbols are mired in ambiguity. On the one hand, their inclusion into religious systems across different geographic zones allows them to transcend the limits of their stone representation and their temporal association with a particular grave. On the other, they stamp the stones with an optical effect and significance, steering the viewer's mind to the question of intentionality and purpose. The viewer and the artisan are thus caught up in the dynamic of perception and reception. If the sun has a specific purpose, does that purpose change in relation to the religious identity of the dead, from stone to stone? Should the image of the sun on a Christian tombstone be taken through a different sequence of meanings from the sun on a Muslim tombstone? Is the artisan, who carves these images, aware of such differences – does she affirm them, ignore them or subvert them? By contrast, meanings appear interlinked in a way that defies religious boundaries and expands the symbol, rather than constricting it to exclude other meanings. Otherness is thus likely to be conceived not against different religions but rather against death, which is common to all.

While no answer can ever been ascertained, it can be pondered that such tombstones mitigate cultural divides with the contribution of new and imported elements to a regional funerary repertoire. The formal differentiation founded on the *millet* criterion did not preclude the fact that the internal boundaries of belonging remained in flux. Conversion was an ongoing process and it was multidirectional. Besides, the *millet* lines of delineation, as mentioned earlier, were not firmly drawn until the late seventeenth century. Religious communities had access to each other and moved across these lines of official differentiation through various forms of cultural and economic practice, including funerary. Many visual motifs were shared, even if their interpretation differed. The local sensibility was still as resonant, if not more so, than the translocal. The coming together of the two produced vibrant material cultural expressions. The outcome is not plain syncretism, which is generally explained as a blending of two disparate entities. The outcome here is greater than the simple equation of one-plus-one because the range of contributions to this funerary interplay of forms and symbols is considerably more complex and dynamic than the sum of its parts.

---

[48] 'Moon', in J. Campo (ed.), *Encyclopedia of Islam* (New York, NY: Facts on File, 2009), 479.

One of the most poignant examples of this complex interplay is the coming together of the seemingly polarised symbols of the cross and the crescent on the same gravestone. The few studies done on it, mainly by Bešlagić but also Mazalić, and more recently by Ivan Lovrenović, important as they are in drawing attention to this phenomenon, also demonstrate unease about the incongruity of the symbol. Branded as an expression of funerary confusion rather than a purposeful commemorative act, they seem to be nothing but historical error. Bešlagić emphatically contends that such tombstones cannot belong to a Muslim person and must be branded as Christian *nišans* rather than Muslim. Indeed, there is no reason to assume that the cross was but the symbol of Christ's sacrifice. But that should not be the focus of our attention, especially as we operate with fixed assumptions that almost invariably condition us to polarise the two symbols. Rather, we need to try to unpack the meaning a tombstone like this may have carried for the viewer engaged in the acts of mourning and remembrance of the dead. In a more complex world in which theological and religious demands may not have been fully aligned with lived emotional and psychological effects of death, the funerary text required a more personalised reception than is possible through a polarised Muslim/Christian binary.

According to the evidence at hand, the cross/crescent tombstones appear in various locations: in the picturesque village of Žunovi, near Sarajevo, there is a still-active Eastern Orthodox cemetery. No larger than a football field, the cemetery contains densely populated Orthodox Christian graves, a few well-preserved *stećaks* placed around the edges, one old uninscribed, massive early *nišan* in the middle, bearing a couple of typical features such as a large turban and a roughly incised sword on one side, and finally, another typical *nišan* of the early period in the shape of a tall slim stela, this one over three metres in height, with a truncated pyramidal top seating an orb. On the upper part of one side, chiselled in a shallow relief, stands a conspicuous, albeit faded, image of the cross. The image is modelled on a stylised anthropomorphic crucifixion motif, with a circular top, resembling in shape the Egyptian *ankh* and folkloric Mediterranean cross rather than the official symbol of the Catholic or Orthodox Church. Such types of cross also exist on *stećak* reliefs. Within a short driving distance, two other cemeteries display similar visual motifs and artefacts: in their case, however, the cemeteries are Muslim, and both sprawl around well-crafted but ill-preserved medieval *stećaks*. In the first, by the rustic village of Imamovići, stand two slabs, reaching as high as the one in Žunovi and displaying crosses in the same anthropomorphic shape, likely wrought by the same mason or school. The other one is a still-active Muslim cemetery in Kalimanići. Here, next to an imposing *stećak* and several sunken small younger *nišans* barely visible in the tall grass, soars an elegant *nišan* with all the same features as the aforementioned ones except for a considerably smaller orb shaped as hemisphere. In addition to the cross, however, this *nišan* is more carefully decorated, with a discrete braid framing the line joining the pyramidal top and the tall rectangular sides. The *nišan* contains three other images: on the back of the slab a delicate crescent points upwards and is positioned roughly at the same height as the cross, and above

Figure 3.19 Muslim *nišan* with a cross, Imamovići.
Photo by Amila Buturović

the crescent, a finely executed relief of a small grounded bird. Beslagić is quick in connecting the *nišan* in question to the feudal Kalimanić family, some members of which were among the earliest converts to Islam. In his opinion, however, the person buried under the cross-marked *nišan* is likely to be a

Figure 3.20a Muslim *nišan* with a cross, Kalimanići.
Photo by Amila Buturović

Figure 3.20b Recto, a crescent and a bird, Kalimanići.
Photo by Amila Buturović

remaining Christian elder who was buried along with his children converts rather than other Christians in the nearby cemetery.[49] While acknowledging the unresolved mystery surrounding the Kalimanići *nišan*, Bešlagić concludes

[49] Š. Bešlagić, *Nišani XV i XVI vijeka u Bosni i Herzegovini*, 38.

that here the bird may reflect Christian symbolism of the soul, which cannot be the case with similar avian representations on other Muslim *nišans* because 'the Muslims would categorically reject any Christian symbols'.[50] The irony of this statement which juxtaposes simultaneous rejection and acceptance is a perplexing one: if a Christian was as readily accommodated into the intimate space of death of another religious community, would there be no space for sharing the symbols in the act of commemoration? If theological essentialism is the principle that guides the attitude towards funerary symbols, should we not expect the same application to the burial act?

Again, we may never know the answer. In all four aforementioned examples images replace texts. The *nišans* are silent, not revealing the identity of their residents and not addressing the passers-by with words. Yet in their looming presence they do announce death and the resting place of the local dead. We are thus entrusted with the task of interpreting the language of images in lieu of words, visual metaphors instead of verbatim explications. Yet, as any other cultural text, it requires us to re-examine our prejudices, loosen our interpretation and readjust our perspectives when other data are amiss.

Social history, especially of the *defter* kind, does not provide much analytical help or any substantial information on the circumstances of conversion beyond the statistical. What we should recognise, however, is that regardless of the broader political and social changes brought by the Ottoman administration, cultural shifts occasioned by the conversion had immediate effects on funerary culture but by no means a singular one. We can therefore neither speak of imposition nor uniformity of Islamic values at this period, at least in matters of material funerary expression. Rather, the best we can do is recognise that in this transformative terrain memory of the dead was continuously drawn between personal and collective considerations, not prioritising religious over other aspects of the dead's identity, including spatial, cultural and filial. In the case of the cross on a Muslim *nišan*, we must not rob this quintessential Christian symbol of the cultural meaning it may well have posed to those Christians who embraced Islam.

These examples are not unique. They bear similarities to many Catholic graves throughout central and southwestern Bosnia and Herzegovina. Both Đoko Mazalić in the 1950s and Ivan Lovrenović more recently[51] have emphasised the importance of the Catholic and Franciscan connection in maintaining the link between the two symbols. Indeed, in numerous Catholic cemeteries one can witness the reversed coexistence of the cross and crescent in the funerary forms typical of Muslim graves but also Christian ones. Mazalić is undoubtedly correct in pointing out the divergent meanings of these symbols, including the possibility that at least one of its types, which

---

[50] Š. Bešlagić, *Nišani XV i XVI vijeka u Bosni i Hercegovini*, 39.
[51] I. Lovrenović, 'Bosanski križ', http://ivanlovrenovic.com/2012/01/bosanski-kriz/.

Figure 3.21 Catholic cemetery with amorphous, cross-shaped tombstones ('*bosanski križ*') in the foreground and a Muslim cemetery below. Both cemeteries still active. Brajković, Vitez.
Photo by Velibor Božović.

he refers to as the cross on the stand, or a mounted cross, is in fact a stylistic skullcap representation of the hill of Golgotha where Jesus was crucified.[52] Because their usage seems not to be singular, we have no reason to assume that the crescent formations on these Catholic graves drew inspiration from the Islamic crescent. On the contrary, given that by this time the Ottoman state had rendered the crescent as its official emblem and used it on all state-related insignia and institutions, the awareness of a possible conflation of meanings must have been heightened. In the zone of cultural overlaps, then, funerary and religious symbols were not exclusive properties even when their usage was normative. The location of meaning could therefore be found neither in the artefact itself nor in some enclosed cosmology, but in the process of its reception, specifically, in the act of commemoration. The relationship between history and cultural text has thus continued even though exclusivist religious and political forces began to bifurcate funerary symbols and texts. Both Mazalić and Lovrenović rightfully lament the loss of cultural memory regarding these distinctive tombstones that can be considered neither fully Ottoman Muslim nor Christian. Lovrenović, who refers to them as *bosanski križ* (Bosnian cross), speaks of their surfacing in the wake of 'the Turkish tsunami'

---

[52] Đ. Mazalić, 'Hrišćanski nišani u okolini Travnika', 115.

which had brought about a complete disconnect from Bosnian medieval identity, and discredits the Ottomans for showing no appreciation for either the *stećak* tombstones or these new upright subforms. The artefacts were, and still are, 'the invisible element of the Bosnian landscape', writes Lovrenović, yet he acknowledges that they emerged and persisted precisely within the Ottoman historical and cultural framework. The disinterested Ottomans, Lovrenović implies, inadvertently facilitated the emergence of this funerary subform in the cracks of their religious and administrative tapestry, where it endured for the next several centuries and, like the *stećak*, gained cultural recognition only when Austro-Hungary took over the rule over Bosnia and Herzegovina at the turn of the twentieth century. Notwithstanding the all too common criticism of the Ottomans for not showing interest in the *stećak* as a distinctive cultural heritage, the assumption that this funerary form emerged as an epiphenomenon, and not as a direct effect of historical context, undermines its representational value.

To start with, the Ottomans provided an imperial umbrella and not – at least for the first couple of centuries of rule over the Balkans – a colonial one. They integrated the population and ensured mobility in ways that did not resemble colonial-style exploitation of human and natural resources and division of power. They recognised the religious diversity of their subjects and were not particularly involved in their internal affairs except through the ecclesiastical appointees. In contrast, Austro-Hungary had a colonising, civilisational mission woven into a divide-and-rule policy. Regardless of their potential fascination with it, their interest in studying the *stećak* was motivated not by a spontaneous fascination with local culture but by a geopolitical interest to curb external, especially Serbian, national ambitions over Bosnia by means of fostering an indigenous Bosnian identity authenticated through its long heritage and culture. Therefore, the regret for the tombstones' 'invisibility' in the Ottoman period is somewhat misplaced: the tombstones were not invisible to those who erected them to bury and mourn their dead, especially as they were still common in the early Ottoman times. They were active places of memory, to paraphrase Pierre Nora, where memory was experienced rather than mediated, as would be the case when, centuries later, they were housed in the museums. In fact, with their extraordinary physical presence as material markers of death they fulfilled their main purpose of giving cultural landscape a spatial value, embodying grief, connecting the cosmos with the earth and facilitating memory. By extension, the fact that *'bosanski križ'* and related *nišans* were neither a simple repetition of earlier forms nor a generic response to an imperial demand suggests that these forms evolved through a creative process of cultural exchange and translation among the living who, against the imperial segregation of its population into fixed religious moulds, negotiated mutually beneficial funerary forms and imagery.

Figure 3.22a Solitary cross/crescent tombstone at Janjići, Zenica, recto. Photo by Amila Buturović

Figure 3.22b Solitary cross/crescent tombstone at Janjići, verso. Photo by Amila Buturović

Figure 3.23 A tombstone at the 'Wedding Martyrs' cemetery, with a cross and a downward crescent on the same side. Rostovo, Novi Travnik. Photo by Velibor Božović

Figure 3.24 A downward crescent arches above a solar sign; an anthropomorphic cross below. Muslim cemetery in Lisac, Novi Travnik. Photo by Velibor Božović

Chapter 4

Islamising Memory, Framing the Community: Funerary Text in the Religious Imagination

> I do not hesitate about anything as I hesitate about seizing the soul of my faithful servant: he hates death and I hate hurting him
>
> Hadith Qudsi

A striking feature of the earliest Ottoman Islamic funerary inscriptions in Bosnia is a lack of explicit concern with God. Most early funerary texts neither mention nor evoke Him. He is not remembered or saluted, praised or challenged. If and when epitaphs suggest divine presence or agency it is done in vague and non-proprietary terms. Confessional loyalties do not seem to be the priority. Rather, commemorative pleas are directed in a horizontal trajectory towards the living, articulated as requests for remembrance and gestures of honour and respect. As such, the early markers of death hardly manifest any Islamic character. Death had not been fully converted despite all nominal formalities associated with the acceptance of the new religious creed in the first two centuries of the Ottoman rule. In the cemeteries in larger urban centres such as Sarajevo, Mostar or Travnik, particularly in the *harems* of their main mosques, the situation was different as the people of affluence and influence followed the Ottoman Islamic funerary standard more closely, but such tendencies were still not discernible in smaller town and village cemeteries across the countryside.

In the eighteenth century, however, commemorative culture of Bosnian Muslims changes with the drawing of clearer lines of differentiation among the religious groups. What had begun as a distinctly urban funerary style evolving in congruity with the imperial centre since the early sixteenth century became, by the late eighteenth century, the ostensible standard in the areas which had until then prioritised local funerary and eschatological sensibilities over the prescribed norms. The spread and consolidation of the Ottoman cosmopolis in terms of literary culture and epigraphic preferences allowed for the Ottoman Islamic funerary style, in form and content, to expand into rural areas. Here, despite relatively low literacy and a lack of connection with the imperial capital, Islamic knowledge was gradually transmitted along different epistemological trajectories. As discussed in Chapter 1, these trajectories comprised legal, theological, Sufi, administrative and literary modes of knowledge. Amidst this multifaceted dissemination and consolidation of mainstream religious values and teachings, memory practices gained a more recognisable Islamic form and content. Whereas in the early periods of conversion Bosnian Muslims had reached into the shared pool of commemorative culture, including both epigraphic and iconographic tropes familiar to the local environment despite the adoption of Ottoman-style upright stelae and turbans, the eighteenth century witnessed a shift towards a more salient Islamic textual expression of grief and memory. The Islamic community increasingly anchored its eschatological and commemorative priorities away from their immediate non-Muslim neighbours – just as non-Muslims were in turn becoming enclosed into their own – gradually harmonising them with other Muslims of the Empire and indeed, the *ummah* at large.

The fact that such a process began to be more noticeable in the eighteenth century is hardly a coincidence. Much has been written regarding the imperial state of affairs during this period. To most scholars in general, the eighteenth century marks a continued decline of the Imperial prosperity that had begun shortly after the heyday of Suleiman the Magnificent (d. 1566) and gradually spread over most aspects of social and political life. Exhausted militarily from the outside through the wars with Europe, Russia and Safavid Persia, and, from within, by internal discord and decentralisation of power, the Ottoman Empire became destabilised by a diminished authority of the Sultan; increased influence of local governors; continuous local strife and revolts which exhausted the resources financially and socially; population increase; the pressure of modernisation which much of the West had by now embraced; intellectual stagnation and many other factors. All in all, the Empire is said to be set on a downhill course with nothing rerouting it from certain and absolute demise. The Tanzimat reforms after 1839 may have deflected and slowed it down, but the 'Sick Man of Europe', as the Empire became contemptuously referred to, was in no position to be restored.[1] In the Balkans, the continuous redrawing of borders and the shift of authority to local notables not only weakened the central power but also occasioned new economies, acquisition of wealth and new alliances to which the central power was not always privy nor a relevant or participating party.

---

[1] The literature on the subject is as vast as is its scope. Commonly, it tends to focus on the social, political and economic factors of the decline, while revisionist works have also emerged to challenge such deterministic narratives of rise and decline. For a comprehensive review of the scholarly state of affairs see V. Aksan, 'Theoretical Ottomans', *History and Theory* 47 (2008), 109–121. Some of the many historical analyses of the period in question include S. Shaw, *History of the Ottoman Empire and Modern Turkey. Vol 1. Empire of the Gazis: The Rise and Decline of the Ottoman Empire, 1280–1808* (Cambridge: Cambridge University Press, 1976); D. Goffman, *The Ottoman Empire and Early Modern Europe* (Cambridge: Cambridge University Press, 2002); D. Quataert, *The Ottoman Empire 1700–1922*, 2nd edn (Cambridge: Cambridge University Press, 2005); Ş. Pamuk, 'Institutional Change and Longevity of the Ottoman Empire, 1500–1800', *The Journal of Interdisciplinary History*, 35:2 (2004), 225–47.

This grand and well-articulated thesis of decline has now been challenged and even discredited on the grounds that it privileges Eurocentric expectations of historical movement and progress and isolates the Ottoman Empire from broader intra-regional and trans-regional variables. While political and economic life did suffer significant shifts and the conventional locus of authority was diffused, other processes were at play and not all corroborate the linear and analytically restrictive thesis of rise and decline. To that end, Dana Sajdi, after a careful cross-disciplinary review of the most important revisionist interventions in the theory of the Ottoman decline, pursues the question of cultural life in the period under study and argues that the sources on cultural history, traditionally absent from conventional discussions about the decline, offer alternative views of the Ottoman subjects as productive and creative agents rather than objects of political stagnation, social degeneration and economic corruption.[2] Although most of the articles in Sajdi's collection relate to the lifestyle of the urban elite through the theme of tulips and coffeehouses as the defining cultural activities of the period, the collection releases cultural history from the shackles of conventional historiography and opens it to the discussion of various dynamic urban institutions and spaces of interaction within and outside political boundaries. There is, of course, no ground to fully dissociate culture from political and social life just as there is little value in reading cultural currents as a simple reflection of political affairs. But, given the overwhelming tendency to read conditions of the Empire through the lens of available sources on social history, it seems especially important to bring out other sources and perspectives, including funerary texts and practices in the areas that were certainly affected by the diffusion of central power, such as the Balkans.

In Bosnia, the available material is unfortunately too fragmented to fully explain the shifts in religious trends of the eighteenth century.[3] An insightful if partial argument points to the influence of the puritanical Kadizadeler movement that had spread from Anatolia into Bosnia and worked to disrupt the dominance of the established Hanafi Islamic and Sufi teachings and practices. In her analysis on the writings of eighteenth-century Bosnian chronicler Mula Mustafa Bašeskija (Basheski), Kerima Filan discusses Bašeskija's dislike of religious fanatics (*müteassıblar*) in general and Kadizadeler in particular, whose activities he first mentions, with considerable contempt, in 1766.[4] Filan points to the similarities between several infamous altercations between the

---

[2] D. Sajdi (ed.), *Ottoman Tulips, Ottoman Coffee: Leisure and Lifestyle in the Eighteenth Century* (London: IB Tauris, 2007).

[3] For some late eighteenth-century examinations of the boundaries of religious practices in Ottoman Bosnia, see S. Zecevic, 'On the Margin of Text, On the Margin of Empire: Geography, Identity and Fatwa-Text in Ottoman Bosnia', (Columbia University: Unpublished PhD Dissertation, 2008), 284–91.

[4] K. Filan, 'Sufije i Kadizadelije u Osmanskom Sarajevu [Sufis and Kadizadeler in Ottoman Sarajevo]', *Anali Gazi Husrev-begove biblioteke* 29–30 (2009), 169–70.

Kadizadeler and Sufis in the capital Istanbul and environs several decades earlier and the first incident recorded by Baseskija in Sarajevo. In all these instances the altercations happened in or around mosques, which testifies to a close relationship that the different movements had with these places of worship, so the dominance over ritual space may have played a great role. Although Baseskija concluded, with much content and praise for God, that the Sufis won the debate, he worried that the Kadizadeler activities would persist (he was correct, they would). Baseskija continued expressing concern about their interference with public religiosity through preaching and action, and especially the fact that the movement was gaining local followers, including some of high stature and affluence. Unlike the previous century in Istanbul where the movement had been limited to low-ranking clerics, in Bosnia they seem to have attracted a much larger network of religious and lay supporters. Baseskija scornfully notes the persistence of the Kadizadeler's disruptive behaviour in the life of ordinary Muslims who are often harassed and asked to explain their actions if they did not conform to the more puritanical interpretation.[5] To that end, Zecevic points out that while the Kadizadeler focused greatly on discrediting and treating the Sufis as outcasts, in Bosnia they had in fact encountered a more complicated profile of the religious elite with a number of its important members being tied to Sufi orders and teachings. This rendered the divide on matters of religious truth and authority not applicable to the Kadizadeler and Sufis per se but to the local norms of orthodoxy and the Kadizadeler's interpretation thereof.[6] As the Kadizadeler's teachings and interpretations increasingly infiltrated religious schools' curricula and libraries, affecting religious discourse in many circles of teaching and preaching, a number of religious officials were compelled to address contentious issues, including matters of everyday piety and religious practice. One such response came as a series of epistles written by the mufti of Aqhisar/Prusac, Muṣṭafā al-Aqḥiṣārī (d. 1755) who, basing his arguments on the works of many influential Hanafi jurists, opines about a wide variety of subjects, including funerary prayers, grave visitations and related funerary rites, cautioning against those that seemed religiously improper and deviant.[7] The epistle was clearly aimed secondarily at a general audience and primarily at religious scholars and students in an attempt to identify proper norms and authoritative texts on the subject and demarcate the dos and don'ts in Islamic death culture.

Although the impact of these multifaceted debates and interactions in the matters of religious authority and interpretation are not fully accounted for, it is clear from the few studies that the presence of conservative teachings

---

[5] K. Filan, 'Sufije i Kadizadelije u Osmanskom Sarajevu', 174–82.
[6] S. Zecevic, 'On the Margin of Text', 290.
[7] M. al-Aqḥiṣārī, *Risāla al-dhākir fī ziyārat ahl al-maqābir*. MS. 154 (Bratislava: The University Library of Bratislava), 29b–41b.

as exemplified by the Kadizadeler galvanised different spheres of religious learning and expression across Bosnia. In terms of intellectual and religious affairs, then, the eighteenth century witnessed a proliferation of debates rather than a stagnation of intellectual output. It also resulted in revisions and re-articulations of 'orthodoxy' in a way that Zecevic suggests to be a form of re-Islamisation, especially as regards the delineation of religious boundaries in the matters of law and theology. The fact that the religious conservatives sought to affect public life as well, targeting not only Sufi practices of shrine visitations, chanting and *dhikr* rituals, but also popular practices of smoking and drinking coffee,[8] indicated that the boundaries of public and private religiosity was equally destabilised. No wonder, then, that funerary culture underwent changes as well. Here, however, this process can be referred to as the first comprehensive wave of Islamisation of funerary memory and its transformation from hybrid and vernacular to unmistakably Islamic. While this shift should not be put in a direct causal link with Kadizadeler's activities and influence, it temporally coincides with their influence and suggests that the Kadizadeler may have contributed to the increased absorption of the Ottoman Islamic norms in the countryside as much as the urban context.

Message in the Stone: Faith, Memory, Liturgy

Changes in commemorative practices left a noticeable impact on material culture in several ways. To start with, the congregation of tombstones within the bounds of distinctly Islamic cemeteries became the norm. The dead began belonging to spatially identifiable zones. While land continued to be shared as deathspace across different religious communities that lived in close proximity, the lines of territorial demarcation among specific cemeteries became more pronounced. The dead of one group could no longer socialise as freely with the dead from other groups. The intimate social fabric of afterlife started to unravel. Cemeteries became spaces ritually and symbolically recognisable as Muslim, Catholic, Orthodox and Jewish, discontinuing the heterotopic, cross-confessional memory characteristic of the early period. Although many cemeteries grew out of previous shared formations and still included material residual signs of earlier splicing, most new cemeteries became erected within a reasonably sufficient distance from the 'other'. In modern times, nationalism and religious exclusivity would further fortify the lines of separation as new roads and fences sprawled among many rural cemeteries like buffer zones, making each a little less ambiguous and ensuring that no transgression would ever again be possible. This differentiation was to be diffused among civic cemeteries during the Yugoslav times, especially

---

[8] S. Zecevic, 'On the Margin of Text', 293–4.

in relation to the increasingly agnostic and secular burials of the socialist period, but the traditional material markers of faith-based memorialisation were ostensibly enshrined by the late eighteenth century. In contrast to the historical continuum within which they were once amalgamated, the old tombstones that do not share the new designation and spatial patterning appear displaced and exotic rather than historical and authentic, as if they no longer have any kinship with the cultural landscape they inhabit.

The eighteenth century thus brought about a form of demarcation that left a lasting impact on commemorative space and ritual action. Islamic tombstones turned to religious language and ritual invocations to specify the community's modes of mourning and memory practices. Funerary language, initially shy and scant, began to convey clearer and longer-lasting liturgical messages. As noted earlier, the introduction of Arabic, although not consistently used, had already marked the beginnings of a new form of funerary literacy. While most tombstones of the earliest period were not inscribed, the ones that were had little to say. Numerical literacy using Arabic script seemed to precede linguistic literacy. Numerous mute tombstones of the early times occasionally indicate the year of either the death or erection of the tombstone, or both. The numbers stand alone, without much commentary, in some ways enhancing the mystery that shrouds the biographical profile rather than divulging it. The most common period of numerical epigraphy is mid to late 900s of the Hijri calendar, namely, the second half of the sixteenth century. Most numbers are crudely and randomly incised and the epigraphic hand is awkward, still adjusting to the writing of numbers in a foreign script. The numbers are often placed in obscure spots on the stone as if considered irrelevant, or as if intended to remain a secret, which is a practice often noticeable on dated *stećak* tombstones of the pre-Ottoman period. There are few exceptions to this rule. One is found in the cemetery of the village of Podvinjci near Visoko where the Hijri year one–thousand–three (1593 CE) is spelled out and executed in unusually graceful calligraphic style emulating the Ottoman urban standard. The same cemetery contains other examples of the most rudimentary date-centred inscriptions: 1034 (1624 CE); 1040 (1630 CE); 1066 (1655 CE), all found on simply decorated male tombstones with turbans. There is one female headstone embellished with three graceful small rosettes etched on a stucco background shaped like a *mihrab* niche with a pointed arch. The Islamic elements are visually and orthographically implied and the date etched below the rosettes reads: year 1067 (1656 CE).

Although the bias against funerary inscriptions dates back to early Islamic polemics and continues to be reinforced by Muslim traditionalists in general,[9] the Ottomans paid no heed. The practice of tomb writing was well-formed

---

[9] L. Halevi, *Muhammad's Grave*, 34–6. For a general overview of Islamic inscriptions, their forms, content and textual variations, see S. Blair, *Islamic Inscriptions* (New York: New York University Press, 1998).

and cultivated across Ottoman lands. In that sense, the lack of inscriptions in Bosnian rural cemeteries and especially the lack of a more explicit attachment to Islamic identity of the early stones ought to be placed in the context of local rather than broader theological factors. First, as discussed in the previous chapter, there is a widespread legacy of funerary anonymity characteristic of *stećak* tombstones. Inscribed, they only convey commonplace identifications such as the name, date or place. The great majority mark the landscape silently, without any appeal to personal identification. Moreover, given the lack of customary epitaphic formula or benediction, the tombstones mask individuality and at once stimulate individual expressions of commemoration, including at the level of visual representations. In the first two centuries after the Ottoman consolidation in Bosnia, the graves of Muslim converts exhibited similar characteristics regarding epigraphic expressivity: some are inscribed without common denominators except those pertinent to official tradition; the majority lack inscriptions and many contain common images. The inscriptions neither beg salvation nor do they express awe before the finally revealed secret of death. Rather, they plea for simple remembrance and marking, in space, of their existence and the final resting ground. After all, they now own the land, as expressed in the aforementioned common phrase, *ṣāḥib hādha al-maqām*, namely, 'the resident of this spot is so-and-so'.

The second factor is a slow and uneven penetration of Arabic language into the cultural practices of commemoration. Although folded into the Ottoman polyglot cosmopolis, the commemorative culture of Bosnian Muslims was slow in becoming. Remembering the dead is a highly personal and intimate issue. We expect to speak for and with the dead in the language in which they can continue knowing us, and we them. Remembering in one language and marking that memory in a different language requires a cognitive leap of faith as it assumes that we can experience and express sorrow in one and seek consolation in another, foreign, language. Without downplaying the authenticity of the new religious identity, we can nevertheless appreciate the difficulty of translating a highly personal sense of loss into a public text by using a foreign and unfamiliar language, despite the fact that God spoke in that language and asked for our obedience in it. It is hardly surprising then that the entry of Arabic into the funerary writings was uneven and slow. In most cases the Arabic language was only nominally taught, hardly by native speakers but mainly through the mediation of the Ottoman religious scholars, so it had little purpose, other than liturgical, in everyday life. With the knowledge trickling to the stonemasons only in a rudimentary fashion, funerary literacy remained basic, austere and inexpressive for a long span of time, especially where commemorative idiom was concerned. By the seventeenth century we only gradually witness the insertion of Islamic messages into memorial stones along with a more explicit biographical profile of the deceased, commonly the name and the date of death. However, this is still done sporadically and unsystematically.

172 CARVED IN STONE, ETCHED IN MEMORY

Figure 4.1 Year 1003 AH/1593 CE,
Podvinjci.
Photo by Amila Buturović

Figure 4.2 Year 975 AH/1567 CE,
Hlapčevića brdo.
Photo by Amila Buturović

Figure 4.3 Year 976 AH/1568 CE,
Podvinjci.
Photo by Amila Buturović

Figure 4.4 Deer image, 1015 AH/1606 CE,
Seonica.
Photo by Amila Buturović

Across rural cemeteries, then, more explicit biographical information becomes available in the late sixteenth and seventeenth centuries. Commonly, the name is volunteered without any introduction or excess information, unless the name comes with a professional or honorific title. As the formulaic expressions such as 'the resident of this grave' or 'the resident of this marker' become common, names are more consistently introduced. To better establish identity, the first name is attached, in a patrilineal fashion, to the name of the father. The year of death follows the term *wafāt/vefat* (death in), or *tuwuffiya* (died in ...). Even when unmarked, graves are typically singular properties, marking a specific individual's resting place. This represents a break with the Bosnian medieval tradition where, in the past, we occasionally see shared cenotaphs or examples of memorial marking of spots where a person may have died but not been buried.[10] In contrast, the Islamic graves mark individual burial spots because, as the teaching has it, each person has to face his or her own predicament in their own individual grave. Unless in exceptional circumstances, two or more bodies cannot share the same grave just as two or more souls cannot share the same punishment or reward. Individual graves, even the unmarked ones, allow the soul to distinguish itself from others and witness God and the beyond on its own terms. While funerary rituals require a careful process of preparation and disposal of the body, memorial markers do not necessarily have to reflect the confessional aspect of one's life. God, as far as Islamic teaching goes, does not make such a demand. The graves need to be simple. That said, Islamic societies across the world have nevertheless developed rich practices of marking death through material culture, and the Ottoman obituary styles and practices excel in this respect. We have already noted that the difference in the spread of funerary and commemorative practices in Bosnia's urban centres and rural areas created a gap in the way the dead are prayed for and remembered. Vernacular practices absorbed pre-Ottoman Christian and popular customs to rework them through new funerary architecture. But the self-identification of the dead as Muslims by using Islamic messages only gradually infiltrated even the most remote of the areas.

The early explicitly Islamic phrases used are canonical and declarative, not concerned about death as a personal experience. Probably the earliest and unique example, in that it has not been recorded later or elsewhere, is the rough insertion of the names of the Rashidun, or the first four 'Rightly Guided' caliphs in Islamic history following the name of the prophet Muhammad. Situated at

---

[10] The practice of marking a gravestone for someone buried elsewhere was not completely abandoned in the Ottoman times, as demonstrated by a number of tombstones dedicated to individuals whose burial place is unknown because they died away from home. One such example is a nineteenth-century *nišan* in the Herzegovinian town of Blagaj, dedicated to Veli Bey who is said to have 'died while travelling and is buried near sheikh Qadri'. Similar examples are mentioned in M. Mujezinović, 'Epigrafika i kaligrafija pjesnika Mehmeda Mejlije [The epigraphy and calligraphy of the poet Mehmed Mejli]', *Naše starine* 4 (1957), 131–68.

Figure 4.5 Vefāt Ahmed, 1080 AH/1669 CE, Džindići. Photo by Amila Buturović

a scenic location by the small village of Dobrun near Višegrad in eastern Bosnia, the *nišan* is plain, without turban and is otherwise undecorated except for a crude (and correct) inscription of the five names: 'Muḥammad, Abū Bakr, ʿUmar, ʿUthmān, ʿAlī'. Based on the stylistic and material evidence, Mujezinović dates the tombstone to the seventeenth century.[11] Although the evocation of the historical and formative religious tradition, rather than God, seems like an unusual statement of belonging, one that evokes a sense of kinship with the community through its founding fathers rather than to God as the creator, the practice of including the names of the Rashidun was common. In the Ottoman art their names appear on tile panels, ceramic work, calligraphic *hilye* 'portraits' of Muhammad and other craft and art surfaces.[12] The political context behind this practice is linked to the self-representations of the Ottomans as the champions of Sunni Islam against the Shi'i oriented Savafid Empire in the east. In that spirit, a visual promotion of Sunni symbols of power and inspiration by means of calligraphic placements of the names on objects of art and architecture intensified in the course of the sixteenth century. Probably the most famous and visible example of this practice is inside of the dome of the Haghia Sofia, where the names of Hasan and Husayn, as well as Muhammad, are added to the Rashidun as inscriptions on large medallions attached to the base of the dome on all sides to demonstrate the full glory of the early Islamic tradition. This, however, was not common practice on tombstones. There are few examples, and the inscriptions of this kind do not necessarily serve the same commemorative value. On the other hand, one may suggest that the articulation of historical and communal identity is as valid as the confessional one. After all, the invisible, transcendent God is a *sine qua non* entity for all monotheists. In the process of transition from Christianity to Islam, the supreme being remains unchanged, but it is His intervention in history that differs. Thus, the change from being a Christian to a Muslim, both of whom worship the transcendent God, is first and foremost stamped by the authenticity of the community to which one belongs in this world. The founding fathers mark that authenticity, and more narrowly, the Rashidun are pivotal for Sunni Islam. However, in terms of personal remembrance, the

---

[11] M. Mujezinović, *Islamska epigrafika*, 2: 122.
[12] S. Blair, 'An Amulet from Afsharid Iran', *The Journal of the Walters Art Museum* 59 (2001), 90–91.

inscriptions of this kind did not probably draw wide interest because faith rather than history increasingly became the symbol of bereavement.

In a more common version of confessional belonging in the seventeenth century, Islamic orthodoxy is further prioritised. An exemplary graveyard in Podvinjci contains a tombstone, amongst several dating back to an early period, with a brief and unskilfully incised epitaph to a certain 'mendicant Husein efendi, year 1053 (1643 CE)', with the verso stating the *shahada*, or the first article of Islamic faith: 'There is only one God and Muhammad is His prophet'. The assertion of the absolute unity of God and the commitment to the validity of the scripture as transmitted via God's prophet, Muhammad, undoubtedly authenticates such tombstones as Muslim. After all, the articulation of *shahada* always locates its speaker within the Islamic community, when one first enters it and throughout one's life as a Muslim. Although the formal act of conversion necessitates witnesses for such a declaration and conversion to be stipulated as valid, the sheer utterance of *shahada* is recognised and celebrated as a statement of belonging. It reflects a simultaneous relation to oneself, God, and the community. In that sense, the function of *shahada* is to provide guidance during the rites of passage in one's life and grounding when one needs it. As Toorawa points out, it is invoked at 'liminal moments: converts pronounce it when they accept Islam; it is whispered in the ears of newborns; it is recited to those on their death-bed; and many Muslims recite it upon waking so that they will instinctively also do so when they are roused in the grave on Judgement Day'.[13] In funerary epigraphy, however, the ambiguity of etching the *shahada* onto tombstones needs to be noted: the inscription invites the visitor to the grave to utter it. It does not make a plea for an intercessory or other prayer; it merely begs witness. One may wonder if the witness is to be borne by the deceased or by the visitor to the grave. If the epigraphic text is a way of establishing a connection, then in this case the connection is mediated by the first article of faith and thus indistinguishable from any other possible interaction with the dead. The *shahada*, it seems, implicates the respondent into its worldview and scope as much as it incorporates the resident of the grave.

Throughout the seventeenth century and even later the *shahada* was placed on a sizable number of Bosnian tombstones, albeit sporadically and inconsistently and with or without a date and name. It is not ubiquitous but is noticeable across rural cemeteries. Recognisable to an even illiterate eye, the *shahada* convokes the community of faith in ways that are probably only experienced through ritual prayers and other normative practices. Visiting the graves, as we have seen, is not a religious obligation in Islamic tradition. The prayer at the grave (*qabur duası*) is done once the bier is laid in the ground and before it is covered with soil and, in Bosnia, after interment, additional recitations were traditionally performed but in a less formal fashion to see off

---

[13] S.M. Toorawa, 'Prayer', in J. Elias (ed.), *Key Themes*, 265.

Figure 4.6 *Shahada*, 1144 AH/1731 CE, Fojnica.
Photo by Amila Buturović

Figure 4.7 *Shahada*, n.d., Visoko.
Photo by Amila Buturović

Figure 4.8 *Shahada*, n.d., Janjići, Zenica.
Photo by Amila Buturović

Figure 4.9 *Shahada*, 1027 AH/1618 CE, Glamoč.
Photo by Velibor Božović

'the soul of the deceased'. They commonly consisted of the last two verses of the second *sura* of the Qur'an, a triple recitation of the *sura Ikhlāṣ*, and additional Qur'anic verses that are left to the discretion of the mourners, all of which are completed by the recitation of the *Fātiḥa* and *Alif-Lam-Mim*.[14] Subsequently, the grave is there to commemorate and associate with the dead, and salute them in the way they can hear and respond to, as per the Prophetic teaching.

Because many gravestones under consideration bear the testimony of faith but do not include the name of the deceased, memory is tempered by anonymity so its focus is placed on the recognition and remembrance of communal rather than personal identity. In fact, the invitation to remember *faith* rather than the individual seems to be the commemorative principle of these tombstones. Even when the names follow the *shahada*, as is the case in some but not all inscriptions, they appear marginal to the religious dictum that dominates the stone, as if the gravestone is first and foremost tied to faith rather than the deceased. It can be argued that the common assumption that tombstone inscriptions are primarily concerned with making a personal statement ignores the fact that the inscriptions resonating with Qur'anic worldview and ethics carry an expansive and communal sensibility rather than one focusing attention on the individual. While this may appear disorienting, the practice has an important cultural and commemorative dimension. The aim is not to ignore the memory of the individual but to imprint the orthography of the holy word into the life of non-native speakers and remember the individual through its framework.

This gradual and uneven entry of Islamic expressions of grief and remembrance on funerary stones peaked in the eighteenth and early nineteenth centuries when Islamic epigraphy comes of age across the Islamic deathscape of Bosnia. The most important of these changes include the prefacing of the name of the deceased with salvific hopes of mercy and forgiveness; the formulaic reference to *al-Fātiḥa*, the opening chapter of the Qur'an, and the invocation of God through (some of) His 99 Beautiful Names, known in the Scripture and tradition as *al-asmā' al-ḥusnā*. These changes increasingly conformed to the Ottoman standard which is associated with memorial stelae and systematically found across main urban centres, and which also includes biographical and professional reference after the name of the deceased and the date/year of death.[15]

As noted earlier, the name was commonly introduced with *vefat/wafāt*, the deceased, or with *ṣāḥib maqām/qabr/nishān*, 'the resident of the place/grave/marker'. None of these terms has an explicit religious or confessional connotation and can be deemed secular in terms of their expectations from death. None implies a relation to God as a creator or a supreme being on

---

[14] S. Sokolović, *Islamski Propisi*, 54–5.
[15] E. Eldem and N. Vatin, *L'épitaphe ottoman musulmane*, 12.

178 CARVED IN STONE, ETCHED IN MEMORY

Figure 4.10 'The resident of this spot (*maqām*) is Aisha', 1177 AH/1753 CE, Ćatići. Photo by Amila Buturović

Figure 4.11 'The resident of this is Mustafa Aga ... ', 962 AH/1555 CE, Šetići. Photo by Amila Buturović

Figure 4.12 'The resident of this *nišan* is sheikh Hajji Ibrahim, the imam and preacher ... ', year 1132 AH/1719 CE, Uskoplje. Photo by Amila Buturović

Figure 4.13 'The resident of this grave (*qabr*) is Osman b. Salih Beg ... ', n.d., Fojnica. Photo by Amila Buturović

whom the deceased must now rely for salvation. No binding responsibility or accountability is placed on either party. With the more widespread usage of the Islamic terms *marḥūm* and *maghfūr* the quality of that relationship changes. The deceased is no longer rendered simply dead, but becomes a recipient of divine mercy and forgiveness. Death is a gift, not a threat, and the deceased, having died in the true faith, can now receive that gift in the form of eternal bliss. Rooted in Arabic *r–ḥ–m*, the term *marḥūm* is semantically related to *al-raḥmān* and *al-raḥīm*, both of which constitute divine names and references to God as the source of mercy and beneficence, as well as to the term *raḥmat*, which alludes to the compassion and tenderness emanating from God as an aspect of his quintessence. Ibn ʿArabī, for example, explains that divine mercy is twofold:

> [it is] the mercy of the gratuitous gift and the mercy of obligation corresponding to the name *al-raḥmān* and *al-raḥīm* respectively. God exercises mercy as a gratuitous gift under the name of *al-raḥmān* while He obligates Himself [to requite] under the name *al-raḥīm*. This kind of obligation, however, is part of the gratuitous gift so *al-raḥīm* is contained within *al-raḥmān*. God has prescribed for Himself mercy (Q. 6:12) in such a way that mercy of this kind may be extended to His servants in reward for the good work done by them individually.[16]

This intimate relationship between the two terms both separates them and places them in an ontological and functional interdependence and, as Rizvi puts it, ascribes universality to one – *al-raḥmān* – and particularity to the other – *al-raḥīm*.[17] The word *raḥmat*, with its many different derivations frequented in the Qur'anic text, encapsulates God's willingness to relieve the soul from the anxiety of death and place it within His providential care. As a Qur'anic exegete succinctly puts it as he explains the two terms, 'The Compassionate, the Merciful: that is to say, the One who possesses mercy, which refers to the desire to wish good for those who deserve it'.[18] Accordingly, if God is essentially the source of mercy and dispenses it in time and place as per His decision, then the commonplace expression of condolence among Muslims, *raḥmat Allah ʿalayhi/ʿalayhā*, may God have mercy on him/her, is not merely a supplication to God to grant mercy but also an expectation of the dead to earn the gift of mercy rather than abdicate that responsibility entirely to God. In a similar vein, God forgives and protects the deceased from punishment, giving them the gift of forgiveness. The dead are those pardoned *maghfūr* (*lahu/lahā*). In both cases, the assertion of mercy and forgiveness procures good fortune when Muslims die. The tombstone no longer marks the place of any human being; it marks the location of salvation where Muslims are liberated of their apprehensiveness about death and absolved of sins.

---

[16] Quoted in S. Rizvi, 'The Existential Breath of *al-raḥmān* and the Munficent Grace of *al-raḥīm*, the *Tafsīr Sūrat al-Fātiḥa* of Jāmī and the School of Ibn ʿArabī', *Journal of Qur'anic Studies* 8:1 (2006), 71.
[17] S. Rizvi, 'The Existential Breath', 74.
[18] Tafsīr Jalālayn, online: http://www.altafsir.com/Tafasir.asp?tMadhNo=0&tTafsirNo=8&tSoraNo=1&tAyahNo=1&tDisplay=yes&UserProfile=0&LanguageId=1.

Figure 4.14 'Kara Osman *marḥūm*', n.d. Kopčić, Bugojno.
Photo by Amila Buturović

Remembering the soul

Once the name of the *marḥūm* and *maghfūr* person is stated, sometimes briefly and at other times in a lengthier familial and professional genealogy, the visitor at the grave is asked to say the prayer for his or her soul. Expressed in Turkish, the distinctly Ottoman phrase *ruhiçün (al)-Fātiḥa* invites the passers-by to engage in a communication with each individual on whose tombstone the phrase is inscribed. In certain cases, the abbreviated version invoking the name of the *sura* is placed instead of the whole phrase. Whether written in full or shortened, the phrase ensures that visiting the grave is no longer a simple act of remembrance. It involves the recognition of responsibility to read the inscription and respond to its demand to intercede on behalf of the dead. Of course, making a demand to recite a chapter from the Scripture assumes not only its visual recognition and identification but the knowledge of its text as well. The Qur'an is memorised and recited in Arabic. For the beginners who attend the *mektebs* (also known as *mejtef*), the primary schools where the Qur'an is taught, the memorialisation of the text is accompanied by its visual recognition. Non-native speakers of Arabic are not taught the language at any considerable length in *mektebs*; rather, they are schooled to visually identify and liturgically vocalise the divinely revealed word in the form of lines, parts of chapters, then full chapters. Memorisation of the Qur'an is paramount because it places, as Walid Saleh argues, 'the Qur'an inside the believer instead of the believer being placed outside the text',[19] although the process presents a particular challenge for the non-native speaker. The Arabic language, while submitted as an entirely unfamiliar semantic field, is approached visually and experientially. Associations and meanings seep in non-verbally. Religious message and scriptural intricacies are absorbed and understood by passing the conventional acquisition of meaning through language. As the result, the non-speaker of Arabic who studies the Qur'an is challenged to perceive the text as both image-word and sound-word, that is, to recite it and experience it rather than read it.

Memory is thus predicated on visual and non-verbal intimacy with the text, formed scholastically but absorbed and stored through a repetitive liturgical and embodied experience thereof. As a result, when imprinted on the tombstone, the name of the opening chapter, the *Fātiḥa*, appears as an image-sound referent to be visually acknowledged, recollected and recited in full.[20] The body is repositioned so the recitation is done with hands raised and palms turned towards the face, as a form of both offering the prayer and receiving the blessing, which is common for other prayers of supplication too.[21] The visual allusion to the *sura* is thus sufficient. Putting the text in its entirety would be redundant, because the visitor to the grave is either included in the

---

[19] W. Saleh, 'Word', in J. Elias (ed.), *Key Themes*, 370.
[20] The chapter reads, in English translation: 'In the Name of God, the Merciful, the Compassionate. Praise belongs to God, the Lord of all Being; the All-Merciful, the All-Compassionate; the Master of the Day of Doom; It is You we worship and You we ask for help; Guide us in the straight path, the path of those on whom You have bestowed favour, not of those who have angered You or of those who are astray'.
[21] S.M. Toorawa, 'Prayer', 277.

company of its knowers or excluded from it. The act of visiting the grave is therefore a multifaceted process which renders commemoration of the dead contingent on a tripartite relationship, involving the inscription which asks for intercession on behalf of the dead, the respondent/visitor who vocalises it and God who accepts it.

In early days of Islam, much opposition arose against the inclusion of the Qur'anic text onto the tombstones. The *basmala*, the verse which opens all but one of the Qur'anic chapters and reads 'In the Name of God, the Merciful, the Compassionate', and the *shahada* can be found sporadically on the earliest funerary records, but other Qur'anic segments are absent. It is only in the eighth century that excerpts from the Scripture became common in Islamic epitaphs, albeit informally in the beginning and later with a certain degree of formalisation.[22] As of the tenth century, 'Sincerity' (*Ikhlāṣ*, Q 112), one of the most compact and expressive chapters regarding God's ontological status as one, undivided and unbegotten entity, became most popular, although debates regarding the permissibility of using the Qur'an in this particular fashion remained strong.[23] Despite the fact that a number of influential jurists and theologians showed unequivocal opposition to tombstone inscriptions in general and those including the Qur'anic text in particular, the practice continued in flexible and changing ways across old and new Islamic lands. Counter-arguments varied from a contention that the Prophet himself disallowed the practice, as attested by the *hadith*, to dissatisfaction with non-egalitarian aesthetics of cemeteries where both opulence and modesty inform the decorum of the tombstones, to the basic bias against epitaphs as attention-seeking texts. Abū Ḥanīfa himself, the Kufan jurist and founder of the Hanafi school of law to which the Ottoman Empire subscribed, spoke out against the practice, asserting grave inscriptions promoted individualisation and inequality among the dead rather than rendering them indistinguishable.[24] Regardless, the Hanafi jurists in the centuries to come consented to the practice or simply turned a blind eye to it and, as material evidence shows, the Ottomans indulged. The invocation of the *Fātiḥa* on graves remained the practice throughout the Ottoman period among the Muslims who were converted through their form of Sunni Islam.

Though commonplace, the placement of the *Fātiḥa* on memorial stones has somewhat obscure historical and theological origins. As earlier noted, the Prophet is said to have recited it in the funeral prayer, and commanded his community to do the same. According to a prophetic instruction recorded in Ibn Majah's *Kitāb al-janā'iz* and similar sound compilations of prophetic utterances, the funeral prayer was to be said for all Muslims, and could be recited by day or night. In the early Islamic period, the *basmala* and the *shahada*

---

[22] L. Halevi, *Muhammad's Grave*, 21–7.
[23] L. Halevi, *Muhammad's Grave*, 32–40.
[24] L. Halevi, *Muhammad's Grave*, 34–5.

were the most common epigraphic identifiers of Muslim graves, but not in a consistent or formulaic fashion. In his study on ninth-century epitaphs found in Aswan and Akhlat, for example, Rogers points out the absence of both scriptural and non-scriptural prayers (*duʿāʾ*). The Qurʾan is only sporadically used, represented by two verses, Q9:33[25] and Q23:7[26], rather than the most prominent *Āyat ul-Kursī* (Q2:255), which is during this period considered the most appropriate Qurʾanic citation for tombstones.[27] Regardless of its obscure epigraphic origins, the *Fātiḥa* is one chapter that has occupied a prominent place in both formal prayers and the everyday religious atmosphere of Muslims across time and place. At times referred to as *umm a-kitāb*, the Mother of the Book, the *Fātiḥa* is in fact considered to be the single most repeated chapter of the Scripture in Muslims' communal and personal life. Because of its ubiquitous usage and spiritual virtue the *Fātiḥa* has been compared to the Lord's Prayer in Christianity. Its text contains a number of key religious and liturgical elements, including the *basmala*, praise to God's mercy and compassion, and two verses of supplication.[28] A prophetic tradition holds it that the omission of the *Fātiḥa* from the prayer ritual renders the ritual invalid and another one stipulates that the recitation of even one letter of the *Fātiḥa* ensures an answer to the prayer.[29] Therefore, its usage in remembering the dead seems to appropriately unify the *Fātiḥa*'s various functions, including ablutionary, protective, curative, devotional and invocative; these have all permeated Muslim daily life since early times. Moreover, the Islamic tradition maintains that *Fātiḥa* stands out among other chapters because it is evidently meant for human articulation rather than divine, as it is based on the prayer for first person plural – a contention attested by the practice among the Sunnis (though not Shiʾis) to end *Fātiḥa*'s recitation with *amīn*, which is not done with other chapters.[30] Despite this prominence, the *Fātiḥa* does not have a ubiquitous epigraphic presence in pan-Islamic terms. It was popularised primarily through the Ottomans. Beforehand, it seems to have been only sporadically recorded in some parts of pre-Ottoman Syria in the thirteenth and fourteenth centuries and, in the fifteenth, in Iraq, Egypt and even Malaysia.[31] In most of these cases, all written in Arabic, the full phrase is the Arabic variation of 'recite for him/her the *Fātiḥa*', clearly suggesting a petitionary plea. The Ottoman formula, established by the sixteenth century and used across much of the Empire, however, standardises it as the Ottoman

---

[25] 'It is He who has sent His Messenger with the guidance and the religion of truth, to prevail above all religions, though the unbelievers may reject'.

[26] 'Those whose seek to exceed those limits are transgressors'.

[27] J. M. Rogers, 'Calligraphy and Common Script: Epitaphs from Aswan and Akhlat', in P. Soucek et al. (eds), *Content and Context of Visual Arts in the Islamic World* (University Park, PA: Penn State University Press, 1988), 107.

[28] S.M. Toorawa, 'Prayer', 266.

[29] W. Graham, 'Fātiḥa', *Encyclopaedia of the Qurʾan* (Leiden: Brill, 2006), 2:190–92.

[30] W. Graham, 'Fātiḥa', 192.

[31] *Thesaurus d'Épigraphie Islamique*.

184 CARVED IN STONE, ETCHED IN MEMORY

Figure 4.15 The gigantic tombstone of Omer AgaBaš ić in Jakir, Glamoč (4.35m tall, turban alone 2m). The inscription reads: 'The year of death of the deceased and pardoned (*marḥūm wa maghfūr*) is 1213 AH/1798 CE. [Say] the *Fātiḥa* for his soul'.
Photo by Velibor Božović

Turkish phrase *ruhiçün al-fātiḥa*, for her/his soul [say] the *Fātiḥa*, which further consolidates this chapter as fundamentally tied to Islamic identity, in both life and death. It also ascertains that the visit to a grave is conceived as numinous moment of connection in which meaning and blessings are bestowed on both the dead and the living through the liturgical act of remembering God's words.

Remembering God

The second symbolic element in the Islamisation of Bosnian tombstones is the multiplicity of qualities that have been used to invoke His greatness. In the Islamic tradition, God possesses epithets that are indivisible aspects of His nature. Through these epithets, He discloses attributes by which we shall know Him. The names are thus self-designated and self-revealed. Although enduring theological debates in the early centuries of Islam fuelled many doctrinal dilemmas about some of God's anthropomorphic self-representations, the ultimate victory of traditionalist theologians and Muslims in general allowed the portrayal of God by using human language. As Elias argues, it is by and large Sufi metaphysics that provided a solution for the different levels of discourse on this conundrum. It recognised God as a combination of His essence, which is entirely transcendent and therefore incomprehensible to human cognition, and His attributes, which allow him to be known. It is at the intersections of the intellectually knowable and the essential that creation takes place.[32] In the act of creation God make His attributes manifested and manifestable in humans as well. Through them God acts and influences the world. The attributes are commonly divided into two categories: one of 'Beauty', which includes qualities with a nurturing function, and the other of 'Majesty', which have an authoritative purpose.[33] Individually, they are like riddle pieces that have a holistic purpose; a mosaic fragmented through language so as to allow human beings to better understand God. Their essence, individually and collectively, is unchangeable and undeniable. They are usually referred to as the 99 names, with the greatest name being hidden. There is no definitive tally of the names and occasional variations do not present a theological challenge. The understanding of the names is contingent on our experiential and intellectual engagement with them; the Qur'an repeatedly affirms that God is known through His beautiful qualities, as in 'God has most beautiful names so invoke Him by them' (Q7:180). But neither our invocations nor understanding of those qualities affects God in His essence. This is why we are supposed to preface each of the names of God, when it stands alone, with the prefix '*al*', or the Arabic equivalent of 'the', making God's name unique and incomparable to any other – 'the

---

[32] J. Elias, 'God', in J. Elias (ed.), *Key Themes*, 167–8.
[33] J Elias, 'God', 168.

Compassionate'; 'the Merciful'. A person can be referred to, or named, *karīm* (generous) but only God is 'the Generous One' (*al-karīm*).

The scriptural command to invoke God by his epithets as popularised through Sufi teachings greatly enriched everyday religiosity. God could be mentioned and adored in more varied, approachable terms. His qualities, many of which we admire and strive to cultivate both in ourselves and others, enable more personal interactions with God. They are at once transcendent and immanent, able to link metaphysical and physical facets of the universe. By means of the names, our capacity to understand and appreciate Him has expanded and become more intimate. God tells us in the Qur'an to frequently remember Him, so He may remember us (Q2:152); and He wishes us to address Him using the Beautiful Names (Q20:8). With each repetition of a beautiful name we please God and regenerate our encounter with Him on lasting spiritual terms. In calligraphy, representing God's name with a pen is a form of sacred art. Usually used for curative, talismanic and other devotional purposes, the inscriptions of God's names, one or several in a single composition, invoke what we believe to be the most significant aspect of His essence condensed in a visual clue and expanded through the devotional act of remembrance. Some of the meditations and prayers focused on God's names have a practical function, and need to be executed a specific number of times, depending on the numerical value of the name – for example, the numerical value of *raḥmān* is 299 so the name needs to be repeated as many times.[34]

The mediums used to express God's glory are manifold: they can be immaterial, as sounds articulated during meditative chants, breathing exercises and ecstatic utterances. In the Sufi tradition, the ritual *dhikr*, or remembrance, of God's names is performed with the help of a rosary containing either 33 or 99 beads. The ritual count commonly begins with '*yā raḥmān, yā raḥim*' (Oh Merciful, oh Compassionate) and ands with '*yā ṣabūr*' ('Oh Patient'). Although the conception of the rosary as a mnemonic and inscriptive device for the recollection of God's names is specific to the Sufis and is usually carefully choreographed as an aid in one's own spiritual labour,[35] the practice has spread over into non-Sufi practices, connecting the embodied and spiritual value of the names. Their representation can also be material, embedded in public and private buildings, textiles, household objects, pendants, and, most relevant for this study, gravestones.

Here too, Ottoman funerary culture has left a lasting impact. In addition to textual references to the Qur'an, which, as seen above, permeate funerary texts across the Muslim world in abbreviated, expanded or metonymical ways, Ottoman tombstone inscriptions commonly include invocations of God's beautiful names. In more stylised versions of such invocations, a divine name

---

[34] A. Schimmel, *Mystical Dimensions of Islam*, 161.
[35] A. Schimmel, *Mystical Dimensions of Islam*, 177–8.

or phrase is etched as a medallion arched over the funerary text. Executed as figural calligraphy, it often leaves the impression of a rosette. More modest invocations lack this stylistic flourish but nevertheless serve as a prelude to the inscription both visually and devotionally. In Bosnia, the invocations are relatively limited and standard. Introduced with either '*huwa*/He [is]' or with the vocative '*yā*/Oh' to request God's presence directly. In the case of funerary texts, most names patterned on the tombstones are drawn from the aforementioned category of Majesty rather than Beauty. Most frequently they are *al-ḥayy* (the Ever-living) and *al-bāqī* (the Ever-lasting), appearing separately or together. Occasionally, only *huwa*/He is etched, akin to the Sufi ceremonies of remembrance where the simple use of the grammatical pronoun suffices to intimate divine presence. Of other names, *al-ghaffār* (the All-Forgiving) is common, alone or paired with *al-dhunūb* to form *ghaffār al-dhunūb* (Forgiver of misdeeds); *al-hādī* (the Guide); *al-fattāḥ* (the Solution Provider, Reliever) and, although rarely, *al-nūr* (the Light) and *al-ḥafīẓ* (the Guardian). In Herzegovina, a number of tombstones are inscribed with *yā Allah al-bāqī* (Oh Allah, Who Lives On); *yā Allah al-wāḥid* (Oh One and Only God); and *yā sattār* (Oh Concealer), a name not consistently included in the list of the 99 names but still found in popular religious idiom for its multiple meanings and interpretations. The repertoire in other Ottoman examples,

Figure 4.16 'He is the Ever-living, the Ever-lasting', executed in the form of the Imperial Monogram, Fojnica.
Photo by Amila Buturović

especially Istanbul, is much wider, including *al-qādir* (the All-mighty), *al-qayyūm* (the Self-Subsisting), *al-karīm* (the Generous).[36]

In such a memorial spectrum, God is always first and last to be remembered according to a markedly different criterion than the one applied to the earliest graves. Elevated from the rest of the funerary inscription, His name stands etched high on the gravestone, preceding the rest of the text yet permeating it as connective tissue, just as He stands ontologically apart but spiritually linked to the living. The deeper, more personal memory inscribed in the epitaph follows, revealing biographical information – at the least the name, family ties, and date of death – to be completed with another remembrance of God, this time by reciting a supplication prayer for the soul of the dead so that it may receive divine protection. The commemorative act of visiting the grave and responding to the funerary text activates intimate connections between God, the dead and the living, whilst unifying disparate aspects of a person's existence – the worldly and otherworldly, both of which belong to the same continuum of infinite divine power.

Remembering life

In between the textual evocations of God stands the epitaph that succinctly identifies the occupant of the grave and his or her immediate lineage. Familial ties, if mentioned, are patrilineal. The epitaph also presents an opportunity for the deceased to be distinguished as a person amidst the anonymity and uniformity of death. Tension between a desire to be remembered as a specific individual and the cultural practice of being designated to the collective dead is evidenced by variations in epitaphic messages. The reasons behind such variations are also historical, resulting from the confluence of separate funerary cultures, vernacular practices and uneven linguistic and eschatological acculturation. The eighteenth century presented a mishmash of epitaphs as the inscriptions moved into a more Islamic style of commemoration. An epitaph in a small cemetery near the town of Glamoč in Herzegovina reads:

> 1146 (1733 CE)
> The deceased (*marḥūm*)
> al-Fātiḥa

Or, in the village of Ćatići near Sarajevo:

> The resident of this place
> Is ʿAisha
> 1177 (1763 CE)

---

[36] E. Eldem and N. Vatin, *L'épitaphe ottoman musulmane*, 59–60.

While it is possible that the deceased was a stranger or traveller who had no family ties, such epitaphs epitomise, probably inadvertently, the Islamic ideal of not binding the person in the grave to worldly associations. As noted, the prophetic tradition recommends avoiding individualisation of the grave. The marker is to be inconspicuous and the grave itself respected but not ostentatious, epigraphically or otherwise. This, however, is not followed closely in either Bosnia or the rest of the Ottoman world. As discussed earlier, by the time of the Ottomans the prophetic recommendation had already been eclipsed by more individualised modes of commemoration.[37] Rarely does one find graves that bear no personalised inscriptions. The majority of cases at least mention the name, such as in this typical example from a village near Bihać in northeastern Bosnia:

Allah
The resident of this spot
Is ʿUmar b. Qāsim
May God grant him
Generous mercy
al-Fātiḥa for his soul
Year 1125 (1714 CE)

The austerity of such epitaphs is not unusual. In contrast to the pre-Ottoman burial culture that rendered the epitaph in the first-person singular to intimately reflect a sense of regret, despair and hope for fair(er) treatment in death, everyday Ottoman epitaphs in Bosnia and Herzegovina appear more restrained and less conversant. They are not laden with emotion nor do they strive to express singularity of experience. In general, life vignettes are absent from the message. Furthermore, pre-Ottoman epitaphs exhibit dual awareness of delight and fright as they reflect on life. In the Ottoman Islamic context, the tone is more subdued and is presented in the third person, mediated by the scribe, mason, or a relative commissioning the tombstone. They generally avoid excess heroic or epic representations. On rare occasions they provide a glimpse into life or the cause of death. A tombstone of a suburban cemetery near Sarajevo reads:

This is the place of
Imam Ahmad
He died of plague
Year 1177 (AH 1763)

Mustafa Bašeskija, the aforementioned eighteenth-century necrologist and chronicler, lists death records from Sarajevo by recording only the name and most immediate relation of the deceased, with a few exceptions. Like in

---

[37] Mentioned earlier in chapter, see note p. 8.

most epitaphs, expanded lineage is omitted. The tone is at once perfunctory and familiar, without extensive narrative input, as if expecting the reader to exercise his or her own recollection as to who is who, and where and why they died. Encrypted thus in neighbourly intimacy and oral communication, Bašeskija's death records, like most epitaphs, rarely unfold into stories of either life or death. He does emphasise if the death is a result of foul play, unusual circumstances or, in the mid and late 1700s, the plague that had swept the city and the region.[38] Like today, only sensational death seems to deserve special mention in Bašeskija's obituaries. Yet even in that semi-anonymity which inevitably transitions into complete anonymity with the passage of time, the deceased is, ideally, graced with all future visitors' recitation of the *Fātiḥa*. The continuity of faith and community is ensured through vigilance over the wellbeing of each individual soul. The danger lies not in forgetting the name or the genealogical and professional placement of an individual life, but rather in forgetting to care for the soul as it continues its journey in death.

Speaking the words of God at someone's grave has both socio-cultural and spiritual significance. First, it brings ritual and liturgical practices into non-canonical spaces, making them sacred and solemn. It makes them meaningful and intimate, even when the familial or social relations with the dead are otherwise not present. Whether one knows the dead or not, one should stop at the gravesite and say a prayer. A dialogue with the dead is thus ensured beyond the familiarity of blood or social ties. Second, as Halevi suggests, it opens up the space for illiterate members of the society to participate in the literate culture.[39] This, as has been seen, is especially significant in the context of non-native speakers who nevertheless contributed and participated in the promulgation of Arabic, Persian and Turkish literacy within the Ottoman cosmopolis. Through their liturgical and poetic participation they nurtured the spread of Ottoman linguistic networks but also the expansion of the vernacular vocabulary of the local Slavic idiom. The formation of such diverse polyglot culture left its effects on local popular and written literature, poetry and prose. Third, it deepened the sense of confessional belonging by drawing clearer lines of demarcation of ritual space within a religiously plural milieu. In contrast to the tombstones that bore no inscriptions or those that emulated texts and images from the earlier heritage, the Islamised tombstones set clearer boundaries of religious belonging. As the vernacular modes of commemoration among Bosnian Muslims took on a more normative content while, at once, more pronounced adoption of Christian memorial forms evolved among the local Orthodox and Catholic communities, the deathscape of Bosnia and Herzegovina continued to change although it never eschewed the possibilities, even contradictions, of placing the dead in visible if not

---

[38] M. Mustafa Başeski, in K. Filan (ed.), *Mecmua* (Sarajevo: Connectum, 2012).
[39] L. Halevi, *Muhammad's Grave*, 28.

ritual proximity to each other. Thus, even as commemorative orthodoxy and orthopraxy within each religious tradition grew stronger, accentuating the internal lines of separation, and as the wresting of control from the Ottoman centre occasionally manifested itself as a joint struggle and at others as mutual bigotry and intolerance, the religious communities saw no contradiction in marking the landscape of death across confessional lines. This cultural vision of death as transcending difference but also as disentangling the ritual behaviour of individuals and communities left enough room for enriching the shared vocabulary and praxis while at once setting the boundaries to pursue one's own sense of eschatological truth.

Figure 4.17 (left) 'Woe upon us is death', a 'secular' elegiac invocation on Ottoman Islamic gravestones, usually replacing a divine name.
Photo by Amila Buturović

Poetic deaths

The epitaphs, it needs to be emphasised, were not all austere and straightforward. Within affluent social circles, some doubled as literary texts, renowned for their authorship and finesse. The increasing sophistication of Ottoman literary culture in Bosnia, its polyglotic repertoire and intersections with highly spiritual lyrics on the one hand and popular tradition on the other led to the production of elegiac and commemorative poetry intended as funerary epigraphy. The poet-epigraphers in question were thus not committed to only writing funerary texts; rather, many were established poets and renowned on a par with the poets of the Ottoman *divan* lyric.

Although associated with Ottoman nobility and enjoyed among highly literate circles of the Ottoman court, *divan* poetry had its authors and consumers in the provinces as well, including Bosnia. Spanning both secular and sacred themes, this poetry is highly stylised and formal, demanding imagination and skill from the poet to navigate its numerous rules. Composed in Ottoman Turkish, it is interspersed with Arabic and Persian rhetoric, grammar and vocabulary, requiring proficiency in Arabic and Persian to be understood and enjoyed in full. Because many poetic rules and norms remained static and arduous yet fully appreciated by the audience, the poets had to resort to creative and clever tweaking of the rules and resist this seeming discouragement of spontaneity. Therefore, the originality of the poem was mainly appreciated through the poet's ability to infuse vitality into such a strict formal structure and awaken passion and enthusiasm about both mundane and sacred matters. Originality was prized inasmuch as it reflected creativity within the prescribed norms.[40]

Figure 4.18 Old Ottoman tombstones in Sarajevo's central park.
Photo by Amila Buturović.

---

[40] W. Andrews et al. (eds), *Ottoman Lyric Poetry: An Anthology* (Seattle: University of Washington Press, 2006), 8.

Among the different genres and elements comprising Ottoman poetry, the art of inscription writing gained an important place. Commonly known as *tārīkh*, or chronogram, this literary genre entails encoding the date into a poetic composition on the basis of the numerical value of the letters used. Chronograms are thus poetic and algebraic riddles, requiring the reader not only to enjoy the poetic text for aesthetic and informative value but also to mathematically decode a hidden date. Chronograms exist in many ancient literary cultures – Indonesian, Hebrew, Roman, Greek and others – but have limited reception. They are first and foremost intended for commemorative purposes in that they mark an important date – of construction, birth, death, military victory, or any momentous event. Chronograms are commonly inscribed on a public object – mosque, bridge, fountain, gravestone – although many poetic chronograms are compiled into anthologies and never epigraphically used. In terms of their literary composition, they require specific skills in both execution and interpretation. Ottoman chronograms drew on the Arabic alphanumeric *abjad* tradition according to which each letter of the alphabet possesses a numerical value. In combining and organising particular letters into a meaningful poetic or narrative sequence one encrypts the desired number/date. Historically, until the number symbols were introduced into Arabic from India, *abjad* letters were used for mathematical calculations. In the religious tradition, particularly in alphabetic mysticism and numerology, numerical values are also assigned to the names of God and key liturgical phrases with the belief that universal secrets could be decoded through alphanumeric calculations.

In Bosnia, many poets writing in Ottoman languages tested their skills in alphanumeric lyrics. Such poems, composed primarily in Ottoman Turkish and – especially in the case of epitaphs – Arabic, engage a variety of themes, and it is commonly in their last, or in the penultimate and last line combined, where the chronogram is executed. Of course, not all chronograms are created equal in terms of their type, quality and merit. The successful or complete chronogram manages to create a full overlap between the verse and intended date. A next-to-complete chronogram requires adjustments, commonly signalled by the poet, which may entail adding an additional letter or more, with the poet's instructions, to arrive at the right number. There is a type of chronogram which requires counting both letters and diacritical dots, each of which has a numerical value. In contrast, there is also a type of chronogram that does not assign numerical value to the diacritical dots at all. Some chronograms involve reaching double the numerical sum of the date, and others require adding up all words and each individual letter.[41]

---

[41] L. Hadžiosmanović and E. Memija, *Antologija tariha Bosne i Hercegovine* [An anthology of the chronograms of Bosnia and Herzegovina] (Sarajevo: Connectum, 2008), 6–7; H. Šabanović, 'Izrazi evā'il, evāsit i evāhir u datumima turskih spomenika [The terms evā'il, evāsit i evāhir in the Dates of Turkish Monuments', *POF* 2 (1951).

Given these variations and possibilities, the poet is bound by specific rules of alphanumerical arithmetic but is also allowed a flight of creative imagination to come up with his or her own relationship with the language.

Given the skill and talent required to piece together an artful and mathematically valid chronogram, it is understandable that composers were held in high esteem and commissioned by a select few who could in fact benefit from being remembered through such a rhetorical device. Public and religious buildings across Bosnia and Herzegovina abound in elegant chronograms. Their proliferation in the eighteenth and nineteenth centuries testifies to the increased sense of ease Bosnian poets had in moving through and contributing to the sophisticated, polyglotic and culturally plural poetic heritage. In this regard it is also important to note their usage of motifs, imagery and sentiments across cultural conventions and lines that divide local and foreign literary elements or sacred and profane themes. It is clear from the chronograms – and in fact their poetic legacy at large – that the poets' self-identification included different strands and sensibilities; this multifaceted heritage of the body of poets enhanced the verse produced and did not diminish the quality of resultant alphanumeric epitaphs in Ottoman languages.

Based on architectural epigraphy found on mosques, bridges, schools, public fountains and other objects, we can glimpse the rich and diverse repertoire of chronograms by a number of different Bosnian authors. Their biographies indicate that many poets held day jobs, as it were: among them were religious scholars, Sufi wayfarers, and prominent individuals who occupied public offices, scribes and calligraphers. This variety of professional backgrounds suggests that being a poet-epigrapher was not necessarily reserved for the talented few but rather that the enjoyment and production of literary culture were accessible across boundaries of professional and religious self-identification. Already in the sixteenth century there are epigraphers who rose to prominence: Nihadi (d. 1587), Nerkesi (d. 1635), Gaibi (d. 1609), Deruni (n.d.). Nerkesi is credited with writing the funerary chronograms on the *nišans* of two prominent Sufis, Ayni Dede and Shamsi Dede, whose arrival in Bosnia is connected with the spread of the Ottoman campaigns. Originally placed in a separate *turbe*, their *nišans* were later removed and are currently located in the precincts of the Ali Pasha mosque in Sarajevo (see Figure 1:1). The chronogram-epitaph dedicated to Ayni Dede starts with a common poetic opening, in lieu of the invocation of a divine name, and reads:[42]

> Woe upon us is death (*ah min al-mawt*)
> The door of this abode leads to Paradise
> For here lies the prince of God's mercy
> A close companion of Sultan Fatih
> Whom he coached on the etiquette of war

---

[42] Translation based on the transcription by M. Mujezinović, *Islamska epigrafika*, I: 404.

[*Say*] *al-Fātiḥa* [*for his soul*]
As he strove to reflect in the divine mirror
His soul became one with God
His pure self now lies in the grave
After he died a martyr's death.
O heart, as you fly through seven heavens
Look for the chronograph of his demise
In the vast sea of God's divine grace.
Year 866 (1461 CE)

Although evidently not written as elegy in the formal sense of the term, poems like this evince sorrow and mourning to commemorate the dead and exalt in his worldly excellence. They tend to express comfort and familiarity, as if the person knew the deceased intimately, and often transition from sombre to hopeful feelings as they reflect on the deceased's life. Biographical information is inserted gently, in this case mentioning Ayni Dede's military engagement in Sultan Mehmed the Conqueror's expeditions as well as his Sufi beliefs exemplified in the metaphor of the mirror, self-reflection and union with God. The last two lines are phrased as a chronogram, and confirmed numerically in the year inscribed at the bottom of the text, 866 AH (1461 CE). The epitaphs, however, are unlikely to be written at the time of death. In this case, the author lived considerably later, in the seventeenth century.[43] His own death happened, rather indignantly, when he fell off his horse during the expedition of Sultan Murat IV where he recorded the course of events. Occupying such a responsible position implied he was highly educated, well integrated in the imperial intellectual elite, and also skilful in different styles of writing. All of these features were sparse in the late fifteenth century when Bosnia only started to be integrated into the Ottoman cosmopolis. Yet the poet's skill in conjuring the immediacy of grief and lamentation nearly two centuries after the recorded death points to the vitality of the genre and its efficacy at re-animating the memory of grief and loss.

Building thus on an already evolving literary tradition, the most acclaimed masters of epitaphic chronograms appear in the eighteenth and nineteenth centuries. They include Abid (n.d.), Mehmed Meyli al-Kurani (d. 1780), Nazari (d. 1817), Fadil (d. 1882), Hilmi (d. 1874), Vehbi (d. *c*. 1817), Shakir (d. 1858) and others. In all these examples, the ability to navigate the challenges of elegiac expression with the arithmetic of the date continues to impress. Abid thus composed an exquisite epitaph to commemorate Arifa, the daughter of a certain Abdullah Efendi, who died in 1172 AH/1758 CE. The *nišan* is no longer preserved but its epitaph was recorded by early twentieth-century chronicler

---

[43] M. Mujezinović, 'Nekoliko nevjerodostojnih turskih natpisa u Sarajevu [A few apocryphal Turkish inscriptions in Sarajevo]', *Naše starine* 2 (1954), 218–19.

and poet in his own right, M. Enveri Kadić (d. 1931). The last several lines of the epitaph read:

> In the sorrow of parting patience is the best comfort
> May her residence be the abode of joy for good
> May her companions be the maidens of Eden
> May she forever be immersed in God's grace
> Abid, now say a prayer as a chronogram:
> Arifa, may in the Garden the chosen be with you.
> Year 1172 (1758/59 CE)

Although this epitaph has in fact been questioned in terms of its alphanumerical accuracy,[44] its composition reflects well the creative efforts of the poets entrusted by the family to lace together images which encompass both grief and hope. In Abid's case, evoking the young woman's beauty, youth and passion for life as she passed and linking it to God's bountiful mercy in the hereafter masterfully weaves different realms of being, natural and mundane, with invisible and eternal. The grave, placed in the earth, is but a portal to otherworldly gardens, rendering poetically the Prophet's saying that the grave is the first stage of the afterlife. This association between beautiful gardens and eternity is a common trope in Ottoman poetry, and indeed Islamic poetry at large, both mystical and profane. As we look around into the beauty of the natural world, we are enjoined to recognise the workings of God and remember His rewards in the afterlife. No wonder, then, that the graveyard is commonly associated with green spaces, shaded away from the clamour of everyday life and suggestive of the beauty of eternity. After all, God Himself refers to Paradise as a garden, *al-janna*.

Of all the Bosnian poets who wrote poetic epitaphs, Mehmed Meyli al-Kurani certainly stands out as the most successful and prolific. Author of some 50 chronograms, mainly in Sarajevo but elsewhere as well, he was an acclaimed author in different poetic styles and a well-renowned calligrapher. His career as a poet was enmeshed with his complex background: although not much information exists about his early days, his poetry reveals an erudite, well-educated, and well-known figure who, based on epistolary evidence, had good relations with the ruling elite. He was a Sufi associated with the Qadiri order, and he was a *timar* holder, which implies a certain level of military involvement and responsibilities.[45] The epitaph on Meyli's *nišan* located near the city of Travnik, which was composed by the poet and judge Vehbi, indicated that Meyli died in 1195 (1780 CE), in good social standing. Another

---

[44] M. Mujezinović, *Islamska epigrafika*, I: 94
[45] S. Bašagić, *Bošnjaci i Hercegovci u islamskoj književnosti* [Bosniaks and Herzegovinians in Islamic Literature] (Sarajevo: Svjetlost, 1986); M. Mujezinović, 'Epigrafika i kaligrafija pjesnika Mehmeda Mejlije [The epigraphy and calligraphy of the poet Mehmed Meyli]', *Naše starine* 4 (1957), 131–68.

poetic tribute to Meyli, also composed as a chronogram but by a different author, praises his gentle and trustworthy disposition, the purity of his soul, his generosity and similar strands of his personality that, poetic hyperbole aside, made him a well-respected figure.[46] In addition to composing funerary chronograms, Meyli also completed a dozen or so chronograms dedicated to important events, such as those honouring the incoming or outgoing governors, religious officials, military successes, and others.[47] His funerary chronograms are as diverse, dedicated to a variety of individuals, and thus oscillates in degrees of formal accolade and lyrical intimacy depending on the identity of the deceased. Here are examples of the latter style, dedicated to a young woman:

> Al-Fātiḥa
> The fair daughter of Muhammad Chelebi
> Departed, sadly, young to the other world
> The plague descended on her reverently
> It crawled in slowly under her armpits,
> Lifted her humbly to her eternal rest.
> When Meyli heard of this relocation,
> He wrote a chronogram, which goes like this:
> May Atiya's soul be worthy of nearness to His.
> Year 1176 (1763/64 CE).

In contrast to this melancholic depiction of death where even the devastating plague is subdued by the finesse and frailty of young Atiya, and where the cruelty and injustice of her premature death yields to the comfort of her transition to eternal nearness to God, beautifying the ugly memory of her illness, the epitaphs dedicated to public officials tend to have a more prosaic style and content. Thus, instead of the focus on grief, the poet praises the deceased's prowess before he shifts focus to traditional references to divine bounties and hopes of salvation. For example,

> Hafiz Mustafa of Mostar
> Decided to move to the other world
> May God make the gardens of Eden
> His eternal and joyful abode
> He dedicated his honourable life
> To pursue knowledge and education
> And wasted no time gaining wealth and fame.
> ...
> When his soul heard the call 'Return!'
> He let go and lovingly passed to eternity
> Meyli! I phrased the chronogram of his death

---

[46] M. Mujezinović, 'Epigrafika i kaligrafija pjesnika Mehmeda Mejlije', 135.
[47] M. Mujezinović, 'Epigrafika i kaligrafija pjesnika Mehmeda Mejlije', 136.

In *jawhar* letters[48] that I put forth like this:
May Paradise be the refuge to Hafiz Bosniak
Year 1178 (1765 AH)[49]

These examples are but a small sample of the poetic skills associated with the writing of alphanumerical epitaphs in which Meyli excelled. Their function is culturally complex since they must intervene where forgetfulness may be a risk. Poetically mediating memories, they present them as both distant with the usage of third person and familiar with the recollection of personal vignettes. In contrast to pre-Ottoman epitaphs, which are mainly written in the first person and composed as dialogues between the deceased and the visitor to the grave, the Ottoman epitaphs are phrased as mediated conversations. This form of mediation, through poetic chronograms or basic biographical inscriptions, removes the voice from the dead and assigns responsibility to the living to speak on their behalf. God is the necessary party in the equation, and commemorating the deceased cannot happen without remembering Him. As the dead drift away from us in space and time, we hold them back and renew their memory by evoking His name.

The practice of writing poetic epitaphs continued well through the nineteenth and also the early twentieth century although they were never popularised beyond narrow social and cultural circles. While grounded in the Ottoman tradition, many chronograms in these later periods departed from their strict norms and opened up to a more local poetic sensibility. In addition, some nineteenth-century epitaphs began to use Alhamiado, local Slavic language written in Arabic script, which testifies to the funerary text's openness to yet another layer of literacy generated under the imperial aegis. Despite its restrictiveness, the funerary text kept expanding to accommodate novelties and varieties in commemorative imagination but it never shook off the main elements of the Ottoman Islamic standard: the basic biographical information introduced with the term *al-marḥūm/al-marḥūma* framed between the evocations of the *Fātiḥa* and God incised on an upright white stela. The local practice of placing a hemisphere and some other visual components inherited from the pre-Ottoman times have recently made a comeback as well, but their usage has been relatively limited. Thus, although the processes of de-Ottomanisation, Austro-Hungarian colonisation, and nation building within the two Yugoslavias brought about important changes in all religious cultures due to the demands of westernisation and secularisation, these basic funerary

---

[48] *Jawhar* chronogram refers to the sum value of the letters that have diacritical dots only.

[49] Hafiz is the honorific title of someone who knows the Qur'anic text by heart, a skill highly valued in Islamic tradition. This particular chronogram seems not to have been etched onto a funerary stone but preserved as a MS folio. M. Mujezinović, 'Epigrafika i kaligrafija pjesnika Mehmeda Mejlije', 151.

carvings have signified a remarkable continuity in the commemorative sensibilities of the Muslims of Bosnia and Herzegovina.

Figure 4.19a and 4.19b Alhamiado inscription, erected in 1924 by Ibrahim Haki Galijašević to commemorate the execution of 12 landlords during the first incursion into Bosnia by Eugene of Savoy in 1110 AH/1697 CE, Tešanj.
Photo by Velibor Božović.

Figure 4.20 Stylised Alhamiado from Mostar: 'Here lies … (*ovde leži*)', 1969(?). Photo by Amila Buturović.

ISLAMISING MEMORY, FRAMING THE COMMUNITY 201

Figure 4.22 *Al-Fātiḥa*, in transliteration. Sarajevo. Photo by Velibor Božović

Figure 4.21 'With God's mercy (*Allah rahmet ile*)', in Cyrillic script. Vragolavi, Sokolac. Photo by Amila Buturović

Figure 4.23 'He is the Creator, the Everlasting. Death is a drink that all shall taste; the grave is the door that all shall pass through; [Say] *Fātiḥa* for her soul'. Faletići. Photo by Amila Buturović

Figure 4.24 *Al-Fātiḥa* in Bosnian translation. Sarajevo. Photo by Velibor Božović

Conclusion

'The dead as memory,' Jon Davies contends, 'as internalized spiritual inheritance, are a vital part of the bonds of the community of the living'.[1] While somewhat self-evident, this observation contains several important points this study has sought to explore in the context of Bosnian Islamic funerary culture. The relationship between the dead and the living is continually shaped and restored through memory, more specifically through a variety of commemorative practices embodied in rituals and retold in stories, funerary inscriptions and images. For all its transcendental and totalising quality, death is only immanently known, galvanising a host of responses and reflecting myriad sensibilities. In Bosnian Islam the process of commemoration relies on multidirectional dynamics: historical permutations converge with eschatological ideals; modernity equipped with secular attitudes introduces new modalities of memory but never fully discards tradition; personal loss merges with public participation; theology is humbled by private choices of mourning; the landscape is culturally transformed as it embraces the dead; bonds with the dead are sustained beyond language and funerary markers, and so on. Death is never isolated from other realms of cultural expression nor is it ever constrained by them. Discourse on death is inevitably shaped by cultural representations and the history thereof. To account for these ongoing dynamics, this study has traversed various disciplinary bounds, surveyed religious, literary and material sources associated with Bosnian Islamic funerary culture and arrived at several observations.

To start with, memory of the dead does not operate in a single direction. Although we tend to speak of memories in proprietary terms as our possessions to be retrieved and calibrated in controlled ways, the dead are not passive objects of our subjectivity. They animate us and summon us in a reciprocal fashion, making demands from us, bestowing favours or inflicting harm. Subjectivity inheres in their identity as human beings but it is obscured

---

[1] J. Davies (ed.), *Ritual and Remembrance*, 14.

by our ambiguous attitude towards human remains. Howard Williams's argument that the dead possess a double identity as persons and objects prompts us to explore the ways in which their personhood persists. They continue to have agency which may qualitatively vary but which endures as a necessary facet of social relations. Thus, in normative Islam, the institution of *waqf* endowments established across Bosnia and Herzegovina functions to maintain the identity and influence of the dead by ushering descendants into action. The living are assigned the responsibility to vicariously carry on post-mortem tasks in a deceased person's name and on his or her terms. In Sufi Islam, the saints and friends of God bequeath grace on visitors to their shrines as intermediaries between this and the other world. Here, the Bosnian tradition of *dobri*, the good ones, merges with this Sufi concept of *awliyā/ evliya*. Not being anchored to the shrine in terms of their spiritual grasp, the good ones visit dreams and memories to offer advice and avert harm. In popular religiosity across Bosnia and the Balkans, the living derive healing and comfort from the dead. They protect and seek protection shortly after the fateful moment of death and they repeatedly return to the dead, in reverence, to remember and be remembered. The dead exercise inimical sway if rules of conduct are not respected. The bond between the dead and the living is thus governed by a particular ethical and behavioural code, which is safeguarded in both religious and secular acts of commemoration. Finally, in Islamic funerary texts guided by the Prophetic tradition, the demand to recite the *Fātiḥa* for the soul of the deceased regenerates Islamic values and perpetuates connections with a universal community of believers.

Second, Bosnian Islamic views about death and commemoration are simultaneous and plural in origin rather than successive in action. The diverse channels through which Islam spread across the region, the endurance of Christian and Slavic customs inherited from pre-Ottoman times, the confluence of modern secular and traditional religious eschatologies and the influence of other cultural and metaphysical views on death and dying, have all left an eclectic mark on funerary culture among the Muslims of Bosnia and Herzegovina. Therefore, while one can speak of a recognisable set of beliefs and practices associated with normative Sunni Islam, there are many other practices and attitudes that expand the norms into a rich interplay between what Smith terms 'utopian' and 'locative' norms, or 'prescribed' and 'performed' praxis in Campo's words. Rather than attracting ire for 'incongruity' or 'syncretism', this interplay ought to be valued as an important hybridity of different teachings and cultural practices, collective humbleness before death, and a desire to provide the dead with a sense of continuity and stability. Shifts and changes in cultural reactions to death are understandably slow and uneven: after all, as Berger reminds us, the challenge of turning something as anomic – and, one might add, unknowable – as death into something meaningful and knowable is a challenge for all religious teachings,[2] but it is an equal challenge for secular philosophies. Through complex exchanges and adaptations, Bosnian Islamic funerary culture accumulated a rich repository of views and practices to cope with death and memories of the dead.

Third, an important aspect of commemorative culture is space. Practices and beliefs surrounding death and memorialisation are explored through embodied rituals and gravestone records. Burial is the adopted mode of disposing of the dead in both Islamic and local Christian traditions. As Bosnians embraced Islam, their graves became marked with upright stelae emulating the Ottoman standard. As aspects of material culture, the gravestones convey important textual and visual clues to help us unlock individual biographical data and decipher collective eschatological sensibilities. However, commemorative space has occupied an ambiguous position in local culture: at times it is considered sacrosanct, especially at crucial historical moments of modern identity formation and in the context of traditional saintly figures whose shrines, during visitations, ascertain a flow of supernal energy with curative and therapeutic powers. These spatial posts are not inherently sacred as per Eliade's suggestion; rather, they are activated through commemorative action, striving for meaning and other forms of creative expression such as elegies, legends, myths, music and the like, all of which facilitate and sustain memory and access to the dead in spatial terms. Likewise, while not a sacred location per se, a common tombstone can become sanctified if the Qur'an is recited at its side or if the name of God incised on it is invoked. Liturgical practices consecrate space for ritual and spiritual purposes while at once creating a commemorative bond with the dead in their resting place. The gravesite thereby becomes meaningful and intimate, even if personal relations with the dead are absent.

Fourth, Bosnian Islamic funerary culture offers important clues on identity formation and group demarcation. Using funerary text as a primary source, the study has sought to unpack the epigraphic and visual components so as to explore vocabulary and techniques used to direct and ritualise the relationship between the dead and the living. Rejecting the assumption that the tombstone is only valuable for social historians because of the biographical data it contains, the study foregrounds the tombstone's significance for reconstructing the history of religious and cultural identities, specifically in the process of transition to Islam and spread of Ottoman Islamic values. Central to this exploration is the translation and interpretation of symbols and eschatological norms from one religious system to another, specifically, from Christianity to Islam and from one language to others. Remaining in dialogue with the vernacular tradition and imperial funerary norms, the nascent Bosnian Islamic community continued hybridising its funerary styles over a long period after

---

[2] P. Berger, *The Sacred Canopy*, 40–42.

the consolidation of the Ottoman rule. By embracing Islam the Bosnians did not abandon their dead ancestors who had died as non-Muslims. To facilitate the remembrance of the ancestors in this transitional period a familiar idiom was needed to reassure the dead that their beliefs and identities would be honoured and that they would continue being connected rather than become detached and forgotten. Native language was only gradually challenged by the introduction of a new linguistic culture of death in this capacity. Translation was instrumental in bridging eschatological gaps: the meaning of death needed to be gently transferred into a different yet sufficiently familiar vocabulary in order to comfort the dying, secure a bond with the dead and nourish memory. The presence of many solitary, anonymous tombstones in the landscape dating from the earliest period of Ottoman military campaigns broadened the commemorative repertoire with stories and legends that have enabled this memory to endure against oblivion. The visual symbols on the gravestones, be they images or Qur'anic invocations, coexisted with the text as part of the same solicitous vocabulary, enabling illiterate members of the society to take part in funerary expression. In contrast, the literate and high society indulged in poetic expressions of grief and ornate elegies through which themes from other literary genres were employed to enhance beautiful if sad memories. Funerary text is thus significant for reflecting a wide range of participants and contributors, and a spectrum of identities borne within the polyglot Ottoman cosmopolis.

Lastly, the physical presence of the dead, in solitary locations and clustered graveyards, offers insights into the history of shared space. The first Muslims of Bosnia were rarely segregated from non-Muslims. There was no taboo associated with placing religiously differentiated dead in close proximity and intensifying their spiritual intimacy. The sense of familial social bonds overrode any practice of confessional, and by extension administrative, separation among different *millets*. This was aided by the Ottoman policy of burying the dead outside city walls so many existing remote locations continued accommodating the dead, including those who had embraced Islam. Many cemeteries to date reflect this history of boundary crossing in death, suggesting such crossings may have been as common in life. This practice would gradually change after the eighteenth century when cemeteries became increasingly confessional and the symbols on the tombstones highly distinguishable. There was no longer ambiguity as to the religious identity of the deceased, although this clarity would again be challenged by the Yugoslav policies of secularisation and de-nationalisation. In that sense, within the provincial context of the Empire, religion was not necessarily a defining criterion for organising necropoleis. Except for mosque yards where the dead were ostensibly all Muslim, the living did not deem it necessary to define the deathscape in exclusive terms. Cemeteries were mixed spaces until the eighteenth century when an impetus for stricter religious observance began to inculcate physical segregation, which was to be amplified by modern attempts at nation building. Nevertheless, the surviving material evidence abounding in many cemeteries, along with an ever more eclectic commemorative praxis, prevent us from establishing a linear narrative of how identities were shaped and memories formed. In our age dominated by a search for unambiguous identities, these ancestors modestly remind us not to forget their own entanglements and challenges in becoming who they were and not to ignore the legacy they left of a complex universe which, from their perspective, would not cease even when life did.

Figure C.1 Old turbans mushrooming in Travnik.
Photo by Velibor Božović.

Appendix
STONE SPEAKER

A visual and reflective travelogue through the deathscape of Bosnia and Herzegovina.
Text by Amila Buturović.
Photographs by Velibor Božović.
www.stonespeaker.ca

Ravne Bakije, Sarajevo

Figure A.1 Ravne Bakije, Sarajevo

Not long ago, an acquaintance told me about his first visit to Sarajevo in the 1980s. Impressed by the proximity of green mountains to Sarajevo's core, he spent a day exploring the steep fringes where the city meets the countryside. A local bus left him at the top of a hillside neighbourhood filled with clean air, fruit trees, hens and rowdy children. On his way back, he followed no particular route, letting himself be rolled like a pebble down the narrow roads. To his dismay, all seemed to wind up at one cemetery or another. 'Sarajevo,' he declared to me, 'is a graveyard jungle!' Indeed, an aerial snapshot of the city reveals a ring of cemeteries spreading over every hill and girdling the rim of the uneven bowl that encompasses the city. The dead, so it seems from this perspective, have the privilege of being elevated above the living. They may occupy a marginal social place, but they are rewarded enchanting vistas that the living can't share, especially in cold months when fog descends. In this picture, taken from an old graveyard called Ravne Bakije that rolls over Sarajevo's southeast hills, the gravestones vigilantly lean over the city. One legend has it that the name of the location dates to the period of the Ottoman conquest when the Ottoman Sultan, enchanted by the view, dismounted the horse and called his entourage to share the pleasure: 'Bak, bak,' he shouted in Turkish, 'look, look!' For anyone who has glanced at Sarajevo from this angle the Sultan's enchantment should come as no surprise. But if for a moment we consider how the city might look from the perspective of these gravestones, inspiration would likely join desperation. Breathtaking beauty and heartbreaking pain follow each other closely in this city, taking turns in unpredictable ways. So do war and peace, violence and romance, prejudice and harmony. How disheartening it must be to stand witness to such opposites lurking in human beings. The city of tensions has graced its dead with an exquisite view but has hardly allowed them to rest in peace.

Malo Polje, Blagaj

Figure A.2 Malo Polje, Blagaj

In his *Requiem for a Nun* William Faulkner wrote, 'The past is never dead. It's not even past.' Cynics would remark that Faulkner must have been speaking of the Balkans where everyone talks about the past as if it were their muse and property, and where the past is so often appropriated to fuel the language of hatred and acts of violence. But the past persists in creative ways too. In the Herzegovinian village of Malo Polje, two old *stećaks* live on as a useful present/presence on someone's land. Here, as in many farms and gardens across Bosnia and Herzegovina, they are recycled and recast into a role not originally intended – as foundation stones, a wall for the shed, or a supporting post for a haystack. Necessity, not invocation of prestige, underpins this kind of appropriation. And so, viewed from this farmer's perspective, the past is indeed alive. It is a real and concrete tool for building and reshaping, not a metaphor tossed around for dividing and destroying.

Dobro, Livno

Figure A.3 Dobro, Livno

Although the village of Dobro ('the Good'), near Livno in western Herzegovina, seems to have been depopulated in recent times, the growing number of modern family homes indicates seasonal presence of its diaspora. Summers must be busy here, certainly busier than when we arrived one October day and found more graves than inhabitants. The main Catholic cemetery that stretches across the arid landscape houses many family and individual tombs and glitters with unforgiving intensity under the Herzegovinian sun. In contrast to slender upright white slabs typical of Islamic gravestones, modern Catholic cemeteries tend to be horizontal, geometrically precise blocks, commonly crafted from black granite and exuding a sense of stability and permanence. Their undiluted blackness may be at odds with the pasty Herzegovinian landscape, but their shape fits well in this open, flat horizon where the shrubs are low, trees stunted, and verticality exists only chimerically. But it has not always been this way. In the middle of the cemetery's undeviating lowness, an anomalous, tall, cross-shaped gravestone draws our attention. This is what we had hoped to find. Though centuries old, it still stands perky and playful like a cocky young man with his arms on his hips and chest puffed up, as if showing off his fancy tattoos. One is a striking cross, carved elegantly as a miniature version of the gravestone itself; the other, a thin crescent arching delicately above the cross. An instance of intense spiritual intimacy between two symbols which our contemporary political imagination has sullied with blood and mutual intolerance. Yet here they are, in the middle of a war-shattered, religiously divided, ethnically cleansed land, basking together in the sun, waiting to be noticed and recognised for the intricacy and creativity of their interaction that once was but is no longer here. May the village of the Good be better appreciated for the goodness of its goods!

Jakir, Glamoč

Figure A.4 Jakir, Glamoč

Occasionally, one comes across such disproportionately large tombstones in the Bosnian landscape that it is easy to think one has walked into a land of giants. Who else would need headstones over four metres tall? Of course, this may not be just another Bosnian eccentricity. In *Mecca and Eden*, Brannon Wheeler explains that many Biblical figures not only lived to be hundreds of years old but were also giants who needed large tombstones. We are told in Deuteronomy, for example, that for some of these trolls, regular-sized men appeared as small as grasshoppers. In the Islamic tradition, Adam – the first man and prophet – is reported to have been of remarkable stature. Muhammad himself described Adam as a very tall palm tree, nearly 60 cubits in height. In metric terms, that makes Adam over 27 metres tall. In nineteenth-century European travel literature into eastern lands, we read of many giant tombstones erected for Biblical and Islamic prophets. One such tombstone in southern Arabia allegedly belongs to the prophet Salih and is some 20 metres long. The tomb of Hud was even 27.5 metres long. Similar reports of funerary extravagance exist elsewhere in the world. So what of Bosnia? Bosnian tradition claims few giants, but it seems to bolster the size of many men in its commemorative imagination. An unusual variety of tombstone sizes, especially the slender turban-topped ones that leave little to the woman's imagination, seem to be a local speciality. Here, the field of Jakir, near Glamoč in western Herzegovina, nests one such example of a supersized headstone: standing over 4 metres tall and capped with a 2-metre turban, it towers over the field and other tombstones as a gargantuan mushroom under whose cap, local rumours have it, eight adults can find shelter from rain. All agog to find a cryptic prediction of Armageddon carved in its stone, we encounter instead a plain epitaph: 'The year of death of the late Omer Aga Bašić, for whom we say our prayer, is 1213 AH' (1798 CE). It is unlikely that Mr Bašić was a colossus. But he must have been a very important man, or at least must have thought of himself as such, to be rewarded with such a large grave marker. There is probably nothing more to it. In the country which currently fetishises larger-than-life expressions of authenticity, to the point of unearthing its own pyramids, building huge medieval monasteries and ethnic theme parks, and claiming its own Marian apparitions, occasional oversized tombstones of pre-modern times seem like a harmless prank on our imagination.

Presjeka, Goražde

It is often tempting to anthropomorphise objects and animals, ascribe to them human-like characteristics as if to make them less alien and enigmatic. In the anthropomorphic vocabulary we construct the dolphin's smile, the sky cries, the sea gets angry and cats exhibit arrogance. Even here, as we study the tombstones, we are guilty of evoking their 'speech' so as to bridge the gap between what we know and do not know about them. For the great Bosnian poet Mak Dizdar the tombstones enhanced intimacy – 'In the sleeper beneath the stone I recognise myself' – and inspired him to transform stone silence into poignant poetry. If the gravestones can speak, what do we imagine them to say? Something sublime to transcend our human condition or something banal to ground us even deeper? What may the monoliths captured in this picture be saying to us, to you and to each other? When we first found them,

Figure A.5 Presjeka, Goražde

ensconced comfortably on the edge of a cliff and facing the mist-shrouded abyss, there was something mischievous and defiant about their whereabouts and disposition. Shortly before we found them, we had attempted to inspect a larger burial ground in the lower parts of the valley, which, according to a plaque standing at its foot, had been declared a national monument in 2004. Our plan was cut short, in what seemed like a movie twist, by a providential phone call from Velibor's brother beseeching us not to go further because of the residual landmines deposited throughout the burial complex. Little had we known, and the timely phone call informed us, that this area, known as Presjeka, had served as a bitter front line during the 1992 war. Did these five *stećaks* peeking from the cliff spy on our naïve stroll into the minefield? Did they secretly hope for more death or were they our guardian angels propitiously inspiring Velibor's brother to make the call? Common sense that the stones were mute objects bore no relevance at this moment. Inexplicable distrust and anxiety crept in, deflating any desire, at least temporarily, to hear them speak. We were both glad to leave this haunting location and return home safe and sound.

Jazići, Kalinovik

Figure A.6 Jazići, Kalinovik

We stumbled upon this old graveyard in the karstic town of Kalinovik, in Republika Srpska, quite by accident. We had enquired with the local residents for directions, but few knew its whereabouts, replying with a vague hand gesture that there were a few 'Turkish' graves at a downtown intersection but they didn't really know where. A patch of land overgrown with thick brush and thorny mulberry bushes caught our attention: it was neither a park nor a groomed path; just a neglected, overgrown scrap of vegetation bulging like an unattractive smudge in the new asphalt. We pushed our way through thorny branches and noticed, further below, several stone mushrooms peeking shyly through the brush. Our explorative presence unsettled a few local men who strolled over, projecting suspicion and bewilderment. 'What's so interesting about these stones? Wouldn't you be more keen to visit Hitler's fort instead?', they asked. We were genuinely intrigued by the news that Hitler had been stationed in Kalinovik as a recruit of the Austro-Hungarian army. That moment in history apparently ranked highly in the local lore; the one we were interested in was better off abandoned to the elements and thorny shrubs.

Varošnice, Jajce

Figure A.7 Varošnice, Jajce

In the picturesque city of Jajce it is easy to trace layers of history at every corner. This ancient city and its environs have housed pre-historic people, welcomed Roman temples, accommodated Slavic settlers, revelled as the royal stronghold for medieval Bosnian kings, and persisted as an important urban centre in Bosnia and Herzegovina to date. In its history, Jajce has hosted many pivotal events, including the coronation and the execution of the last Bosnian king Stjepan Tomašević and, much later, in 1943, the key session for the formation of the Socialist Federal Republic of Yugoslavia. But the beauty of Jajce is not only historical; it is also timeless, manifested in its transcendental nature as much as historical sites. It is here that two majestic Bosnian rivers, Vrbas and Pliva, converge, then free-fall into the city centre as a clamorous, 20-metre deep white curtain before they continue a scenic journey in and out of space and time. Amidst Jajce's ancient catacombs, Roman ruins, regal fortress, old-style Bosnian houses and modern buildings, there lay one of the oldest and largest of Bosnian Ottoman cemeteries. The cemetery, Varošnice, once contained thousands of graves dating back to between the early sixteenth and twentieth centuries and guarded the history of local families. Anticipating a long day of research in the green field overlooking the river below and the fort above, we equipped ourselves with enough *bureks* and *kiflas* to eat, high-SPF creams and notepads, chalk and camera lenses, and headed northwest to Jajce. What we encountered, alas, was not what we had hoped for. A vast, uneven, and overgrown field welcomed us, barely offering any readable gravestones. Some had sunk deeply into the soil, creating a subterranean limestone universe we could not access, while others had long been evicted by urban and industrial expansion. Many, however, seemed newly destroyed and uprooted, leaving sore cavities in the landscape that spring grass could only partly blanket. Disfigured and abandoned, this important location chronicling the life and death of Jajce seemed banished from the city's historical (and tourist) map, cast away like bad apples among good ones worthy of keeping. As we left the site, the dilemma remained: is the selection of some and the elimination of other cultural artefacts an inevitable result of historical and urban development – teleology of sorts – or is it a staged form of alienation from a particular historical moment, even its stigmatisation? Neither option seems satisfactory.

Alifakovac, Sarajevo

Figure A.8 Alifakovac, Sarajevo

It is said that Alifakovac is the most enchanting Ottoman cemetery in the region. Slanted on a hill overlooking Sarajevo, it flickers with hundreds of slender tombstones dating as far back as the fifteenth century, and hundreds more erected since then. Also known as the travellers' cemetery where people with no kin in the city were buried, Alifakovac holds many layers of history in its limited space. The older stones seem frivolous, eccentric and even clumsy in comparison with the new ones, which stand tall, stylised, and orderly. What they all have in common are the stories they tell, through an inscription, image or both. Sadly, not all stories can be told all the time. As old stones sink into the ground, bidding a slow farewell to the city that has accommodated them for so long, some deposit their stories into collective memory and others into collective oblivion. Hardier stones, distrustful of such a repository, stubbornly persist: they hold on, as if keeping together the past and the present in the hope that, even in a mutilated condition, they won't be cast to forgetfulness.

Šetići, Rogatica

Figure A.9 Šetići, Rogatica

Deep in the woods of eastern Bosnia, amidst ancient oaks and looming chestnuts, hides a lonesome stone warrior. Legends have it that Sultan Mehmet the Conqueror included in his military entourage numerous stonemasons to erect proper headstones for his fallen heroes. Dubbed in local folklore as '*šehitski nišani*', or 'martyrs' headstones', and recognised by their turban-topped, upright slabs, these stones usually abide alone, mute to history and deaf to their surroundings. This one in the village of Šetići, tucked away in a patch of pristine forest trespassed only by the occasional shepherd and his flock, fills us with awe. Standing calmly over four metres tall, with an equally colossal footstone, the *nišan* competes with the trees for a ray of distant sunlight. Unlike its silent kith and kin elsewhere which reveal no epitaphic detail, this *nišan* is given a voice to speak through an inscription, allowing us to place it on the historical map rather than relegate it to foggy uncertainty. So what does it say and to whom does it speak? The language of the inscription is rudimentary Arabic, carved sloppily and with a few typos. It identifies the dead man as Mustafa Aga, and the date of his passing as the year 962 of the Islamic calendar, which corresponds to 1555 of our era. Under the inscription is a simple carving of a sword, an obvious testimony to Mustafa Aga's military prowess. Though communicative, the stone is by and large inaccessible to the local audience, both physically because of its location and linguistically because hardly anyone outside the nascent Ottoman centres of learning would have been literate enough to understand its text. Thus, this precious early memorial, which actually raises more questions than provides answers, has lived on in solitude, announcing to the forest and its creatures the story of his sacrifice for a new religious culture that was taking root across Bosnia and the Balkans.

Dobrače, Rogatica

Figure A.10 Dobrače, Rogatica

On the plains of Dobrača, which stretch along the road from Sarajevo to Rogatica in eastern Bosnia, history and nature work in sinister ways. Far away in the field, a small *stećak* necropolis lies embedded in the grass, projecting perfect stillness and isolation. Around it, herds of wild horses graze quietly, not letting out a sound with either hooves or grinding teeth, as if patiently sketching an impressionist painting. Suddenly, they pierce the deafening silence with a thunderous gallop, transporting us from the painting into a movie set somewhere in the Russian steppes. The landscape, abandoned by humans, seems to exist out of time. But that is only an illusion: a shepherd we encounter tells us the horses became wild after their owners were ethnically cleansed from the area. He points to some faraway ruins – of a school, a mosque without a minaret and several burned houses. The clock, which seems to have stopped when we set foot into the fields of Dobrača, came back to tick again once we realised that violence may have produced some of this boundless harmony. How unsettling.

Fatnica, Bileća

Figure A.11 Fatnica, Bileća

In the small village of Fatnica, in southeastern Herzegovina, an elegant upright monolith – *stećak* – adorns the playground of what used to be the village school but is now yet another desolate war ruin. Both objects, the school and the *stećak*, invoke memories of death but the *stećak* seems to be doing it in a more dignified and subtle manner. It is adorned with a delicate pattern with miniature yet majestic arches and a necklace of perky rosettes. The school children coming out to play during recess may have thought of life in its presence, not of death. But its epitaph, inscribed in medieval Bosnian script, offers no kind words: 'May the one who razes and steals this stone be cursed!' Is that what has made it stand still in place for all these centuries? Perhaps the same message should have been carved on the entrance of the school.

Rostovo, Novi Travnik

Figure A.12 Rostovo, Novi Travnik

At the plains of Rostovo, not far from the glorious city of Travnik, the vast sky folds gently into the rolling fields. Here lies a late medieval necropolis which marks, according to one legend at least, the tombstones of a bloody wedding procession. The legend says that a brawl took many Muslim and Christian lives on a day when senseless violence ruled instead of amity. Now, every tombstone in this breathtaking necropolis displays a harmonious carving of the cross and the crescent on its front. The dead are labelled for posterity as all the same. We can assume that those who erected the tombstones here, far away from any settlement, thought of the seamless transition between the earth and the sky when they immortalised their dead in this timeless landscape with such harmonious symbolism. They did not imagine, as they were not privy to modern science, that the world had a beginning and an end. They also did not know that future generations, who would sneer at the medieval imagination, would imagine another kind of infinitude, in which the cross and the crescent would be eternally incompatible. Irony is at work.

Lisac, Novi Travnik

Figure A.13 Lisac, Novi Travnik

Returning from the wonderfully successful treasure hunt at the plains of Rostovo, we drove through the village of Lisac where, sadly, large new houses eclipse any charm a remote mountain village may possess. Unexpectedly, a patch of land thickly overgrown with ferns promised to hide old graves. Yes! Our excitement was momentarily dampened by the same awkward dilemma we face at any unforeseen location: who do we approach to ask about the graves? Is it impolite to extract people out of real time to indulge us in the village's history and memory? Besides, who here 'owns' the history and memory? Who 'owns' the dead?

Tomislavgrad

Figure A.14 Tomislavgrad

In Tomislavgrad, the town once known as Duvno, the morning was bright and sunny but the street atmosphere felt lukewarm. Our short visit involved a hike to an old Muslim cemetery, then to a chic Italian-style pizzeria for lunch. At the cemetery, numerous stone slabs graced the hill but they seemed oddly disconnected. In fact, the cemetery and the town appeared faintly aloof, as if living through an uneasy truce in the current political situation in which the Catholic symbols began to overpower the Islamic and Orthodox ones. On the way out we noticed a turban-capped male slab and a smaller one leaning into each other, in a scene that resembled an intimate moment between a father and a son. Are they bidding farewell to the town or admiring the Catholic basilica dedicated to the allegedly first Croatian saint, Nikola Tavelić? Are they contemplating the changing times when the basilica takes centre stage and the cemetery retreats? Perhaps it is unfair to ascribe to the dead the observations and sentiments of the living.

Dujmovići, Bjelašnica

Figure A.15 Dujmovići, Bjelašnica

Bjelašnica, or the White Mountain, has a special standing in the Sarajevan cultural imagination. Its massive summits and harsh winters had long kept it physically distant and inaccessible yet ostentatiously present in the local lore. Until the 1984 Winter Olympics when Bjelašnica hosted men's Alpine skiing events, it had hardly been a destination for the faint-hearted urbanites; only the brave, robust climbers and experienced hikers dared explore its inhospitable, if stunning, terrain. Whether because the Olympics tamed it or the 1992 war made everyone more resilient to environmental peril, Bjelašnica has recently become a much safer landscape to enjoy, offering ample opportunities for risk-free, all-season adventures and picnics across its vast solitudes. And to us, interested in the intersections of landscape and memory, Bjelašnica has served the most delectable of platters: a vast rolling plain replete with clustered cemeteries – medieval *stećaks*, Ottoman *nišans*, Catholic roods and Orthodox crosses – which speak to the fact that Bjelašnica had been tamed long before the modern Olympics were ever conceived. Like the fields in which they lie, these funerary markers expand and roll into each other, making us feel scattered and confused as much as thrilled and authenticated. How do we even start to reconstruct meaning in such diversity of memorial signs? Should we attempt a chronological narrative and sort out the gravestones in a linear pattern? Or, should we respect their non-linear arrangement and think of a model that can encompass multiple memories, including new ones produced by the picnickers as they spread their blankets and eat their sandwiches in the vicinity of the graves, thus tying, perhaps unconsciously, new bonds with those for whom Bjelašnica too had been a favourite destination, but on their final journey.

Božine, Rogatica

Figure A.16 Božine, Rogatica

One early morning, the road we travelled wound to its very end. Normally, roads connect into each other, joining elaborate multidirectional webs of movement that rarely have a visible beginning or end. In this case, the road simply dissolved into grass. On the right stood a plain house with its front door wide open; on the left, a makeshift basketball post leaning against a wooden fence that followed the contours of the hill and descended into the field. We had read in an old study that somewhere in this village – which, we now found out, consisted of this one house and its field – there was a necropolis of unusual-looking Ottoman gravestones. An unexpectedly well-dressed boy peeked his head through the door and answered our query affirmatively. Behind him, several more men of different ages showed up, all equally stylish. As it happened, we chanced on an Orthodox Christian/Serb 'slava', the annual feast honouring a patron saint, in this case St George.

Inside, a lavish table spread included pork and lamb roasts, steaming baked potatoes, fresh cheese, pies of different kinds, baklavas, and jugs of home-made plum brandy. The elderly male host let us explore the yard only after we promised we'd join the feast. The sight outside was surreal: amidst yard tools and fruit trees slender old stele, some leaning into the fence and others sinking into the soil, lay scattered all over the field, revealing rough reliefs of mythical-looking birds and large animals in motion. Like an abandoned exotic zoo, the gravestones inhabited the field in full harmony with the livestock and crops. Ravaged by time but preserved by this fecund natural environment, they showed atypical but befitting faces of death. 'Tell us, what ancient civilisation may have built these odd stones?' a young man hoping for the news of some glorious history asked as we joined the table. 'They go back to the Turkish time,' I said awkwardly. Evoking the infamous Turks at the feast honouring an Orthodox saint who died for his faith may have been a tactless remark, but the elderly host graciously settled the matter: 'We all have been known to build great tombstones,' and filled my glass with home-made elixir.

Bibliography

Abiva, H. 'Survey of Sufi Orders in the Balkans'. Online <http://bektashiorder.com/sufism-in-the-balkans-1>.
Abiva, H. 'The Poems of Mulhid Vahdeti', Online <http://bektashiorder.com/poems-of-mulhid-vadeti>.
Abou-Lughod, L. 'Islam and the Gendered Discourses of Death'. *International Journal of Middle East Studies* 25:2 (1993).
Abu Dawud. *Sunan: kitāb al-janā'iz*. Vol. 20. http://www.sunnah.com/abudawud.
Abu Hanifa. *Al-fiqh al-akbar*. Trans. I. Ninowy. Online <http://fahadmahdi.webs.com/Other%20Books/Fiqh%20e%20Akbar%20By%20Abu%20Hanifa.pdf>.
Agnew, J.A. *Place and Politics: The Geographic Mediation of State and Society*. Boston: Allen and Unwin, 1987.
Agoston, G. and B. Masters (eds). *Encyclopedia of the Ottoman Empire*. New York: Facts on File, Inc., 2009.
Aksan, V. 'Theoretical Ottomans'. *History and Theory* 47 (2008).
Al-Aqḥiṣārī, M. *Risāla al-dhākir fī ziyārat ahl al-maqābir*. MS. 154. Bratislava: The University Library of Bratislava. 29b-41b.
Al-Bukhari. *Ṣaḥīḥ: Kitāb al-janā'iz*. Vol. 23. Online http://sunnah.com/bukhari.
Algar, H. 'Some Notes on the Naqshbandi Tariqat in Bosnia'. *Die Welt des Islams* 13: 3–4 (1971).
——'The Hamzeviye: A Deviant Movement in Bosnian Sufism'. *Islamic Studies* 36:2 (1997).
Anderson, B. *Imagined Communities*. London: Verso, 1991.
Andrews, W., N. Black and M. Kalpakli (eds). *Ottoman Lyric Poetry: An Anthology*. Seattle: University of Washington Press, 2006.
Assmann, J. *Cultural Memory and Early Civilization*. Cambridge: Cambridge University Press, 2011.
Atçıl, A. 'The Formation of the Ottoman Learned Class and Legal Scholarship (1300–1600)'. PhD Dissertation, University of Chicago, 2010.
Balivet, M. *Romanie Byzantine et Pays de Rum Turc*. Istanbul: Isis, 1994.
Bašagić, S. *Bošnjaci i Hercegovci u islamskoj književnosti* [Bosniaks and Herzegovinians in Islamic literature]. Sarajevo: Svjetlost, 1986.
Başeski, M.M. *Mecmua*, edited by K. Filan. Sarajevo: Connectum, 2012.
Bejtić, A. 'Jedno vidjenje sarajevskih evlija i njihovih grobova kao kultnih mjesta [One perspective on the saints of Sarajevo and their graves as veneration sites]'. *POF* 31 (1981).
Berger, P. *The Sacred Canopy*. New York: Anchor Books, 1967.

Bešlagić, Š. *Stećci, katološko-topografski pregled* [The stećaks: a topographic catalogue]. Sarajevo: Veselin Masleša, 1975.
——*Nišani XV i XVI vijeka u Bosni i Herzegovini* [The nišans of the 15th and 16th centuries in Bosnia and Herzegovina]. Sarajevo: ANU, 1978.
Blair, S. *Islamic Inscriptions*. New York: New York University Press, 1998.
——'An Amulet from Afsharid Iran'. *The Journal of the Walters Art Museum* 59 (2001).
Bogićević, V. *Pismenost u BiH* [Literacy in Bosnia and Herzegovina]. Sarajevo: Veselin Masleša, 1975.
Boym, S. *The Future of Nostalgia*. New York: Basic Books, 2001.
Busuladžić, M. 'Nekoliko protuvjerskih običaja kod nas [A few of our superstitious practices]'. *Novi Behar* 3 (1945).
Buturović, A. *Stone Speaker: Mediaeval Tombs, Landscape and Bosnian Identity in the Poetry of Mak Dizdar*. New York: Palgrave, 2002.
——'Love and/or Death: Conflict Resolution in Traditional Bosnian Ballad'. In *Women in the Ottoman Balkans*, edited by A. Buturović and I. Schick. London: IB Tauris, 2007.
——'Death'. In *Key Themes for the Study of Islam*, edited by J. Elias. Oxford: Oneworld, 2010.
——'Bosnia and Herzegovina, Between Loss and Recovery. *Descant Canadian Literary Journal* 156 (Spring 2012), 10–15.
——'Sufi Orders and Movements: Balkans', *Encyclopedia of Women and Islamic Culture*, 2014. Brill Online <http://www.paulyonline.brill.nl/entries/encyclopedia-of-women-and-islamic-cultures/sufi-orders-and-movements-balkans-COM_0149a>.
Campo, J. 'Muslim Ways of Death: Between the Prescribed and the Performed'. In *Death and Religion in a Changing World*, edited by K. Garces-Foley. Armonk, NY: M.E. Sharpe, 2003.
Campo, J. (ed.). *Encyclopedia of Islam*. New York, NY: Facts on File, 2009.
Chapman, J. 'The Living, the Dead and the Ancestors: Time, Life Cycle and the Mortuary Domain in Later European Prehistory'. In *Ritual and Remembrance: Responses to Death in Human Societies*, edited by J. Davies. Sheffield: Sheffield Academic Press, 1994.
Clayer, N. and A. Popovic. 'Le culte d'Ajvatovica et son pèlerinage annuel'. In *Le Culte des Saints dans le Monde Musulman*, edited by H. Cambert-Loir and C. Guillot. Paris: École française d'Extreme Orient, 1995.
Ćehajić, Dž. 'Društveno-politički, religiozni, književni i drugi aspekti derviških redova u jugoslavenskim zemljama [Social, political, religious, literary and other aspects of the dervish orders in Yugoslav lands]'. *Prilozi za Orijetalnu Filologiju* 34 (1984).
——*Derviški redovi u jugoslovenskim zemljama s posebnim osvrtom na Bosnu i Hercegovinu* [Sufi orders in Yugoslav lands with special emphasis on B-H]. Sarajevo: Orijentalni Institut, 1986.
Connerton, P. *How Societies Remember*. Cambridge: Cambridge University Press, 1998.
Ćorović, V. 'Prilog proučavanju načina sahranjivanja i podizanja nadgrobnih spomenika u našim krajevima u srednjem vijeku [Contribution to the study of burial practices and erection of tombstones in medieval times]'. *Naše starine* 3 (1955).
Coşgel, M. 'Ottoman Tax Registers (*Tahrir Defterleri*)'. *Economics Working Papers* (2002) 200–47. Online http://digitalcommons.uconn.edu/econ_wpapers/200247.
Ćošković, P. 'Veliki knez bosanski Tvrtko Borovnić [The Great Bosnian Duke Tvrtko Borovnić]'. *Croatica Christiana Periodica* 20: 37 (1996).
Davies, J. (ed.). *Ritual and Remembrance: Response to Death in Human Societies*. Sheffield: Sheffield Academic Press, 1994.
Dickie, J. 'Allah and Eternity: Mosques, Madrasas and Tombs'. In *Architecture of the Islamic World*, edited by G. Michell. London: Thames & Hudson, 1995.

Dobrača, K. 'Tuhfetul-musallin ve zubdetul-haši'in od Abdul-Vehaba Žepčevije Ilhamije [A gift and treat for those who pray to God by Abdul-Vehhab Ilhami of Žepče]'. *Anali Gazi Huserv-Begove Biblioteke* 2–3 (1974).
Đozo, H. *Fetve.* Srebrenik: Ilmijja BiH, 1996.
Eklund, R. *Life between Death and Resurrection according to Islam.* Uppsala, Almqvist & Iksells, 1941.
Eldem, E. 'Urban Voices from Beyond: Identity, Status and Social Strategies in Ottoman Muslim Funerary Epitaphs of Istanbul (1700–1850)'. In *The Early Modern Ottomans: Remapping the Empire*, edited by V. Aksan and D. Goffman. Cambridge: Cambridge University Press, 2007.
Eldem, E. and N. Vatin, *L'épitaphe otomane musulmane, XVIe–XXe siècles*. Paris: Peeters, 2007.
Eliade, M. *The Sacred and the Profane.* Trans. W.R. Trask. New York: Harcourt Brace Jovanovic, 1961.
Elias, J. 'God'. In *Key Themes for the Study of Islam*, edited by J. Elias. Oxford: Oneworld, 2010.
Faroqi, S. *Approaching Ottoman History: An Introduction to the Sources.* Cambridge: Cambridge University Press, 2000.
Filan, K. 'Sufije i Kadizadelije u Osmanskom Sarajevu [Sufis and Kadizadeler in Ottoman Sarajevo]'. *Anali Gazi Husrev-begove biblioteke* 29–30 (2009).
Filipović, N. *Islamizacija u Bosni i Hercegovini* [Islamisation of Bosnia and Herzegovina]. Sarajevo: Armis Print, 2008.
Fine, J. *When Ethnicity Did Not Matter in the Balkans.* Ann Arbor: University of Michigan Press, 2006.
Fusch, A., M. Cosgrove and G. Grote (eds). *German Memory Contests: The Quest for Identity in German Literature, Film, and Discourse Since 1990.* Camden: Camden House, 2006.
Georgevitch, T.R. 'Serbian Habits and Customs'. *Folklore* 28:1 (1917).
Gillis, J. (ed.). *Commemorations: The Politics of National Identity.* Princeton: Princeton University Press, 1994.
Goffman, D. *The Ottoman Empire and Early Modern Europe.* Cambridge: Cambridge University Press, 2002.
Graham, W. 'Fātiḥa'. *Encyclopaedia of the Qur'an*. Leiden: Brill, 2006, vol. 2.
Granqvist, H. *Muslim Death and Burial: Arab Customs and Traditions Studied in a Village in Jordan.* Helsinki: Helsingfors, 1965.
Hadžibajrić, F. 'Risala Šejha Mustafe Gaibije [Treatise of Shaykh Mustafa Gaibi]'. *Anali Gazi Husrev-begove biblioteke* 4 (1976).
Hadžijahić M. 'Tekija kraj Zvornika – postojbina bosanskih hamzevija [Sufi lodge near Zvornik – the residence of Bosnian Hamzevis]' *POF* 10–11 (1960–61).
——*Predislamski elemeniti u kulturi bosanskih muslimana* [Pre-Islamic elements in Bosnian Muslim culture]. Sarajevo: Institut za društvena istraživanja, 1973.
——'Sinkretistički elementi u islamu u Bosni i Hercegovini [Syncretic Elements in Islam in Bosnia and Herzegovina]'. *POF* 28–9 (1978–79), Sarajevo 1980.
——'Badžijanije u Sarajevu i Bosni'. *Anali Gazi Husrev-begove biblioteke* 7–8 (1982).
Hadžiosmanović, L. and E. Memija. *Antologija tariha Bosne i Hercegovine* [An anthology of the chronograms of Bosnia and Herzegovina]. Sarajevo: Connectum, 2008.
Hafizović, R. 'A Bosnian Commentator on the *Fusus al-hikam*'. *Journal of the Muhyiddin Ibn ʿArabi Society* 47 (2010).
Halebi, I. *Mevkufat Islam Fıkhı*. Istanbul: Sağlam yayınevi, 2003. 2 vols.
Halevi, L. *Muhammad's Grave: Death Rites and the Making of Islamic Society.* New York: Columbia University Press, 2007.

Hallam E. and J. Hockey (eds). *Death, Memory and Material Culture*. Oxford and New York: Berg, 2001.

Handžić, A. 'O formiranju nekih gradskih naselja u Bosni u XVI stoljeću – uloga države i vakufa [On the development of towns in Bosnia in the 16th c. – the role of the state and religious endowments]'. *POF* 25 (1975).

―'O ulozi derviša u formiranju gradskih naselja u Bosni u XV stoljeću [The role of dervishes in the formation of towns in Bosnia in the 15th c.]'. *POF* 31 (1981).

―'Konfesionalni sastav stanovništva u Bosni i Hercegovini u prvim stoljećima osmanske vladavine [Religious composition of Bosnia's population in the first few centuries of the Ottoman rule]'. *POF* 42–3 (1992–93).

Handžić, M. *Književni rad bosansko-hercegovačkih muslimana* [Literature of the Muslims of Bosnia and Herzegovina]. Sarajevo: Državna štamparija, 1934.

―*Islamizacija Bosne i Hercegovine i porijeklo bosanskih Muslimana* [Islamisation of Bosnia and Herzegovina and the origins of Bosnian Muslims]. Sarajevo: Islamska dionička štamparija, 1940.

Hangi, A. *Život i običaji muslimana u Bosni i Hercegovini* [Lifestyle and customs of the Muslims of Bosnia and Herzegovina]. Sarajevo: Naklada Daniela Kajona, 1906.

Hazen, J.M. 'Contemporary Bosnian Sufism: Bridging the East and West'. MA Thesis. Washington DC: American University, 2008. Online <http://eprints.soas.ac.uk/13816/1/Hazen_3369.pdf>.

Herb, G. and D. Kaplan (eds). *Nested Identities: Nationalism, Territory, and Scale*. Lanham: Rowman and Littlefield, 1994.

Hodžić, S. 'Odbacujmo štetne običaje i sujevjerja [Let us discard harmful customs and superstitions]'. *Glasnik VISa* 8–12 (1952).

Huković, M. 'Gaibija, šejh Mustafa – mistik i buntovnik [Sheikh Mustafa Gaibi – mystic and rebel]'. *POF* 41 (1991).

Ibn Majah, *Sunan: kitāb al-janā'iz*. Vol. 6. Online http://www.sunnah.com/ibnmajah.

Ibrišević, S. *Pravi put i stranputice* [The true path and wrong paths]. Sarajevo n.p., 1990.

Ilić, S. 'Hamzevijska i hurufijska jeres u Bosni kao reakcija na političku krizu Osmanske Imperije u drugoj polovini 16. vijeka [The heresy of Hamzevi and Hurufi orders in Bosnia as a reaction on the political crisis of the Ottoman empire in the second half of the 16th c.]'. *POF* 41 (1991).

Ivakhiv, A. 'Toward a Geography of "Religion": Mapping the Distribution of an Unstable Signifier'. *Annals of the Association of American Geographers* 96:1 (2006).

Jezernik, B. 'No Monuments, No History, No Past: Monuments and Memory'. In *After Yugoslavia: Identities and Politics within the Successor States*, edited by R. Hudson and G. Bowman. New York: Palgrave McMillan, 2011.

Kafadar, C. *Between Two Worlds: The Construction of the Ottoman State*. Berkeley: University of California Press, 1995.

―'Self and Others: The Diary of a Dervish in Seventeenth Century Istanbul and First-Person Narratives in Ottoman Literature'. *Studia Islamica* 69 (1998).

Kalus, L. (ed.), *Thesaurus d'épigraphie islamique*. Geneve: Fondation Max van Berchem, 2013. Online edition < http://www.epigraphie-islamique.org>.

Kemura, S. *Sarajevske džamije i druge javne zgrade turske dobe* [The mosques of Sarajevo and other public buildings from the Turkish period]. Sarajevo: n.p., 1913.

Kiel, M. 'Ottoman Sources for the Demographic History and the Process of Islamisation of Bosnia-Hercegovina and Bulgaria in the Fifteenth – Seventeenth Centuries: Old Sources – New Methodology'. In *Ottoman Bosnia: A History in Peril*, edited by M. Koller and K. Karpat. Madison: The University of Wisconsin Press, 2004.

Kreuter, M. 'Women in Southeast Vampire Belief'. In *Women in the Ottoman Balkans*, edited by A. Buturovic and I. Schick. London: IB Tauris, 2007.

Konstantakopoulou, A. 'Religious Syncretism and Deviance in Islamic and Christian Orthodoxies'. *Turkish Historical Review* 3 (2012).
Kostić, M. 'Gaibijino Turbe kod Stare Gradiške [Gaibi's *turbe* near Stara Gradiška]'. *Narodna Starina* 13 (1934).
Kreševljaković, H. *Esnafi i obrti u Bosni i Hercegovini, 1463–1878* [Guilds and crafts in Bosnia and Herzegovina, 1463–1878]. Sarajevo: Veselin Masleša, 1958.
Krstić, T. 'Illuminated by the Light of Islam and the Glory of the Ottoman Sultanate: Self-Narratives of Conversion to Islam in the Age of Confessionalization'. *Comparative Studies in Society and History* 51:1 (2009).
Kujundžić, E. *Bošnjacka tradicijska kultura: uspomenar* [Bosniak traditional culture: memoir]. Sarajevo: LAPIS, 2009.
Lambourn, E. 'Tombstones, Texts, and Typologies: Seeing Sources for the Early History of Islam in Southeast Asia'. *Journal of the Economic and Social History of the Orient* 51: 2 (2008).
Laqueur, H.P. 'Dervish Gravestones'. In *The Dervish Lodge: Architecture, Art, and Sufism in Ottoman Turkey*, edited by R. Lifchez. Berkley: University of California Press, 1992.
Lovrenović, D. *Stećci. Bosansko i humsko mramorje srednjeg vijeka* [*Stećaks*: The medieval tombstones of Bosnia and Hum]. Sarajevo: RABIC, 2010.
Lovrenović, I. 'Bosanski križ [Bosnian cross]'. Online <http://ivanlovrenovic.com/2012/01/bosanski-kriz/>.
Malcolm, N. *Bosnia: A Short History*. London: Macmillan, 1994.
Margalit, A. *The Ethics of Memory*. Cambridge, MA: Harvard University Press, 2002.
Maroney, E. *Religious Syncretism*. London: SCM Press, 2006.
Mazalić, Đ. 'Hrišćanski nišani u okolini Travnika [Christian *nišans* near Travnik]'. *Naše starine* 4 (1957).
McClelland, B. *Slayers and their Vampires: A Cultural History of Killing the Dead*. Ann Arbor: The University of Michigan Press, 2006.
Mehinagić, I. 'Četiri neobjavljena izvora o hamzevijama iz sredine XVI vijeka [Four unpublished sources on the Hamzawiyya from the 16th c.]'. *POF* 18–19 (1968–69).
Michel, R. *Mostar 1908, with Photographs by Wilhelm Wiener*. Sarajevo: Dobra knjiga, 2006.
Mitchell, W.J.T. (ed.). *The Language of Images*. Chicago: University of Chicago Press, 1980.
—— (ed.) *Landscape and Power*. Chicago: The University of Chicago Press, 1994.
Monumenta Turcica: Vakufname iz Bosne i Hercegovine. Sarajevo: Orijentalni institut, 1985.
Mujezinović, M. 'Nekoliko nevjerodostojnih turskih natpisa u Sarajevu [A few apocryphal Turkish inscriptions in Sarajevo]'. *Naše starine* 2 (1954).
——'Epigrafika i kaligrafija pjesnika Mehmeda Mejlije [The epigraphy and calligraphy of the poet Mehmed Meyli]'. *Naše starine* 4 (1957).
——*Islamska epigrafika Bosne i Hercegovine* [Islamic epigraphy of Bosnia and Herzegovina]. Sarajevo: Sarajevo Publishing, 1998. 3 vols.
Mulahalilović, E. *Vjerski običaji Muslimana u Bosni i Hercegovini* [Religious customs among the Muslims of Bosnia and Herzegovina]. Tuzla: Hamidović, 2005.
Nametak, A. *Islamski kulturni spomenici Turskog perioda* [Islamic cultural monuments of the Turkish period]. Sarajevo: Državna štamparija, 1939.
Nilević, B. 'Slika religioznosti srednjovjekovne Bosne pred osmanski dolazak [Religious composition of medieval Bosnia prior to the Ottoman arrival]'. *POF* 41 (1991).
Nora, P. 'Between Memory and History: Les Lieux de Mémoire'. *Representations* 26 (1989).
Norris, H.T. *Islam in the Balkans*. Columbia, SC: University of South Carolina Press, 1993.
Olick, J., V. Vinitzky Seroussi and D. Levy (eds). *Collective Memory Reader*. Oxford: Oxford University Press, 2011.

O'Shaughnessy, T. *Muhammad's Thoughts on Death: A Thematic Study of the Qur'anic Data*. Leiden: E.J. Brill, 1969.
Palavestra, V. *Historijska usmena predanja iz Bosne i Hercegovine* [Oral histories from Bosnia and Herzegovina]. Sarajevo: Buybook, 2004.
Pamuk, Ş. 'Institutional Change and Longevity of the Ottoman Empire, 1500–1800'. *The Journal of Interdisciplinary History* 35:2 (2004).
Quataert, D. *The Ottoman Empire 1700–1922*. Cambridge: Cambridge University Press, 2005.
Radić, R. 'Bosanska Gradiška – nekadašnji Berbir [Bosanska Gradiška – previously Berbir]'. *Politika [Daily]*. 1 September 1936.
Ragon, M. *The Space of Death*. Charlottesville: University Press of Virginia, 1988.
Raudvere, C. 'Claiming Heritage, Renewing Authority: Sufi-oriented activities in post-Yugoslav Bosnia-Herzegovina'. *European Journal of Turkish Studies* 13 (2011).
——'Textual and Ritual Command: Muslim Women as Keepers and Transmitters of Interpretive Domains in Contemporary Bosnia and Herzegovina'. In *Women, Leadership and Mosques*, edited by M. Bano and H. Kalmbach. Leiden: Koninklijke Brill NV, 2012.
Ricci, R. *Islam Translated*. Chicago: The University of Chicago Press, 2011.
Ricoeur, P. *Memory, History, Forgetting*. Chicago: Chicago University Press, 2004.
Risteski, L. 'Categories of the "Evil Dead" in Macedonian Folk Religion'. In *Christian Demonology and Popular Mythology*, edited by G. Klaniczay and E. Pocs. Budapest: CEU Press, 2006.
Rizvi, S. 'The Existential Breath of *al-raḥmān* and the Munficent Grace of *al-raḥīm*, the *Tafsīr Sūrat al-Fātiḥa* of Jāmī and the School of Ibn ᶜArabī'. *Journal of Qur'anic Studies* 8:1 (2006).
Rogers, J.M. 'Calligraphy and Common Script: Epitaphs from Aswan and Akhlat'. In *Content and Context of Visual Arts in the Islamic World*, edited by P. Soucek, C. Bier and R. Ettinghausen. University Park, PA: Penn State University Press, 1988.
Rossington M. and A. Whitehead (eds). *Theories of Memory*. Baltimore: John Hopkins University Press, 2006.
Sajdi, D. (ed.). *Ottoman Tulips, Ottoman Coffee: Leisure and Lifestyle in the Eighteenth Century*. London: IB Tauris, 2007.
Šabanović, H. 'Izrazi evā'il, evāsit i evāhir u datumima turskih spomenika [The terms evā'il, evāsit and evāhir in the dates found on Turkish monuments]'. *POF* 2 (1951).
Schick, I.C. 'The Harem as Gendered Space and the Spatial Reproduction of Gender'. In *Harem Histories: Envisioning Places and Living Spaces*, edited by M. Booth. Durham: Duke University Press, 2010.
Schimmel, A. *Mystical Dimensions of Islam*. Chapel Hill: The University of North Carolina Press, 1975.
Schwartz, S. *Sarajevo Rose: A Balkan Jewish Notebook*. London: Saqi Books, 2005.
Sells, M. *Early Islamic Mysticism*. New York: Paulist Press, 1996.
Shaw, S. *History of the Ottoman Empire and Modern Turkey. Vol 1. Empire of the Gazis: The Rise and Decline of the Ottoman Empire, 1280–1808*. Cambridge: Cambridge University Press, 1976.
Sheldrake, P. *Spaces of the Sacred: Place, Memory, Identity*. Baltimore: Johns Hopkins University Press, 2001.
Sikirić, Š. 'Pobožne pjesme (ilahije) šejh Abdurrahmana Sirrije [Devotional songs of sheikh Abd al-Rahman Sirri]'. *Glasnik Islamske Vjerske Zajednice* 9: 11–12 (1941).
Škaljić, A. *Turcizmi u srpskohrvatskom jeziku* [Turkish loan words in Serbo-Croatian]. Sarajevo: Svjetlost, 1985.

Smith, J. and Y. Haddad. *The Islamic Understanding of Death and Resurrection*. Oxford: Oxford University Press, 2002.
Smith, J.Z. *Map is Not Territory: Studies in the History of Religion*. Leiden: E.J. Brill, 1978.
Sokolović, S. *Islamski propisi o čuvanju zdravlja, posjeti bolesnika i sahrani umrlih Muslimana* [Islamic regulations on maintaining health, visiting the sick and burying deceased Muslims]. Sarajevo: Ahkam al-Islam, 1972.
Stewart, P.J. and A. Strathern, *Landscape, Memory and History*. London: Pluto Press, 2003.
Tafsīr Jalālayn. Online <http://www.altafsir.com/Tafasir.asp?tMadhNo=0&tTafsirNo=8&tSoraNo=1&tAyahNo=1&tDisplay=yes&UserProfile=0&LanguageId=1>.
Thielgaards Watts, M. *Reading the Landscape of America*. New York: Macmillan, 1957.
Thomson, G. 'Irish Discoid Gravemarkers'. *Archaeology Ireland* 20:3 (2006).
Toorawa, S.M. 'Prayer'. In *Key Themes for the Study of Islam*, edited by J. Elias. Oxford: Oneworld, 2010.
Toussilis, Y. *Sufism and the Way of Blame: Hidden Sources of a Sacred Psychology*. Wheaton, IL: Quest Books, 2010.
Trako, S. 'Stećci: božanska igra brojki i slova [Stećak: A divine play of numbers and letters]'. *Soc. ekol. Zagreb* 20:1 (2011).
Traljić, S. 'Muslimanski narodni spomenici [Muslim traditional monuments]'. *Narodna uzdanica* 8 (1940).
Trimingham, J.S. *The Sufi Orders in Islam*. Oxford and New York: Oxford University Press, 1998.
Tuan, Yi-Fu. 'Rootedness versus Sense of Place'. *Landscape* 25 (1980).
Vego, M. *Zbornik srednjovjekovnih natpisa u Bosni i Hercegovini* [Anthology of medieval inscriptions in Bosnia and Herzegovina]. Sarajevo: Zemaljski muzej, 1962–64. Vols. 1–3.
Veinstein, G. (ed.). *Syncrétismes et hérésies dans l'Orient Seldjoukide et Ottoman, XIVe–XVIIIe siècle*. Paris: Peeters, 2005.
Venhorst, C. *Muslims Ritualizing Death in the Netherlands*. Zurich: LIT, 2013.
Vidović, D. 'Simbolična predstava na stećcima [*Stećaks*' symbolic representations]'. *Naše starine* 2 (1954).
Volčić, Z. 'Yugo-Nostalgia: Cultural Memory and Media in the Former Yugoslavia'. *Critical Studies in Media Communication* 24:1 (2007).
Vukanović, T.P. 'Witchcraft in the Central Balkans II: Protection against the Witches'. *Folklore* 100:2 (1989).
Waardenburg, J. 'Death and the Dead'. *Encyclopaedia of the Qur'ān*, edited by J.D. McAuliffe. Leiden: Brill, 2001. Vol. 1.
'Wakf'. in *Encyclopaedia of Islam*, 2nd edn. Brill Online Reference Works <http://referenceworks.brillonline.com.ezproxy.library.yorku.ca/entries/encyclopaedia-of-islam-2/wakf-COM_1333?s.num=66&s.start=60#d17497315e13851>.
Walter, C. *The Warrior Saints in Byzantine Art and Tradition*. Aldershot: Ashgate, 2003.
Wenzel, M. *Ukrasni motivi na stećcima* [*Stećak* decorative motifs]. Sarajevo: n.p., 1965.
Weschke, R. 'Bosnia: 409 dead after Srebrenica massacre buried', <http://www.missingblog.net/409-dead-after-srebrenica-massacre-reburried-in-bosnia/>.
Wheeler, B. *Mecca and Eden: Ritual, Relics, and Territory in Islam*. Chicago: University of Chicago Press, 2006.
White, B. 'A Persistent Paradox'. *Folklore* 83:2 (1972).
Williams, H. 'Death Warmed Up: The Agency of Body and Bones in Early Anglo-Saxon Cremation Rites'. *Journal of Material Culture* 9:3 (2004).
Winter, J. *Sites of Memory, Sites of Mourning*. Cambridge: Cambridge University Press, 1995.

Yankova, V. 'Светци-воини. Балкански легенди за светци кефалофори [Martyrs-Warriors: Balkan Legends of Saints Kefalofori]'. *Ethnocultural Interactions* (2005).
Yilmaz, S. and I. Yosmaoglu, 'Fighting the Spectres of the Past: Dilemmas of Ottoman Legacy in the Balkans and the Middle East'. *Middle Eastern Studies* 44:5 (2008).
Young, J. *The Texture of Memory: Holocaust Memorials and Meaning*. New Haven, CT: Yale University Press, 1993.
Zaman, M.Q. 'Death, Funeral Processions, and the Articulation of Religious Authority in Early Islam'. *Studia Islamica* 93 (2001).
Zecevic, S. 'On the Margin of Text, On the Margin of Empire: Geography, Identity and Fatwa-Text in Ottoman Bosnia'. Columbia University: Unpublished PhD Dissertation, 2008.
——'Islamic Law in the Balkan Peninsula', *The Oxford International Encyclopedia of Legal History*. New York: Oxford University Press, 2009. Online http://www.oxford reference.com/view/10.1093/acref/9780195134056.001.0001/acref-9780195134056.
Zelizer, B. *Remembering to Forget: Holocaust Memory Through the Camera's Eye*. Chicago: The University of Chicago Press, 1998.
Zirojević, O. 'Vjerski sinkretizam: Alahovi hrišćani [Religious syncretism: Allah's Christians]'. *Montenegrina*. Online http://www.montenegrina.net/pages/pages1/religija/vjerski_sinkretizam_alahovi_hriscani_o_zirojevic.html.
Zwierzchowski J. and E. Tabeau, 'The 1992–95 War in Bosnia and Herzegovina: Census-Based Multiple System Estimation Of Casualties' Undercount', 16. Online: http://www.icty.org/x/file/About/OTP/War_Demographics/en/bih_casualty_undercount_conf_paper_100201.pdf.

'Farewell Speech of Reisu-l-ulema Dr Mustafa Cerić at Ajvatovica, Shaban/June, 1433/2012'. Online http://www.rijaset.ba/index.php?option=com_content&view=article&id=14642:govor-reisu-l-uleme-na-ajvatovici-2&catid=40:minine-vijesti.
'Masse Remembers Srebrenica Genocide'. (16 July 2012). Online <http://www.rijaset.ba/english/index.php/template/latest-news/268-masse-remembers-srebrenica-on-the-17th-anniversary-of-the-genocide>.
'Serb President Tomislav Nikolic "Sorry" for Srebrenica Massacre'. *The Australian* (26 April 2013). Online <http://www.theaustralian.com.au/news/world/serb-president-tomislav-nikolic-sorry-for-srebrenica-massacre/story-e6frg6so-1226629769906>.
'Srebrenica Khutba by Ef. Mustafa Cerić'. (11 July 2013). Online <http://www.rijaset.ba/english/index.php/template/latest-news/278-srebrenica-khutba-by-mustafa-ef-ceric>.

Index

a se biljeg/a se leži 135, 137, 146
Abiva, H. 21, 26, 30
abjad 193–4
Abou-Lughod, L. 39
Abu Dawud 37, 38
Abu Hanifa 39, 182
Agnew, J.A. 92
Ahmed Sudi Bosnevi 29
Ajvatovica 71–2, 74–5
Ajvaz Dede 72–5
Aksan, V. 125, 166
Al-Bukhari 37, 38
al-insān al-kāmil 28
Algar, H. 17, 24, 56
Alhamiado 25, 198, 199, 200
Anderson, B. 92, 103
Andrews, W. 192
Antun Hangi 42–7, 49, 51, 52
Aqḥiṣārī, al- 41, 168
Assmann, J. 63, 64, 66, 68, 92
Atçıl, A. 18
Austro-Hungary 26, 42–3, 83, 132, 163, 198, 216
awliya/evliya 27, 53, 76, 204
Ayni Dede 21–2, 89, 194–5
Azrael 35, 41

Balivet, M. 17
Balkans, the 5–6, 16–18, 21, 23, 26, 33, 67, 75, 81, 84, 90, 93, 96, 124, 128, 139, 163, 166, 167, 204, 211
  Ottoman legacy in 139
baraka 133
barzakh 33–4, 36, 41, 88
Bašagić, S. 196
Bašeskija 167–8, 189, 190
Bejtić, A. 76, 77
Bektashi 21, 23, 25–6, 27, 28, 29
Berger, P. 14, 204
Bešlagić, Š. 9, 114, 120, 132, 135, 144, 154, 157, 159, 160
Bhabha, H. 99
Biblical lore 82, 213–14
Blagaj 23, 24, 175
Blair, S. 170, 174
Bogićević, V. 121
Bogomil 112, 120, 151
bones 64, 88
  identity of 88
  materiality of 36
Bosančica 120, 129, 134, 135–6, 144, 145
Bosniak dead 74, 100, 105, 121
Bosniak identity 72, 74

Bosniak nation 74, 100–101
Bosniak people 62, 74, 115
Bosnian Church 53, 112
Boym, S. 97
bula 54
Busuladžić, M. 49

Campo, J. 15, 33, 156, 204
Ćehajić, Dž. 21, 23–5, 29, 30
cephalophory 82–5
Cerić, M. 74–5, 104
Chapman, J. 93
Christians, of Bosnia 1, 11, 13, 17, 32, 71, 77, 83, 87, 110, 123, 132–3, 146, 157, 160–61
Clayer, N. 74
colonial 42, 163
communism 13, 96–7
Connerton, P. 61, 62
conversion 6–8, 10, 15, 21, 35, 110, 112, 122–3, 137–9, 150, 156, 175
  sources of 7–9, 110, 161–2
Ćorović, V. 114
Coşgel, M. 7
Ćošković, P. 52
Crypto-Christians 17–18
Cyrillic script 110, 120, 201

Davies, J. 14, 63, 93, 95, 116, 203
Dayton, the 1–2, 62
dead, the
  and the living 36, 63, 75, 77, 90, 122, 150–51, 185, 188, 203–5
  as ancestors 10, 63, 150–51, 206
  as remains 60, 88–9, 91, 93, 95, 101–2, 109, 204
  as subjects/objects 64, 91
  subjectivity of 14, 60, 68, 88, 91, 95, 100, 203
dhikr 20, 24, 27, 53–6, 169, 186
Dickie, J. 75–6
divan poetry 25, 192
djedovski štap 154

Dobrača, K. 41
dobri 52–3, 76, 77, 83, 130, 204
dova 70–72; see also petitionary prayer
Đozo, H. 49
dvovjerstvo (dual religiosity) 17

Eklund, R. 34, 65
Eldem, E. 124, 125, 128, 132, 177, 188
Eliade, M. 98, 129, 205
Elias, J. 185
eschatology 9, 13
Evliya Çelebi 21

Faroqi, S. 6
Fātiḥa al- 38, 45, 69, 70, 107, 178, 180, 184–6, 188, 191, 192, 193, 198, 201, 204, 206
Fevzi Mostarac 29
Filan, K. 167, 168, 190
Filipović, N. 7
Fine, J. 140
folk 70, 132
  poetry 52–3,
  tradition 42–3, 46–7, 88, 115, 151–2
  lore 4, 51, 82, 84–5, 88, 151–2, 157, 219

Gazi Husrev Beg 24
genocide 1, 62, 74, 97, 101–5
Georgevitch, T.R. 88
Gillis, J. 74, 92
Glagolitic script 120
Goffman, D. 125, 166
Graham, W. 183
Granqvist, H. 39

hadith 19, 34, 36–9, 40, 49, 52, 69, 88, 89, 165, 182
Haddad, Y. 35, 36, 88
Hadži Sinan 25
Hadžibajrić, F. 84
Hadžijahić, M. 17, 23, 49, 54, 77
Hadžiosmanović, L. 193

Hafizović, R. 28
hagiography 7, 72, 82
Halevi, L. 32, 33, 37, 39, 82, 88, 89, 132, 170, 182, 190
Hallam, E. 5
Hamzevi 23, 25, 27, 30
Hanafi 16, 18, 20, 23, 38–9, 167, 168, 182; see also Abu Hanifa
Handžić, A. 16, 19, 30
Handžić, M. 7, 29
harem 125, 148–9, 150, 165
Hasan Kaimi 25, 29, 54, 76
Hazen, J.M. 21, 26
hazire 124, 125, 148, 149
Herb, G. 92
historiography 5, 103, 105, 167
Hockey, J. 5
Hodžić, S. 91
Huković, M. 84

Identity 7–9, 59, 62–3, 71–4, 110, 115–16, 123, 130, 138, 141, 148, 163, 171, 174, 185, 203–5
 and space 3, 8, 57, 60, 92, 141, 205
 and nation 2, 7–9, 11, 59, 61–3, 71–5, 163
 of the dead 36, 60, 78–9, 110, 117, 134, 138, 141, 156, 161, 173, 177, 197, 203–4, 206
Ibn 'Arabī 23, 29, 179
Ibn Majah 34, 37, 38, 182
Ibrahim Halebi 39
Ibrišević, S. 49
Ilić, S. 23
immortality, 102, 115, 122, 140–41, 150–51, 152, 154, 162–3
Islamisation 7–10, 20, 32, 138–41, 169, 185
Ivakhiv, A. 98–9

Jews, of Bosnia 32, 67, 77, 115, 123, 169
Jezernik, B. 96
Jurjev (St. George's) 72,

kabristan 124, 133
kabur 129, 132, 133 ; also see *qabr*
Kadizadeler 25, 26, 167–9
Kafadar, C. 7, 8, 19
Kalus, L. 132
Kaplan, D. 92
Kemura, S. 55
Khalwati/Halveti 24
Khidr 27
Kiel, M. 6
kitāb al-janā'iz 34–7, 51, 182
Konstantakopoulou, A. 17
Kostić, M. 84
Kreševljaković, H. 132
Kreuter, M. 90
Krstić, T. 8
Kujundžić, E. 77

Lambourn, E. 111
Laqueur, H.P. 124
liturgy 55, 56–7, 169, 181, 183, 185, 190, 193, 205
Lovrenović, D. 151
Lovrenović, I. 157, 161, 162–3

McClelland, B. 88
Malcolm, N. 112
Margalit, A. 61
Maroney, E. 16
martyr 33–4, 37, 53, 65, 67–8, 74–8, 87, 100–101, 104–5, 130, 141
martyr's graves/tombstones 75, 85, 101, 219; see also *šehtiski nišan*
martyrdom 78, 82–5, 90, 107, 108, 131, 141
 in Byzantine Christianity 81, 82,
 in Islam 38, 65, 74, 82–3, 85, 100, 104, 140–41
 in the Qur'an 34, 101
 beheaded 82–3, 86–7; also see cephalophory
Mazalić, Đ. 154, 157, 161, 162

Mehinagić, I. 23
Mehmed Meyli 25, 195, 196–7
Mehmet II, Sultan 18, 21, 219
memory
  collective 10, 53, 62–3, 66, 92, 96–7, 103, 145, 151–2, 219
  cultural 60–65, 67, 68, 74–5, 87, 91, 95, 97, 114, 116, 130, 141, 162
  of the dead 10, 14, 33, 63, 65–6, 74–9, 91–2, 107, 109, 162, 205
  funerary 137, 169
  material 5, 10, 163, 170–71
Memija, E. 193
memory studies 10, 61, 109
Mevlevi 25
mevlud 54
mezar 129,133
Michel, R. 75, 83
millet 132, 156, 206
Mitchell, W.J.T. 93, 151
mortality 36, 56, 89, 99, 121
Moshe Danon 77
Mostar 23, 29, 76, 83, 146, 197, 200
Muhasibi 66
Mujezinović, M. 9, 85, 89, 173, 174, 194–8
Mulahalilović, E. 55, 71
Mulhid Vahdeti 29–30
Munkar/Nakir 36, 39, 46

nafs (soul) 89
Nametak, A. 123
Naqshbandi 11, 23, 24, 25, 29, 56
national identity 74
National Museum 135
national myths 101, 115
nationalism 61, 92, 169
nation building 62, 96, 103, 139, 198, 207
nationhood 99
Nilević, B. 112
nišan 129, 133–4, 135, 137, 147, 152, 161, 163, 174, 194–6
  šehitski (martyr's) 75, 85, 101, 219

hrišćanski (Christian) 154–6, 157, 159, 161
Nora, P. 103–5, 137, 163
Norris, H.T. 21, 23
nostalgia 35, 96, 122
  Yugo- 96–7

Olick, J.V. 62
orthodoxy 15, 17, 19, 25, 51, 138, 168, 169, 175, 191
O'Shaughnessy, T. 33
Ottoman cosmopolis 138–40, 165, 190, 195, 206
Ottoman Empire 5–10, 15, 20–21, 23, 28, 39, 42, 124, 132, 166, 167, 182
Ottoman chronograms 193–8
Ottoman culture 7, 18, 41, 72, 74, 84–5, 122–5, 135–8, 148–9, 162, 186
Ottoman epitaphs 186–91, 198
Ottoman Islam 16–19, 20, 23, 27–9, 39, 42–3, 123, 128, 140–41
Ottoman languages 9, 25, 42, 110, 123, 132–4, 139–40, 190, 194
Ottoman legacy 26, 32, 49, 139,
Ottoman literature 110, 138–40, 192
Ottoman tombstones 110–12, 120, 122, 123–5, 128–30, 133–5, 139, 146–8, 152–4, 155–6, 192
Ottomanisation 10, 139–40, 198

Palavestra, V. 90, 115
Pamuk, Ş. 166
Popovic, A. 72
prayer
  commemorative 71
  funerary 9, 39, 45, 54, 168, 182
  Lord's 183
  petitionary 10, 55, 70, 89, 110; see also *dova*
  rain 71

qabr 34, 132–3, 134, 145, 146, 177–8
Qadiri 25, 196

Quataert, D. 166
Qur'an 76, 91, 99, 156
Qushayri 66

Radić, R. 84
Radmilja, 14, 90, 92, 134, 156
Ragon, M. 61
Raudvere, C. 26
Reis ul-Ulema 74
Ricci, R. 138–9
Ricoeur, P. 61
Risteski, L. 90
Rizvi, S. 179
Rogers, J.M. 183
rootedness 92
Rossington, M. 63
rūḥ (spirit) 36, 39, 88–9, 181, 185

Šabanović, H. 193
sacred space 98–9, 129, 150
Sajdi, D. 167
Sarajevo 85, 89, 157, 165, 168, 189, 218
Sarajevo Roses 106
Sarı Saltık 21, 28, 139, 140, 141
Schick, I.C. 149
Schimmel, A. 30, 186
Schwartz, S. 77
secular 13, 28, 32, 59, 63, 65, 92, 95, 99, 111, 156, 157, 180, 194, 195, 205–7
secularisation 26, 47, 198, 206
secularism 103, 117
šehitski nišan 75, 85, 101, 219
Sells, M. 66
sevdalinka 44, 139
shahada 35, 37, 41, 43, 175–7, 182
shahid/šehid 53, 100
Shamsi Dede 21, 22, 89, 194
Shaw, S. 25, 166
Sheldrake, P. 3, 98
Sikirić, Š. 29
Sinan Beg 19, 69
Sirri Baba 24, 29
Sisters of Rum 54, 77

Škaljić, A. 134
Smith, J. 35, 36, 88
Smith, J.Z. 129, 204
Sokolović, S. 47, 49–51, 70, 91, 177
Srebrenica 101, 102, 103, 105
stećak 114–15, 116–20, 130, 135, 138, 141, 143, 147, 151–2, 154, 155, 156, 157, 163, 170, 171, 211, 215, 221, 225
Stewart, P. 95, 122
Stolac 77
Strathern, A. 95, 122
Sufism 20–23, 52–5, 56–7
Sulvadžije (interrogators) 46
syncretism 16–17, 141, 156, 204

tahrir defteri 6; see also tax registers
tariqa 20, 24
tax registers 6–7
tekke 11, 23–6, 29, 30
tespih (prayer beads) 55
tevhid 53–6
text
  cultural 4, 52–3, 141, 161, 162–3
  funerary 8–10, 14, 110–12, 116, 121–2, 127–8, 150–51, 157, 165, 167, 186–8, 192, 198, 204–6
  visual 117, 134
  written 134, 138–9
Thielgaards Watts, M. 93
Thomson, G. 155
Toorawa, S.M. 175, 181, 183
Toussilis, Y. 23
Trako, S. 151
translation 10, 124, 129, 134, 137, 138–40, 146, 150, 205
Travnik 125, 146, 165, 196, 222, 223
Traljić, S. 125, 147
Trimingham, J.S. 53
turbe 75–6, 78, 79, 81, 83, 89, 133, 194

Uhud 37, 38, 104
ulema 18

vampires 50, 67, 88, 90
Vatin, N. 125, 128
Vego, M. 114, 120, 135, 146
Veinstein, G. 16
Venhorst, C. 39
Vidovic, D. 114
Volčić, Z. 97
Vukanović, T.P. 88

Waardenburg, J. 34, 35
Walter, C. 82
waqf 6, 19–20, 24, 30, 68–70, 204
Wenzel, M. 114, 116, 118
Weschke, R. 102
White, B. 81
Whitehead, A. 63
Williams, H. 64, 91, 206

Winter, J. 103, 104

Yā-Sīn 37
Yankova, V. 81
Yediler turbe 76
Yi-Fu Tuan 92
Yilmaz, S. 139
Yosmaoglu, I. 139
Young, J. 62
Yugoslavia 1, 26, 62, 72, 96–7, 198, 217

Zecevic, S. 168–9
Zelizer, B. 152
ZIDRA 26
Zirojević, O. 17
Zwierzchowski, J. 100